Teaching
Multicultural
Literature
in Grades K-8

Teaching Multicultural Literature in Grades K-8

Edited by
Violet J. Harris
The University of Illinois at Urbana-Champaign

Christopher-Gordon Publishers, Inc.
Norwood, MA

Acknowledgements

Chapter 5:

Material from *Black Elk Speaks* used with the permission of the University of Nebraska Press.

"One Great Thing" and "To a Firefly" reprinted with permission of Atheneum Publishers, an imprint of Macmillan Publishing Company, from *The Earth is Sore,* adapted and illustrated by Aline Amon. Copyright © 1981 by Aline Amon Goodrich.

"My Horse, Fly Like a Bird" copyright © 1989 by Virginia Driving Hawk Sneve. Reprinted by permission of Holiday House.

Christopher-Gordon Publishers, Inc.
480 Washington Street
Norwood, MA 02062

Printed in the United States of America

10 9 8 7 6 5 4 3 2 1   96 95 94 93 92

ISBN: 0-926842-13-7

To my parents, Gertrude and Willie Harris, my sister, Patricia R. Harris, my goddaughters Selena Harper and Shana Powell, my special friend Dr. Paul V. Maynard, and my sister friends.

Short Contents

Preface   xv

Chapter 1:   The Politics of Children's Literature: Reflections on Multiculturalism, Political Correctness, and Christopher Columbus   1
Joel Taxel

Chapter 2:   Multicultural Literature for Children: Making Informed Choices   37
Rudine Sims Bishop

Chapter 3:   Contemporary Griots: African-American Writers of Children's Literature   55
Violet J. Harris

Chapter 4:   Turning the Page: Asian Pacific American Children's Literature   109
Elaine Aoki

Chapter 5:   Native Americans in Books for the Young   137
Donnarae MacCann

Chapter 6:   We Have Stories to Tell: A Case Study of Puerto Ricans in Children's Books   171
Sonia Nieto

Chapter 7:   Ideas a Literature Can Grow On: Key Insights for Enriching and Expanding Children's Literature About the Mexican-American Experience   203
Rosalinda B. Barrera, Olga Liguori, and Loretta Salas

Chapter 8:   Caribbean Children's Literature   243
Yahaya Bello

Chapter 9:   Sources for Multicultural Literature   267
            Violet J. Harris

Index   277

Contributors   293

Long Contents ___

Preface   xv

Chapter 1:   The Politics of Children's Literature: Reflections on
             Multiculturalism, Political Correctness, and Christopher
             Columbus   1
             Joel Taxel

   Introduction   3
   The Smithsonian Exhibition   5
   The Politics of Children's Literature   8
   Christopher Columbus and Children's Literature   12
   Christopher Columbus and the Selective Tradition   26
   Summary   30
   References   33

Chapter 2:   Multicultural Literature for Children: Making Informed
             Choices   37
             Rudine Sims Bishop

   Introduction   39
   The Need for Cultural Authenticity   40
   Becoming Informed   43
      Be Aware of Various Types of Multicultural Literature   44
      Read Extensively in Literature Written by "Insiders"   46
   Selection Guidelines   47
      Literary Criteria   47
      Other Criteria   49
      Select a Balanced Collection   49
      Select Individual Books Carefully   50
   Conclusion   51
   References   51
   Children's Books   52

Chapter 3:   Contemporary Griots: African-American Writers of
             Children's Literature   55
             Violet J. Harris

Introduction   57
A Pernicious Tradition   60
   Stereotypes of African Americans   61
In the Beginning: *Clarence and Corinne* and *Little Brown Baby*   64
The Current Status of African-American Children's Literature   68
   Recurring and New Trends and Themes   70
   Other Considerations   74
Contemporary Griots and Word Sorcerers   75
   Virginia Hamilton   76
   Lucille Clifton   77
   Eloise Greenfield   78
   Mildred Taylor   80
   John Steptoe   82
   Walter Dean Myers   84
The Second Wave: Reinforcements   86
   Ashley Bryan   86
   Jeanette Caines   88
   Patricia McKissack   89
The Reinterpreters: No Longer Waiting in the Wings   91
   Angela Johnson   91
   Emily Moore   92
   Patricia Fitzgerald Howard   94
Strategies for Classroom Use   96
   Pre-school and Primary Ages   96
   Intermediate Grades   97
   Upper Elementary   98
   Historical Information   99
Some Final Words   99
Recommended Readings   100
Works Cited   101
Children's Books Cited   104

Chapter 4:   Turning the Page: Asian Pacific American Children's
             Literature   109
             Elaine Aoki

Introduction   111
Asian Pacific American Literature   112

The Evolution of Asian Pacific American Authors and Illustrators   114
What is Being Promoted in the Literature?   116
Effects of Literature   120
Rationale and Goals for Asian Pacific American Children's
    Literature   120
Criteria for Selecting Quality Asian Pacific American Literature   122
Teaching Ideas and Strategies   123
    Folktales   125
    Playing with Language   126
    Point of View   126
    Cross Cultural Experiences Comparisons   127
    Another Look at History   128
    Role Playing   128
Recommended List of Asian Pacific American Children's
    Literature   128
Turning the Page   132
References   133

Chapter 5:   Native Americans in Books for the Young   137
             Donnarae MacCann

Introduction   139
Novels About History   140
Novels About Modern Times   146
Picture Books   150
Folklore and Poetry   153
Histories and Biographies   157
Conclusion   160
Discussion Questions   163
Endnotes   164
References   165
Recommended Titles   168

Chapter 6:   We Have Stories to Tell: A Case Study of Puerto Ricans in
             Children's Books   171
             Sonia Nieto

Introduction   173
A Review of Latino Children's Literature in the United States   174
Puerto Rican Children's Literature: A Case Study   177
Puerto Rican Children's Literature Since 1983   178
Invisibility   179

Absence and Disparagement of the Puerto Rican Family and Recurrent
Use of Stereotypes 182
Defining a Children's Literature: Illuminating the Puerto Rican
Experience 188
The Future of Puerto Rican Children's Literature 191
Whose Responsibility Is It? 191
Using Puerto Rican Children's Literature 193
Conclusion 195
Endnotes 195
Books Reviewed 197
Annotations of Highly Recommended Books 199
References 200

Chapter 7: Ideas a Literature Can Grow On: Key Insights for Enriching
and Expanding Children's Literature About the Mexican-
American Experience 203
Rosalinda B. Barrera, Olga Liguori, and Loretta Salas

Introduction 205
Defining the Mexican-American Experience 208
The Necessity and Challenges of Authentic Portrayal 212
The Vital Role of Mexican-American Voices and Perspectives 218
Literary Potential and Directions for the Future 226
A Source of Learning for All Children 231
Value of Background Knowledge 232
Use of Oral Tradition 233
Literature Study Groups 234
Conclusion 235
Endnotes 236
Children's Book Reviewed 237
References 238
Creative Literature Cited 240

Chapter 8: Caribbean Children's Literature 243
Yahaya Bello

Historical Backgrounds and Introduction 245
Demographics 245
Historical Development of Caribbean Literature 246
Anansi Stories 248
Folk Tales, Legends, and Animal Stories 250

Realistic Fiction   255
Illustrated Books for Early Primary Grades   257
Summary   259
Strategies for Presentation   259
A Supplement for Units in Social Studies and History   259
A Means to Explore Attitudes Concerning Language and Cultural
Diversity   260
A Means to Explore the Similarities in the Responses of African
People to Their Experiences in the Western World   261
Conclusion   261
List of Recommended Books   261
References   263

Chapter 9:   Sources for Multicultural Literature   267
Violet J. Harris

Small Presses   269
Large Presses   270
Organizations   273
Journals   274
Bookstores   275

Index   277

Contributors   293

Preface _____

We are what we read . . . more or less. I am a reader today because my mother purchased books at the supermarket, more than likely Golden Books. She shared them with me and I entered kindergarten a reader. I continued reading because my father took me to sign up for a library card and waited while I selected books, mostly fairy tales. Most of my school reading revolved around basal series and few books stand out until fifth grade. Then, I discovered a new world of literature through two books, *Up From Slavery,* the autobiography of Booker T. Washington and *The Negro in the Making of America,* a history book written by Benjamin Quarles. Both affected me profoundly. I still remember and marvel at the sacrifices Mr. Washington made and the obstacles he overcame. I appreciated his work even more when I made biweekly jaunts to Tuskegee University some years later. Professor Quarles made me aware of Richard Allen, Frederick Douglass, Phylliss Wheatley, Harriet Tubman, and other heroes and heroines, some celebrated, others unsung.

A few years later, I was even more fortunate. It was the late 1960s and the Black Arts Movement was in full bloom and the junior high I attended was located a half city block from Ellis' Bookstore. Ellis' Bookstore was a haven dedicated to African-American, Caribbean, and African literature, history, and periodicals. I spent a significant portion of my allowance there on books such as *The Souls of Black Folk, The Blacker the Berry, Cane, Their Eyes Were Watching God, From Slavery to Freedom* and a host of other books. I especially remember going there one Sunday to hear Nikki Giovanni read poetry. Her poem "Nikki Rosa" remains one of my favorites today.

As I look back, the books I purchased at Ellis' Bookstore were all adult books and some of their multiple meanings escaped me. I did not know that something named African-American children's or young adult literature existed. This lack of awareness was a problem then and now. How many other youngsters go from picture books and series books to adult fiction for some affirmation of themselves? I did not discover African-American children's literature until the mid-1980s while enrolled as a graduate student at the University of Georgia. Professor Ira Aaron gave me two books, Virginia Hamilton's *M. C. Higgins, the Great* and Margo Zemach's *Jake and Honeybunch Go to Heaven;* I then became aware of an extraordinary body of literature. Hamilton touched me in the way that I remember Washington and Quarles had; they each made me feel proud and they gave me some historical memories and knowledge. A course taught by Joel Taxel on women and minorities in children's literature was influential as well. I recount these literary experiences only to convey the lack of awareness many of us possess about children's literature written by people of color and to detail the monumental effects the books can engender.

I became convinced that the literacy achievement of African-American children would improve if they could see themselves and their experiences, history, and culture reflected in the books they read. I still hold firmly to that belief. I want children to discover African-American literature and the literature of other people of color in a more systematic fashion. I want it to become an integral component of schooling. I am hopeful that children will encounter books such as *Me and Neesie, Abuela, Tucking Mommy In,* and *Hawk, I'm Your Brother* with as much ease as *The Tale of Peter Rabbit.*

Now, with the assistance of some remarkable scholars, adults have available a thoughtful and informative guide for the selection of multicultural literature. The book required nearly three years of sustained efforts. First, I had to convince the publishers that a market for this kind of text existed. Second, I had to decide what constituted multicultural literature and which groups to include. This was not an easy task. Some reviewers wanted a chapter on girls and women, others wanted Southern Whites and Jews, and I wondered about the other groups usually placed under the rubric of multiculturalism: the elderly, gays and lesbians, linguistic and religious minorities, and the disabled. Would I include them? In the end, I decided to concentrate on those who are most excluded and marginalized, people of color. Then, I had to find individuals who were familiar with the children's literature of a particular group and members of that same group, whenever possible. This was necessary for an insider's perspective. Joel Taxel, Rudine Sims Bishop, Elaine Aoki, Donnarae MacCann, Sonia Nieto, Rosalinda Barrera, and Yahaya Bello agreed to write chapters. I am eternally grateful to each.

Writing the chapters resulted in prolonged introspection, some pain and anger, a bit of weariness, and ultimately, joy and hope for each author. How do you capture those feelings and condense a group's literary history in so few pages? Is it even possible to make anger and pain palatable and inoffensive for readers who might simply want a listing of multicultural books? Undoubtedly many will conclude that you cannot. I still do not have an answer. Nonetheless, these chapters are not diatribes, nor are they intended to evoke guilt. They are intended to serve as catalysts for sharing the literature. I remain hopeful that readers will understand that the authors and illustrators of the literature struggle to find acceptance and this must become known. Readers should become aware of those struggles because they underscore the reasons why most children will not encounter this literature to any great extent. I hope that those who read this book will effect some kind of change and that more children will discover books that touch their hearts and minds.

Inevitably, when one lists those individuals who were helpful in the creation of a book, someone is excluded inadvertently. Nonetheless, special thanks to Sue Canavan and the staff of Christopher-Gordon Publishers, the reviewers, and other individuals who aided each author.

V.J.H.
March 1992

1

The Politics of Children's Literature

Reflections of Multiculturalism, Political Correctness, and Christopher Columbus

Joel Taxel

INTRODUCTION

Although the idea of multiculturalism in children's literature, and in education in general, is hardly new, it is difficult to recall a time when it was subject to more intense discussion and debate. Essentially a movement to expand subjects like history and literature to include the experiences of previously neglected and oppressed groups, within the past year multiculturalism has attracted the attention of such important shapers and reflectors of opinion as *Time, Newsweek, U.S. News and World Report, The Atlantic Monthly* and *The New Republic.*

Time, for example, ominously prefaced its July 8, 1991, cover story bearing the title "Whose America?" with the suggestion that "a growing emphasis on the nation's 'multicultural' heritage exalts racial and ethnic pride at the expense of social cohesion" (p. 12). *The New Republic* referred to multiculturalism as "one of the most destructive and demeaning orthodoxies of our time" (quoted by Cockburn, 1991, p. 690). In a similar vein, Patrick Buchanan captured the essence of the fears of the most extreme critics of multiculturalism when he stated: "When we say we will put America first, we mean also that our Judeo-Christian values are going to be preserved, and our Western heritage is going to be handed down to future generations, not dumped on some landfill called multiculturalism" (quoted by Kopkind, 1992, p. 21).

President Bush himself entered the fray in a speech at the University of Michigan and interjected a sense of crisis and urgency into the debate that was startling to those who have labored for decades to expand the literary canon to include women and people of color and the range of stories and people deemed worthy of inclusion in our history books. In a sense, authors, literary critics, and historians have struggled to overcome what Adolph Reed referred to as the equation of history (and by extension, literature) with "the narratives of the people in charge" (quoted by Cockburn, 1991, p. 691). While the actual target of the President's remarks was what is derisively labelled "political correctness," a movement that *Time* suggested seeks "to suppress thought or statements deemed offensive to women, blacks or other groups" (Allis, Bonfante, and Booth, 1991, p. 13), it is the case that in "most assaults on 'political correctness,' the bogyman is multiculturalism" (Foner and Weiner, 1991, p. 163).

Close examination of the controversies surrounding political correctness and multiculturalism in art, literature, and curriculum in general reveals that they are centrally concerned with how we define ourselves as individuals and understand our nation's past, present, and future possibilities. Because these controversies involve issues that simultaneously are aesthetic, relate to questions of historical interpretation, and often involve myths that are basic to this country's beliefs about itself, they are profoundly political and increasingly contentious. Because the respective sides in this controversy feel passionately about their positions, there is an intensity to the debates that often precludes reasonable discussion and discourse; the sides talk past one another.

In the pages to follow, I will discuss some of the difficult and complicated social and political factors that need to be taken into account when thinking not only of multicultural children's literature, but all forms of popular culture, literature as well as films, television, painting, and so forth. My focus will be on a handful of picturebook biographies chosen from among the many books published in anticipation of the 1992 commemoration of the 500-year anniversary of Christopher Columbus's voyage from Spain to the Western Hemisphere. This discussion hopefully will support my contention that literature for young people is best understood and appreciated when a wide range of factors, political as well aesthetic, are considered.

I begin by examining the firestorm of controversy generated by the "West as America" exhibition at the Smithsonian Institution's National Museum of Art. Criticism was directed especially at the "revisionist" wall texts that accompanied the paintings and photographs by Jackson, Bierstadt, Remington, and Moran that contain mythic images depicting the conquest of the West that are embodied in countless movies, television programs, and novels. For example, Remington's 1903 painting, "The Fight for the Water Hole," depicts an incident that had occurred 30 years earlier in which some tough and determined Texans defended themselves from an attack by Comanche Indians. The work is interpreted by the wall text "as an allegory in which a native-born white elite is surrounded by menacing and uncivilized immigrants" (Foner and Weiner, 1991, p. 164). According to historians Eric Foner and Jon Weiner (1991), this controversy is but the latest manifestation of "the assault on 'politically correct' thought by long-time conservatives, onetime radicals, and academics" who lament the passing of the days before the advent of large numbers of women and minorities on college campuses and other centers of intellectual and cultural significance (p. 163). Displeasure over the Smithsonian exhibit even led to threats by influential members of Congress to cut off funding for the Institute and to the cancellation of plans for the exhibition to visit a number of major American cities. The furor over the exhibition did, however, make it clear, despite the claims of Dinesh D'Souza (1991) and others, that "thought police" on the left are out to destroy intellectual freedom; it is the political right that possesses the power and actually poses the real danger to these freedoms[1] (Foner and Weiner, 1991).

The Smithsonian controversy is worth exploring in further detail because it provides an almost paradigmatic instance of the contentious and increasingly frequent disputes over significant aspects of the cultural life of our nation. This and similar "culture wars" (Shor, 1986) are in fact "interpretive wars" (Casey, 1992), struggles to incorporate the voices and viewpoints of historically powerless, oppressed, and marginalized groups into the narratives accorded status and respect in this society, and the reaction of dominant social groups to these efforts. That is, attempts to alter or amend particular definitions and conceptions of our nation's experience are understood best as part of the long standing and determined struggle of African and Native Americans and women to wrest control from "the people in charge" of the historical and literary narratives that are so significant to a nation's understanding of itself. Literature written expressly for young people, of course, has been enmeshed in controversies of this sort for quite some time (e.g., Sims, 1982; Taxel, 1981, 1986, 1988).

THE SMITHSONIAN EXHIBITION

The paintings in the exhibition represent the settling of the West as a part of the inexorable, divinely ordained advance of human history across the continent. The obstacles in the way of this inevitable march of history were a massive continent with an "untamed" wilderness that was to give up its treasures to the courageous, enterprising, and ingenious settlers from Europe who moved westward bringing with them Enlightenment ideas of progress and democracy which they perfected as they tamed the savage wilderness. This view is best articulated in Frederick Jackson Turner's "frontier thesis," which saw western expansion:

> As a mystical social process in which European culture was stripped away by settlers' encounter with nature. On the frontier, emerged the quintessential American, cut free from the European past and devoted to individualism, democracy, and equality. (Foner and Weiner, 1991, p. 163)

In these stories, the Native Peoples who had resided for centuries on the continent were regarded as obstacles and inconveniences not all that different from the rivers to be forded, the mountains to be climbed. The richly varied native cultures were reduced to stereotypes such as the noble savage, the violent aggressors, or a race doomed by the advance of history. Such stereotypes were repeated in such well known children's books as Newbery Award winners *The Matchlock Gun* (Edmonds, 1941) and *Caddie Woodlawn* (Brink, 1935) and Monjo's (1968) widely known *Indian Summer.* While such stereotypes have been eclipsed by more positive representations such as those seen in films like *Dances With Wolves,* Paul Goble's many fine interpretations of Native American legends (e. g., 1984, 1985), and Joyce Rockwood's masterful and strangely neglected account of the catastrophic effects the arrival of the Spanish had on a vibrant Cherokee culture, *To Spoil the Sun* (1987), traces of the legitimate claims of Native Americans for the continent they had inhabited for millennia are only rarely in evidence in books for young people. As we shall see, such discussion is absent in most of the new books on Columbus.

Foner and Weiner's (1991) discussion of the Smithsonian controversy provides a useful bridge from that controversy and the primary concerns of this chapter. They suggest that the exhibit's wall texts begin with "the unexceptional premises" that the paintings "tell more about the feelings and ideas of the artists and patrons than about the 'Indians' whose lives they represent." That is, "the nineteenth century paintings do not simply record Western 'reality.' Instead . . . they are 'products of convention' rooted in the dominant ideologies of our time" (p. 163).

That narratives about the past, whether they be history or fiction, often tell us as much about the era in which they were written as they do about the era being recreated is hardly a new or radical thought. Consider the differences in point-of-view and perspective between such novels about the antebellum south and slavery as Mitchell's *Gone With the Wind* written in 1936 and Haley's *Roots* (1976), Walker's *Jubilee* (1975), or Lester's collection of short stories, *Long Journey Home* (1972). Similarly, even the most cursory reading of Elizabeth Yates's' Newbery winning biography, *Amos Fortune, Free Man* (1950), and Virginia Hamilton's acclaimed, *Anthony Burns: The Defeat and Triumph of an Escaped Slave* (1988) reveal as much about evolving societal attitudes toward African-Americans as they do about the lives they seek to portray. Finally, my own study of Revolutionary War fiction (Taxel, 1983) pointed out that the differences between books like *Johnny Tremain* (Forbes, 1943) and *My Brother Sam is Dead* (Collier and Collier, 1976) tell us as much about the attitudes of their respective authors toward World War II and the Vietnam War as they do the American Revolution.

The Smithsonian exhibit wall texts reflect the work of the "New Western" historians who conceive of the West's development as "a complex history, not simple heroic progress." New West History holds that "American history contained many Wests, all more or less "invented," all different and ranging from the prosaic and intermittently violent reality of white settlement and Native American dispossession" (Foner and Weiner, 1991, p. 163). Kathryn Lasky provides a similar glimpse of the west in her novels *Beyond the Divide* (1983) and *The Bone Wars* (1988). Elsewhere, Lasky (1990) discusses the gulf between what her research led her to understand about the history of the West and the "fictions of history" she encountered as a child in the fifties in movies and television programs such as *Gunsmoke* and books that she read. The West as Lasky came to know it, included "consistent and appalling history of violence against women," and had little in common with the enduring fictions of history so favored by guardians of our national mythology such as Patrick Buchanan. For critics of the Smithsonian exhibition, there is no place in the accounts of western expansion and settlement of the genocide against Native Americans that in a very real sense can be traced to October 12, 1492 (Bigelow, 1992, Meltzer, 1990).

What critics of the Smithsonian exhibit, of multiculturalism, and of revisionist approaches to Columbus are seeking instead is "nothing less than an entire interpretation of the American past. What they want is the kind of relentlessly celebratory account of American development so common in the 1950s" (Foner and Weiner, 1991, p. 163). Many of the disputes over the role of art, literature, film, and history (and narrative in general) in fashioning our understanding of our past and present have been clouded and obscured by accusations that particular groups are seeking to impose "politically correct" thinking on society. Despite such claims, the outcome of the Smithsonian controversy (i. e., the fact that the exhibition's planned tour was cancelled) supports the contention Foner and Weiner (1992) and Cockburn (1991) that the current imbroglios over political correctness and multiculturalism are better seen as resentment and resistance of conservative forces to the social changes of the past several decades (e. g., the women's and civil rights movements), and a desire to return to the more tranquil days when mythology passed for history. Cockburn (1991) spoke to this very point when he stated that "the will to retain a useful historical amnesia lies at the heart of the fury about political correctness" (p. 690). As we shall see, many of the recent books about Columbus suffer from just such an amnesia, more precisely, a troubling inability to deal forthrightly with the catastrophic impact Columbus's arrival in the western hemisphere had on native cultures.

THE POLITICS OF CHILDREN'S LITERATURE

Foner and Weiner's (1991) "seemingly unexceptional premise" that art forms, whether they be painting or literature, "are products of convention rooted in the dominant ideology of their time" must not, of course, lead to the reduction of literary works to simple reflections of conventions rooted in ideology. To do so would be to grossly overextend an important theoretical insight and would be bad criticism as well (Taxel, 1983, 1991b). On the other hand, to ignore the influence of larger social, political, and ideological forces on literary creation, production,[2] and consumption (i. e., response to literature), to assume that the authors, editors, and readers are unaffected by such influences, is equally problematic. Despite *this* seemingly unexceptional claim, several decades of research revealing the continued existence of a selective tradition in children's literature favoring the perspectives and world views of dominant social groups (e. g., Apple and Christian-Smith, 1991; MacCann and Woodard, 1972; Taxel, 1981, 1983, 1986), and the increasing influence of innovative approaches to literary and cultural analysis (e. g., Belsey, 1980; Roman and Christian-Smith, 1988), it remains the case that the dominant, if not exclusive, thrust of criticism in children's literature continues to rest on the assumption that literary works are objects to be contemplated, revered, and cherished. That is, literature, like art in general, is believed to exist for its own sake and have little, if anything, to do with politics, let alone ideology. Analysis of literature, above all, involves issues of style, character, setting, plot, theme, point-of-view, and so forth. To mix politics and literature, this viewpoint holds, can lead only to the subversion and perversion of the art from (Townsend, 1969).

Although the books discussed below are biographies, the case I will make for the politics of children's literature primarily is concerned with fiction. Clearly, it is more difficult, perhaps impossible, to deny that biography and other nonfiction are not, in the most fundamental senses, political. The long-standing habit of selecting political or military leaders, white Anglo males, rather than African-American women, movie stars rather than obscure political activists, for biographies makes important political statements about what and who we value. In addition, authors of biography for young people, in varying degrees, take liberties in inventing dialogue and illustrators create graphic images that suggest meanings that go beyond what an historian might feel is justifiable on the basis of this historical record. The point here is that while the political dimensions of biography and history are comparatively easy to establish, it is essential to understand that even pure fiction has that dimension as well. Because it is essential that an understanding of the politics of literature extend beyond the books I have chosen to discuss, I focus my remarks on the most difficult case to make.

An influential and oft-quoted article by Townsend (1969) is representative of the views of those who maintain that "in writing there is no substitute for the creative imagination, and in criticism there is no criterion except literary merit." Although Townsend qualifies his stance somewhat by admitting the relevance of a books' contribution "to moral perception or social adjustment or the advancement of a minority group," he insists that the assessment of a book's racial attitude rather than its literary values is a dangerous step on the road to "literature as propaganda."

Townsend's reiteration of the distinction between a work's aesthetic properties and its social, political, historical, and cultural values was a powerful restatement of the view that literature exists for its own sake, that it was an art form occupying what might be termed an ethereal realm that was beyond politics and ideology, perhaps, outside of history itself. This approach is illustrative of the extent to which discussions about literature for young people are depoliticized. Despite the over 20 years since the publication of Townsend's essay, I submit that the preeminant concern of critics remains with the selection of the "best books," with best being defined in terms of literary and aesthetic values.

In an important discussion of these matters, Kelly (1984) stated that whatever else it might be, literary quality is "that which the world's great books purportedly have in common;" it is timeless and speaks to what is "universal" in human beings. Literary value is believed to be primarily a function of form rather than content; it is believed to reside "in the formal properties of a work rather than in its content" and a literary work can be about anything as long as it embodies appropriately crafted "organic" form. Perhaps Kelly's most significant point for the present discussion is his assertion that the values critics insist are literary are, in fact, based on "a correspondence to things as they are" or "the critic's conception of 'truth.'" Consequently, a purely literary approach to literature is a "chimera" because evaluation based on conventional literary values "may mask what is fundamentally at issue — a critic's acceptance or rejection of the moral and social implications of an author's fictive world." "So-called literary approaches," Kelly concludes, "are specific cultural allegiances wrapped in the mantle of art and labelled handled with reverence" (p. 3).

Eloise Greenfield (1985), a noted author of books for young people, echoed a similar sentiment when she addressed the question of whether art can be justifiably seen as political.

> There is a viewpoint which denies the relevance of this question, that holds art to be sacrosanct, subject to scrutiny only as to its esthetic value. This viewpoint is in keeping with the popular myth that genuine art is not political. It is true that politics is not art, but art is political. Whether in its interpretation of the political realities, or in its attempt to ignore these realities, or in its distortions, or in its advocacy of a different reality, or in its support of the status quo, all art is political and every books carries its author's message. (p. 20)

Kelly (1974) also argued against limiting analysis and criticism of literature to a work's capacity to generate emotional and intellectual responses in readers stating that to restrict analysis to literature's inherent power or ability to evoke responses eliminated the need to examine the complex forces that shape both the creation and effect of literary works. This challenge to the view that literary creation and aesthetic judgements were independent of the author's and the reader's cultural and political context led Kelly (1970) to suggest that children's literature is best conceived of as a symbolic form that functions to reaffirm "the values, principles, and assumptions that structure and give meaning to a specific vision of the world. Literature directs the attentions and questions of young people by providing a statement of 'how things really are'" (p. 25). Sims's (1982) comment that "belief in the power of literature to change the world underlies most of the controversies in the field of children's literature" (p. 1), speaks to the widely accepted view that the values, principles, and assumptions affirmed in children's books are internalized by readers as well.

A significant move away from the exclusively aesthetic approach to the criticism and analysis of children's books was discernible when the civil rights and women's movements were garnering national and international attention. Concerns about the oppression and powerlessness of people of color and women led many, perhaps inevitably, to look at the manner in which these groups were represented in children's books (e. g., Broderick, 1973; Larrick 1972; Lieberman, 1972; MacCann and Woodard, 1972, 1977; Sims, 1982; Taxel, 1978, 1981; Weitzman et al., 1973). The rationale for such studies was the belief that literature was more than simple entertainment and nourishment for the developing imaginations and sensibilities of the young. While no one seriously questioned whether literature should be a source of imaginative pleasure and delight, it also was recognized that literature either implicitly or explicitly provides statements about a host of critically important social and political questions: what it means to be human; the relative worth of boys and girls, men and women, people from various racial, ethnic, and religious communities; the value of particular kinds of action; how we relate to one another, and about the nature of community, and so forth. In their retrospective look at three decades of research on gender stereotyping in children's books, Peterson and Lach (1990), for example, pinpointed what was undoubtedly a central concern of those raising the alarm about various kinds of bias in children's literature:

> It seemed obvious that repeated exposure to these kinds of images [i.e., sexist images] was likely to have detrimental effects on the development of children's self-esteem . . . and on the perceptions children have on their own, and others' abilities and possibilities. (p. 186)

Discussions about the sociocultural and political dimensions of literature have become part of a broader critique of society that, among many things, seeks to explain how and why ideologies such as racism and sexism are so ingrained in consciousness as to become part of our common-sense understanding of how the world works. Although the past several decades have been marked by undeniable improvements in the manner, for example, African-Americans are represented in children's literature, the nature of evolution of the representations of girls and women offer strikingly contradictory evidence. The proliferation of romance novels such as the "Sweet Dreams" and "Sweet Valley High," as well as the enormously popular "Babysitters Club" books, indicate that we often take steps forward only to go backwards. The overt racism of the Duke and Buchanan campaigns, evidence of a massive backlash against the women's struggles for social equality (Faludi, 1991), indicates that it is hardly time to declare victory. The continuing strength of calls for more multicultural children's literature, the vehemence of the reactions against the concept, indeed, the very existence of this volume, are illustrations of the continued importance of this issue.

In light of these all-too-real facts, critics continue to look closely at aspects of the social environment such as children's literature, television, films, and so on, that influences children's developing social constructions of the world. Wexler (1982) is helpful in providing a framework in which to conceptualize the problem. He suggests that studies of cultural forms, such as books, films, television programs, painting, and the like, point to the fact that "social power is culturally represented" and that "knowledge and culture are essential moments in the process of social domination." Because class culture is presented and represented as common culture, "the present order is seen as "natural and eternal" and the cultures of oppressed groups are silenced (p. 279).

Despite the changes referred to above and the existence of what have been referred to as "voices of resistance" (Taxel, 1991a), it remains the case that the selective tradition governing literature and other aspects of culture continues to significantly underrepresent women and people of color, or present them in pejorative and stereotypic ways. Selective traditions are among the critical factors shaping our beliefs, world views, and perceptions of ourselves and the society we live in. In short, the profoundly and unavoidable political nature of culture, whether an exhibition of paintings at the Smithsonian Institute or books about Christopher Columbus, no longer can be denied.

CHRISTOPHER COLUMBUS AND CHILDREN'S LITERATURE

It is neither surprising nor inappropriate that children's book publishers are seizing the Quincentennial anniversary of Columbus's momentous voyage from Spain to the Western Hemisphere as the opportunity to make available a wide array of books on Columbus. Virtually every publisher's catalogue for the years 1991 or 1992 includes at least one book (fiction, as well as nonfiction, in formats suitable for preschoolers to students in high school and beyond) about the man who insisted on the title, "the Admiral of the Ocean Sea."

The question for many of us is not whether it is appropriate to commemorate the arrival of the Nina, the Pinta, and the Santa Maria on the coast of San Salvador on October 12, 1492. Virtually all historians agree that Columbus's arrival on the shores of the "New World" was an occurrence of epochal significance, one that changed the world forever. It is the event that signaled the beginning of the Great Age of Exploration that, in the words of Gardner Soule's 1988 biography, "set in motion the greatest migrations ever, before or since, as European families set out over the entire globe." Columbus's importance in American history certainly derives from the sense that his voyage marks its beginning, what Bigelow (1992) refers to as a "secular genesis" (p. 118). Gray (1991), writing in *Time,* put it this way: "Columbus's journey was the first step in a process that produced a daring experiment in democracy [i. e., the United States], which in turn became a symbol and a haven of liberty" (p. 52). Less well-known, and conspicuously absent from even the most recent of the Columbus books, is an acknowledgement that Columbus's arrival on the coast of San Salvador on October 12, 1492, initiated an "American holocaust" (Rethinking Schools, 1991, p. 2) that resulted in the virtual genocide of the hemisphere's native population. In addition is the fact that central to the great migrations referred to by Soule was the Atlantic slave trade, an enterprise that was unremittingly brutal and resulted in death and enslavement for millions of Africans (e. g., Lester, 1968; Tannenbaum, 1946). Bigelow's (1992) outrage at the persistent silence of Columbus books on these matters is palpable. At the outset of "Once Upon a Genocide: Christopher Columbus in Children's Literature," an examination of a small sample of biographies on Columbus,[3] he asserts that the Columbus biographies "function as primers on racism and imperialism. They teach youngsters to accept the right of white people to rule over people of color, of powerful nations to dominate weaker nations" (p. 112). In a similar vein, Rethinking Schools, a Milwaukee-based organization dedicated to radical school reform, sees the significance of the Columbus story as "the beginning of a winner's history that profoundly neglects the lives and perspectives of all the *Others,* not just people of color: women, working class people, the poor (Rethinking Schools, 1991, p. 3, emphasis in original).

This startlingly frank appraisal may jar the sensibilities of some precisely because the perspective is so at variance with the one enshrined in our national mythology, what I have referred to the dominant selective tradition. According to traditional accounts, Columbus's journey to the New World is depicted "as a 'great adventure' led by 'probably the greatest sailor of his time.' It's a story of courage and superhuman tenacity. Columbus is brave, smart, and determined (Bigelow, 1992, p. 112). Milton Meltzer, author of one of the few books that treats Columbus in a comprehensive and balanced fashion, describes the prevailing Columbus myth as follows:

> Columbus was one of the best and bravest men of his time. Because he loved adventure, he got the king and queen of Spain to provide him with three ships so he could sail across the ocean to open up a new route to Asia — and prove the world was round. Landing on some island in the Caribbean, he "discovered" America and took possession of the land for Spain. He called the red-skinned people "Indians." He gave them some trinkets and returned to Spain with a few of the Indians to show Ferdinand and Isabella. (Meltzer, 1992, p. 2)

According to Meltzer (1992), the danger of providing young people with myths rather than history is that mythology "makes it easier for the people who wield political power to get away with platitudes and pieties they feed to the public so they can carry out their policies at home and abroad. If we do not learn how to ask probing questions about the past, how will we meet the challenges of the present?" (p. 2). Meltzer's (1990) book points to a host of important questions about, for example, the social context of Columbus's world and about the relation between the reasons the myths suggest led to the voyage (e. g., to prove that the world was round) and the motives actually supported by the historical record. Also considered by Meltzer are the peoples and the civilizations that had existed for millennia that Columbus "encountered"[4] at the end of his voyage. Perhaps the most difficult question of all, however, is whether the destruction of so many peoples and cultures who lived, in Rockwood's (1987) words, "on the other side of history" and the initiation of the barbaric Atlantic slave trade that commenced shortly after Columbus's voyage can continue to be justified in the name of "progress."

It is important to note, however, that although Meltzer (1990) goes a long way in demystifying the myths about Columbus, he avoids the temptation to demonize him. His book thus is a balanced point of reference, a benchmark, that I will utilize in my brief sampling of a handful of the recent Columbus books. I have chosen to limit my discussion to a small group[5] of picturebooks about Columbus for two reasons. First, these are the books that are likely to provide children with their introduction to the Columbus myth. Consequently, because these books are likely to provide children with formative impressions about Columbus, it is important to see the relation between the myth criticized by Bigelow and Meltzer and what the newer books have to offer. Second, is the more pragmatic reason that the greater complexity of the longer books raises too many issues to discuss in a chapter of this sort. Suffice it to say, however, that except for Meltzer's book, the problems found in the books to be discussed below invariably are found in the longer books.[6] This is all the more disturbing in view of perhaps the naive belief that greater space and a more mature audience would have led authors to be a bit more daring in raising the difficult issues that Columbus compels us to entertain. Fortunately, there are at least a few books that provide standards of excellence by which to assess the others.

Christopher Columbus and the World Around Him includes ample discussion of Columbus's remarkable skills as a navigator and an account of his epochal voyages (there were four) that are the constants of every book available. The book includes an illuminating discussion of the late 15th century world that gave rise to Columbus, a world moving from medievalism to the world of the early Renaissance and the Age of Exploration and Discovery. Although it is not to be expected that such a discussion be included in the briefer books designed for young children, its absence in the more detailed and comprehensive books intended for older readers is a serious deficiency (e. g., Soule, 1988; West and West, 1991). The brutal treatment of the indigenous inhabitants of the lands "discovered" by Columbus is examined in the context of the prevailing attitudes of his day that automatically viewed Native Americans as inferior beings who could be brutalized, enslaved, and murdered without the slightest pause. As Meltzer (1990) notes, "The idea that the Indians might have a right to determine their own way of life and to govern themselves never occurred to Columbus" (p. 92). We come to see that his treatment of this group of "others" is consistent with that endured by Spain's centuries old Jewish community who were the principle target of the brutal Spanish inquisition that was occurring at precisely this time.[7]

Jews were given the choice of converting to Christianity, leaving their homes, or facing execution. Significantly, Columbus's departure from the small port of Palos on August 3, 1492, rather than Spain's principal Atlantic port Cadiz, was to ensure that his small fleet did not get tied up with the masses of Jews attempting to flee Spain by the August 2 deadline. By providing such historical context, Meltzer makes it possible for readers to understand Columbus's dual mission, the discovery of a sea route to the gold and other riches of Asia and the extension of the "Catholic domain by converting the heathen of Asia to 'our Holy Faith'" (Meltzer, 1990, pp. 73-74). The ultimately genocidal treatment of the native people encountered by Columbus, like the treatment by Ferdinand and Isabella of the Jews of Spain, clearly was predicated on a view that anyone not of his faith were less than fully human "others" who could be pushed around and disposed of with impunity.

A final point of significance about *Christopher Columbus and the World Around Him* is that Meltzer introduces us to contemporaries of Columbus who were as outraged by the heinous actions of the Spanish as we are today. His primary source of information on the tragic fate of the inhabitants of the Western Hemisphere is Bartolomé de Las Casas, the first priest to be ordained in the Americas. In the *The History of the Indies,* Las Casas described Spanish actions as "impious, criminal and ignominious" and decried the "blood stained riches, obtained by theft and usurpation [and] accompanied by [the] slaughter and annihilation of these people" (quoted by Meltzer, 1992, p. 7). Sources such as these make it clear that Meltzer's concern about the tragic fate of the Native Americans is not simply a backward projection of late 20th century ethics and morality ("political correctness" in contemporary parlance) but was shared by at least some of Columbus's contemporaries.

Having considered Meltzer's treatment of Columbus, a book that provides a welcomed reminder that there *are* American writers and publishers willing to ask difficult questions that lead to painful answers, it might be useful to compare it briefly to a book that exemplifies the Columbus myth, Ingri and Edgar Parin D'Aulaire's (1955) picture book biography, *Columbus.* While admitting that learned men said that the world "was not small and flat but a huge ball that spun around in space," (p. 7) the D'Aulaires place great stock in story that Columbus set out to prove the world is round (e. g., pp. 8-9). Columbus's adventurous spirit and desire to prove that the world was round to a skeptical world[8] becomes a substitute for more mercenary motives, such as the desire for gold and fame, as the central motivation for "great enterprise of the Indies" (Meltzer, 1990, pp. 54, 74, 112, 130-31; Zinn, 1980, p. 3). Although the D'Aulaires do not deny that Columbus had mercenary motives, they minimize the possible impact of such baser interests by joining them to religious considerations: "He began to think that the Lord had chosen him to find the riches of the East for himself and to carry the Christian faith to the heathens" (p. 16). Similarly, "the good Queen Isabella" is presented as one who wanted to "share her

Christian faith with the people in the East who had never heard about Christ" (p. 18). No mention is made of the ways such religious zeal fed the murderous intolerance that led the Inquisition, and the previously mentioned expulsion of the Jews, or contributed to the rationalization of the policy of enslaving the native peoples of the "new" world. Finally, the D'Aulaires' characterization of the Moors of Spain as "heathens" (e. g., pp. 16, 17) and their description of Native Americans as "naked red-skinned savages" (p. 34) effectively reduces them to "others"[9] whose lands then can be justifiably seized in the name of Christian sovereigns thousands of miles away: "He stuck the Holy Cross and the banner of Spain into the glistening sand and claimed the land for the Spanish crown" (p. 34).

The possibility that Columbus's arrival on the shores of the Western Hemisphere might be considered the initial step in a European invasion is an idea that never seems to have occurred to the D'Aulaires. Such a formulation, like that offered by the wall texts in the Smithsonian exhibition previously discussed, raises troubling questions of the history that follows (i. e., that of the United States). In my view, this is more than simply a case of the failure of individual authors to imagine alternative explanations for a pivotal episode of history. Instead, the dominant conceptions of Columbus are better viewed as part of the complex process whereby a selective tradition is constructed. Meltzer's book clearly illustrates, however, that this conception now is being challenged and contested.[10] It remains now to be seen what other writers, and their publishers, have chosen to contribute to this critically important interpretive war over how the important story of Christopher Columbus will be presented to our children.

Biographies generally focus on the growth, development, events, and forces that lead their subjects to do whatever it was that deems them worthy of remembering. They usually culminate in accounts of those signal events or accomplishments that mark individual's life as one of distinction. Joan Anderson's (1991) *Christopher Columbus: From Vision to Voyage,* a book that contains photographs by George Ancona of actors and actresses in period dress and settings, is unusual in that it deals exclusively with the events leading to the approval of Columbus's voyage by Isabella and Ferdinand; the voyage itself is not described. "This book," states Anderson in the author's note,

> is about a man of great valor — one who singlehandedly changed the course of world history. So many historical figures seem larger than life. The myths that have grown up around them are so grand that people tend

to see them as almost superhuman. After studying the life of Columbus, it became clear to me that he was in many ways an ordinary man . . . (unpaged)

Despite the intent to provide a portrait of an "ordinary man," the focus on Columbus's single-minded effort to secure funding for his expedition results in a portrait of a man who hardly is ordinary. Further, the absence of **any** real sense of the context of Columbus's era (e. g., Spain's centuries long war against the Moors, the Inquisition, and the expulsion of the Jews, and so forth), gives one the feeling that he stands outside of history. The book's final lines jump ahead to October 12, 1492, and note that when Christopher Columbus sighted land in the "New World" seventy days later he, "without knowing it . . . ushered in the Age of Discovery," again reinforces the view that Columbus stands virtually alone on the stage of history. Finally, and most troubling, is the implied assumption that the Age of Discovery was occurrence without its negative dimensions. As we have seen, such an assessment is a question of perspective or point of view. Anderson's decision to limit her account in the manner just described makes it easy to render those who greeted Columbus when he arrived in San Salvador both voiceless and invisible and seemingly absolves her of the need to raise the sort of disturbing questions posed by Meltzer. Thus, rather than challenging prevailing myths, *Christopher Columbus: From Vision to Voyage* reinforces the traditional story of Columbus as a man of great courage and tenacity and his voyage as a great adventure (Bigelow, 1992, 112).

Four other brief picturebooks also emphasize the drama and adventure that is undeniably central to Columbus's story. Like *Christopher Columbus: From Vision to Voyage,* however, they also effectively transform the native peoples of the Western hemisphere into an "absent presence" whose tragic story is rendered insignificant when compared to Columbus's great adventure. Jean Marzello's (1991) *In 1492* is designed for the youngest readers and begins with the rhyme taught to countless generations of American schoolchildren: "In fourteen hundred and ninety two Columbus sailed the ocean blue" (unpaged). We learn that "he sailed by night; he sailed by day" and "used the stars to find his way" until, finally, on "October 12 their dream came true." We **do** meet the Arawak natives who "were very nice; They gave the sailors food and spice," after which Columbus "sailed on to find some gold to bring back home, as he'd been told." While admitting that Columbus was **not** the first American, he nevertheless 'was brave, and he was bright."

The simplicity of the rhyming text is enhanced by Steve Björkman's energetic, brightly-colored, cartoon illustrations. Despite its disarming simplicity, *In 1492* is a virtual primer into the prevailing myths about Columbus. Marzello does indeed show that Columbus was brave and bright and that his dream came true, but she provides not even the slightest indication that when he was unable to find sufficient gold to satisfy Ferdinand and Isabella during his later voyages, Columbus was "determined to fill up his ships with another source of wealth, human labor." Among those selected were the "very nice" Arawak natives (Meltzer, 1990, p. 141). Eventual Arawak resistance led to a brutal Spanish response: "When the Spaniards took prisoners they hanged them or burned them to death. Among the Awaraks, mass suicides began . . . Infants were killed to save them from the Spaniards. In two years, through murder, mutilation, or suicide, half of the 250,000 Indians on Haiti were dead" (Zinn, 1980, p. 4).[11]

There are similar problems with *The Great Adventure of Christopher Columbus* (1992), a pop-up book that is the product of a collaboration between two of the most respected names in contemporary American children's literature, Jean Fritz and Tomie dePaola. Among the many biographies by Fritz is *Where do you think you're going Christopher Columbus?* (1980), the only book about which Bigelow (1992) has anything remotely positive to say. Written in Fritz's distinctively wry style, *The Great Adventure of Christopher Columbus* packs a surprising amount of text into its tightly designed format. We read, for example, that "like most people," Columbus "knew that the world was round like a ball" (unpaged). We also hear of the outrageous demands Columbus made to the Spanish monarch "in return for a successful voyage. He wanted titles: Admiral of the Ocean Sea, Viceroy and Governor General of the lands he discovered. He wanted top keep for himself one-tenth of all treasure he brought back and he wanted all these rights to be handed down to his family." Although, as the book's title makes clear, the focus is on the adventurous aspects of the voyage, Fritz at least makes it clear that some of Columbus's motives were mercenary.[17]

The book's treatment of the initial encounters between Columbus and the "Indians" is troubling, however, especially as compared to the one contained in Fritz's earlier book. In *Where do you think you're going Christopher Columbus?*, Fritz jokingly asks readers to imagine how the native inhabitants of San Salvador might have perceived the arriving Spanish. After noting that the Spanish were surprised to see the naked natives, she states, "the natives were even more surprised to see the dressed Spaniards. All that cloth over their bodies! What were they trying to hide? Tails, perhaps?" (pp. 31-32). Bigelow (1992) comments that Fritz's recreation of this scene "seems to poke fun at Columbus" rather than "to seriously consider the Indian's point of view." While "this interior dialogue for the Indians" does ridicule the Spanish explorers, it also has the effect of trivializing the Indians' concerns" (p. 115). In contrast, Joyce Rockwood's haunting, *To Spoil the Sun* (1987), which centers on another of the initial contacts between Native Americans and the Spanish, makes clear the catastrophic consequences of this and similar encounters and that they hardly were occasions for jocularity.

Despite this caveat, Fritz's earlier book at least raises the possibility that a reader might attempt to see Columbus's arrival form the Native American perspective. No such possibility is afforded by *The Great Adventure of Christopher Columbus*. On the page containing a pop-up figure of Columbus planting the Spanish flag on the beach on San Salvador, Fritz explains that as the Spanish ships came closer to the shore, "Columbus looked for a glint of gold; there were no glints. There were people, but they weren't dressed in gold-embroidered robes. They weren't dressed at all. Stark naked — that's what they were, so this couldn't be Japan." After "claiming" the land for Spain, Columbus asks the Indians,

> Which way to Japan? They didn't understand a word he said, so he pointed to the gold rings that the men wore in their noses. He motioned to show that he wanted gold. Where was it? .... *That* way, the natives pointed East. So that was the way Columbus sailed. He found more islands but no gold. He wasn't discouraged; he was sure to find gold one day.

Fritz (1992) thus does point to the extent to which a desire for gold drove Columbus; even in this momentous first landing, it is not very far from his mind. What she does not hint at is the lengths he and his crew would go in the face of later disappointments and discouragements over the lack of sufficient gold. During his infinitely more ambitious second voyage, Columbus still entertained the hope that he would be able to carry large amounts of gold home in order to pay dividends to the crown and the others who had invested in his Enterprise of the Indies. Believing that the Indians were concealing rich fields of gold on the island of Hispaniola, Columbus

> ordered all Indians from the age of fourteen up, to collect a fixed amount of gold every three months. Each person who delivered his tribute of gold was given a copper token to hang around his neck. Indians found without that token had their hands and feet cut off and were left to bleed to death. (Meltzer, 1990, pp. 141-42; Zinn, 1980, p. 4)

A final point needs to be made about this and similar recreations of Columbus's initial encounter with the native peoples of the Western Hemisphere. Bigelow (1992) suggests that a variant of this scene is read by virtually every child in the United States and that it

> constructs a powerful metaphor about the relations between different countries and races. It is a lesson not just about the world 500 years ago, but about the world *today.* Clothed, armed, Christian, white men from a more technologically "advanced" nation arrive in a land peopled by darker skinned, naked, unarmed, non-Christians — and take over. (p. 115, emphasis in original)

In journal entries recorded on the very day he arrived in the West Indies, Columbus acknowledged the remarkable generosity of the people he encountered. "Anything they have, if it is asked for they never say no, but rather invite the person to accept it." Despite this gracious behavior, Columbus also notes that "with fifty men they could all be subjected and made to do all that I wished" (quoted by Meltzer, 1992, pp. 4-5). About these thoughts and feelings, the books like *In 1492* and *The Great Adventure of Christopher Columbus,* as well as most of those to follow, say little, if anything. In sharp contrast, Meltzer (1990) strikes a markedly different tone when he connects this statement to the history that follows. Stating that the lands Columbus had "discovered" would soon be called the "New World of the Americas" by Europeans, Meltzer concludes the chapter covering the first encounter with the Native Americans by stating what should be obvious but is not precisely because most of the books about Columbus end before the mythic tale they tell takes its gruesome turn. Those that don't stop usually look the other way, minimize the enormity of the tragedy, or ignore it all together.

> It was not a New World to the millions of dark-skinned Native Americans. They had been there thousands of years before the white man would "discover" them, enslave them, and exterminate them. (p. 86)

Steve Lowe's selections from *The Log of Christopher Columbus* (1992) provide Columbus's own account of the perilous tension-filled voyage into the unknown. Columbus's doubts and fears, his description of breathtaking sites, his concerns about the threat of mutiny among the crew are brought to life by Robert Sabuda's striking illustrations. The combination of words and illustrations is quite powerful but the book unquestionably serves to reinforce, yet again, the mythic tale of the voyage as a great adventure without any damaging consequences. Lowe's introduction fosters as well a misconception about Columbus's motivation for making the voyage: "Columbus had the dream of sailing west to India, but not the money.... He made a last appeal to Ferdinand and Isabella: Pay my expenses, then name me admiral of the not-so-wide ocean, and I will bring you back the gold of India" (unpaged). All accounts seem to agree that Columbus undoubtedly was an adventurous man who sought to do something that no one was known to have done before. However, for Lowe to claim that he was without selfish motives is inexplicable in light of the well-documented fact that Columbus "wanted enormous rewards if his Enterprise should succeed" (Meltzer, 1990, p. 67). Lowe's puzzling treatment of this issue perpetuates the falsehood that gets to the heart of the way readers are asked to understand Columbus.

The next-to-last excerpt is from October 12, 1492, the same day that Columbus wrote that "with fifty men they could all be subjected and made to do all that I wished" (Meltzer, 1992, pp. 4-5). This telling comment is **not** part of Lowe's text. He instead limits the entry to the following: "No sooner had we concluded the formalities of taking possession of the island than people began to come to the beach, all as naked as their mothers bore them. They are well-built people ... their eyes large and pretty.... They are friendly." The comment excluded by Lowe clearly indicates that Columbus's intentions were not quite so friendly, something made painfully clear by Meltzer and others I have referred to.

Lowe's next and final selection is from November 27, 1492. Here, Columbus writes of the marvelous beauty of the new land: "I told the men with me that, in order to make a report to the Sovereigns of the things they saw, a thousand tongues would not be sufficient to tell, nor my hand to write it, for it looks like an enchanted land." Sabuda's illustration depicts Columbus standing under a tree looking in the distance as the sun sets over a distant mountain. This is the final image in the book; in both words and pictures we gain the impression of Columbus as a conqueror well-satisfied with his new domains.

The effect of Lowe's very careful editing, what he chooses to include and exclude, illustrate in microcosm an essential contention of this chapter: that narratives are value-laden selections from a universe of possibilities and that different selections tell different stories. Historically, it has been the case that the narratives selected as most important are those of the powerful, the adventurous, the victorious, of men like Christopher Columbus. Then, as now, the focus usually is intended to show the subject's "best side" and, as we have seen, most of the accounts stop before things get ugly. In contrast, the narratives and voices of the "losers," the millions of Native Americans who did not survive the European onslaught, for example, are all but lost; they remain a barely audible murmur from "the other side of history." While writing biography, especially biography for children, always involves a process of selection and omission, of emphasis and deemphasis, of presence and absence, the nature and significance of the very specific kinds selection and omission, emphasis and deemphasis, presence and absence, I have been considering point to the incontrovertible existence of a politics of children's literature.

Peter Sis's *Follow the Dream: The Story of Christopher Columbus* (1991) is a truly stunning picturebook whose central theme is the pursuit of dreams, the opening up of new worlds. While, of course, the Columbus saga is the book's subject, the project embodies a quite personal statement by the author/illustrator. Its magnificent layout and design, its remarkably skillful incorporation of period maps, diagrams, and symbols, combine to produce a work that demonstrates the enormous artistic potential of the modern picturebook. However, this book is disturbing to the very degree that it is artful. In every important respect, *Follow the Dream* perpetuates romantic myths about Columbus and effectively silences the voices of those he met when his dream finally was realized.

Sis provides us with considerable insight into the book in his "Note to the Reader." "When I came to America in 1982 [from Czechoslovakia], all I knew about Columbus was that he had sailed the ocean blue in 1492" (unpaged). He read many books and studied maps, some of which "showed Europe surrounded by high walls, with monsters standing beyond."[13] It is here that Sis establishes a personal connection to Columbus for he too grew up in a country surrounded by a "wall," a wall known as the "Iron Curtain." As we know, the wall of 15th century ignorance and superstition did not hold back Columbus. "For him, the outside world was not to be feared but explored." In Sis's skillful hands, Columbus's journey becomes a metaphor for those, like Sis himself, who are unwilling to be restrained by the walls that stand in their way. As such, the book provides a paradigmatic instance of the American dream itself; America **is** the land where, with determination, persistence, and steadfastness, anything is possible. Any wall can be climbed, any ocean crossed if only we follow the dream. Because belief in this core tenet of American ideology is so deeply ingrained, it often is difficult to stand back and hold it up to critical scrutiny. When it is embodied in forms as artistically brilliant as those provided by Peter Sis, the difficulties are exacerbated. Thus it becomes especially important to examine the way he represents the realization of Columbus's dream.

Sis begins by informing us that Christopher Columbus was expected to follow in his father's footsteps and become a weaver. However, he had "his own ideas about his future." His reading, observations of ships in the harbor of Genoa, and conversations with merchants and sailors led him to continue "weaving dreams of adventure and discovery." This dream became, with time, "a plan . . . to reach the Orient by a new route." The remainder of the book is a demonstration of the fact that although "fulfilling his dream was not easy," Columbus succeeded. This simple rendering of the Columbus myth is elaborated and extended by Sis's intricately detailed illustrations.[14] The very conscious simplicity of his telling makes any provision of historical context impossible, a fact that serves to heighten the mythic, almost "beyond history" quality of the book.

The last two pages, in significant respects, are mirror images of one another. The left hand page finds Columbus standing and casting a long shadow "on a beach of white coral" which he "claimed . . . for the King and Queen of Spain." The figure of Columbus casts a long shadow that does not quite reach the ten figures who stand facing him in a pose that many readers describe as "awestruck" or "worshipful." They too cast shadows, although theirs are not nearly as long as that of Columbus. Otherwise, the beach is entirely empty. A variety of birds have been sketched into the border that frames the illustration. Significantly, Sis includes not a single word of text explaining who these people are or how they figure into the dream that clearly just has been fulfilled; those who greeted Columbus are visible for only this brief, unexplained moment after which they disappear from the book, as they did from history.

The facing page takes us to the present. A group of children, accompanied by an adult, stand and gaze with reverence at a towering monument to Columbus. The other figures in the previous illustration have disappeared and the once empty landscape now includes an urban scene replete with rush-hour traffic congestion. The borders of the illustration include sketches of many of the trappings of modern day civilization ranging from rocket ships to hair dryers. Perhaps Sis intended these as an ironic comment on how the world has changed in 500 years. The text on this page tells us that "today we know that what Columbus found was not a new route to the Orient but a new continent." Whether ironic or not, this last page hardly lessens the reverential manner in which Columbus is regarded in both the illustrations and throughout the text. Columbus did follow his dream and "he had reached 'America.'" That the complex civilizations populated by millions of individuals who undoubtedly had dreams of their own collided with that of Columbus is not a part of the story that Peter Sis has chosen to tell. As a result, the image of Christopher Columbus as adventurer, dreamer extraordinaire not only remains unchallenged, it is raised to heights without equal in the books I examined.

The final books to be discussed in this section are by David Adler, author of two popular series of biographies for young readers: the "Picture Book Biographies," designed for the children in primary grades, and the "First Biography Series," intended for children in the middle to upper elementary grades. Adler has written books about Columbus for each series and these books shed some interesting light on the issues under discussion. *A Picture Book of Christopher Columbus* (1991b), illustrated by John and Alexandra Wallner, is a straightforward and rather dry presentation of the by now familiar adventure story of the man who "discovered [sic] a land which was later called America" (unpaged). Although Adler does infer that interest in getting to the Indies where one could get "valuable jewels and spices" was an important factor in Columbus's decision to make the voyage, he only hints at the issues concerning the fate of the native peoples of America. Columbus "claims" the island of San Salvador for Spain, gives the "natives of the island" some trinkets and calls them Indians. He later returns to Spain with "gold trinkets, parrots, and a few Indians," a formulation that does little to suggest to the young readers that these are people worthy of the considerations usually accorded to human beings. Upon his return, we are told only that the men in the settlement Columbus left behind were "cruel to the Indians" and that "the Indians killed them all." This is all Adler has to say in this simple book about these complex issues. He quickly concludes by stating that Columbus "had been a great sailor" who had found "his way across unknown waters and back home again. He had found the New World."

Adler's *Christopher Columbus, Great Explorer* (1991a) has the most lengthy and honest discussion of Columbus's meeting with the Indians of any of the books discussed thus far. It is clear that the author is familiar with Columbus's log as some of the material paraphrases excerpts that are quoted above. Columbus sees "the natives" as a "quiet, gentle, and seemingly peaceful people." He describes them as a "generous people . . . willing to share with him everything they had." Despite this assessment, "Columbus decided that the Indians could be easily converted to Christianity and just as easily made to be obedient servants" (p. 30). Then, in a passage that is remarkable amongst these books for its frankness, Adler states:

> The arrival of Columbus was a tragic happening for the Indians. Europeans
> brought unknown diseases with them. Indians were captured by the

thousands and forced into slavery. Many of them committed suicide rather than be taken to Europe. In the years ahead, millions of Indians would be brutally killed by the conquering people from across the sea. (p. 31)

This remarkably blunt and powerful statement is not followed up. The very next sentence describes Columbus's exploration of San Salvador. Native Americans are mentioned briefly and in passing in several other places (e. g., pp. 36, 45) but the mind boggling fact that the reality of the statement quoted above is never referred to again. Most significantly, it is not weighed in Adler's final accounting of Columbus in the final chapter that revealingly is titled, "A Great Seaman." Columbus, we are told in the book's concluding paragraph,

> was a strong willed, determined man, and a great seaman. He died believing he had reached the East. He hadn't, but the voyages he made changed the world. He linked Europe and America. He began a great era of exploration. His bravery at sea and his discoveries encouraged others to sail to unknown lands. (p. 46)

That this great era of exploration was accompanied by the brutal killing of millions of Indians by "conquering people from across the sea" apparently is deemed less significant than Columbus's strong will and seamanship. This thoroughly value-ladened assessment would be remarkable were it not the case that a similar assessment is either implicit or explicit in most of the books I have examined. Thus, a story that historian Howard Zinn (1980) reminds us began with "conquest, slavery, and death" (p. 7) still retains its aura as a great adventure.

CHRISTOPHER COLUMBUS AND THE SELECTIVE TRADITION

It is important to recognize that the treatment of Columbus found in children's books is not all that different from that found in many of the most respected of the books on the subject published for adults. Zinn (1980) discusses this very point in relation to the work of Samuel Eliot Morison who, before his death, was considered perhaps America's foremost Columbus scholar.[15] Morison's treatment of the Native American holocaust initiated by Columbus highlights some of the critical points about selection, omission, emphasis, and the politics of literature I have sought to make throughout this chapter.

In his widely read, *Christopher Columbus, Mariner,* Morison speaks of the death and enslavement of the native peoples of the Western Hemisphere as follows: "The cruel policy initiated by Columbus and pursued by his successors resulted in complete genocide" (quoted by Zinn, 1980, p. 7). Zinn notes that this forthright statement is "buried halfway into the telling of a grand romance." The remarkable fact of the genocide of millions of people is not even mentioned in Morison's final assessment of Columbus. Although Morison admits that Columbus was not without his faults and defects, he insists that these were

> largely the defects of the qualities that made him great — his indomitable will, his superb faith in God and his own mission as the Christ-bearer to lands beyond the seas, his stubborn persistence despite neglect, poverty, and discouragement. But there was no flaw, no dark side to the most outstanding and essential of his qualities — his seamanship. (quoted by Zinn, 1980, p. 7).

A crucial fact for Zinn is that Morison *does* mention the horrifying reality of genocide. He makes no attempt to lie outright or omit important information that could lead to "unacceptable conclusions" (pp. 7-8). Indeed, genocide is perhaps the harshest word can select to denote the idea of mass murder. Similarly, we have seen that Adler (1991a) does not flinch from mentioning "millions of Indians would be brutally killed." Both Morison and Adler, however, adopt a different, more subtle and thus difficult to discern strategy to integrate this horrifying fact in their overall conception of Columbus; they mention the reality of genocide and then move on to matters they feel are more important. That is, they acknowledge the reality of mass murder, but then bury it amidst a mass of other information, a strategy that implicitly tells us that mass murder is not that important. Certainly, it should not bear on our final judgment about the man who, after all, did usher in the great age of exploration that led to the foundation of the United States.

Zinn recognizes, of course, that an historian cannot avoid the selection and emphasis of certain facts and the exclusion and deemphasis of others. He offers an intriguing and illuminating analogy between the selectivity of an historian and that of a mapmaker who, needing to "produce a usable drawing for practical purposes," flattens and distorts the earth's shape and then decides from among the myriad possibilities which particular bits of geographic information he or she will include in the map in question. For Zinn, there is no argument to be made against selection, simplification, and emphasis. They are necessary and inevitable for both the cartographer and the historian. There is, however, a very crucial difference.

> The mapmaker's distortion is a technical necessity for a common purpose shared by all people who need maps. The historian's distortion is more than technical, it is ideological; it is released into the world of contending interest, where any chosen emphasis supports (whether the historian means to or not) certain kinds of interests, whether economic or political or racial or national or sexual. (p. 8)

Zinn notes that ideological interests generally are not articulated by historians. Instead, they are presented as if all readers of history shared a common interest that writers of history "serve to the best of their ability." Zinn concludes that Morison's overriding emphasis on the heroism of Columbus and later explorers, and the deemphasis of the genocide they committed, "is not a technical necessity but an ideological choice. It serves — unwittingly — to justify what was done" (p. 8).

The books I have discussed adopt a similar stategy and thus tacitly justify, primarily through silence, what by any reasonable standard is a human tragedy of staggering proportions. It is this denial, this continuance of a selective tradition in which the cultures of oppressed groups continue to be silenced that is at the heart of the politics of most of the books about Christopher Columbus. While a number of the books do demonstrate the very considerable artistic talents of their creators (especially Sis's, *Follow the Dream*), it is inconceivable that at this point in history we can continue to deny the relevance of the kinds of questions that I have sought to raise in this chapter. It is the raising of these issues that lies at the heart of all of the current furor about multiculturalism.

Meltzer's *Columbus and the World Around Him* (1990), and the dozens of books that he has written throughout his distinguished career, demonstrate that it is possible to write, publish, and sell books that get to the heart of difficult and at times painful questions about the gap between the rhetoric and ideology of American dream, and the realities of our history. Most of Meltzer's books, however, are written for older readers and it is reasonable to ask if it is possible to raise the troubling questions that are central to his biography of Columbus in a format that is both truthful, engaging, and developmentally appropriate for younger readers. I will conclude this chapter with a brief discussion of a book that demonstrates emphatically and unequivocally that it *is* possible to do just this.

Vicki Liestman's *Columbus Day* (1991) is written in an easy-to-read format and contains colorful, if undistinguished, illustrations by Rick Hanson. Although this book does not come close to the aesthetic brilliance of Sis's (1991) book, it is a step in the right direction. The ease with Liestman broches sensitive and complex issues is particularly impressive. The tone is set in her author's note in which she refers to the 1000 A.D. landing of Lief Ericson on the coast of North America where he "was driven away by the Native Americans who already lived there. . . . The word **discover** means to find out something that is unknown. But America wasn't unknown to the Native Americans" (p. 3). After covering much of the territory gone over by Adler, Liestman directly addresses the issue of Columbus's contact with the people he met on San Salvador.

> Columbus thought he was in the Indiea. So he called the people Indians. Of course, the people and the island already had names. . . . The Taino did not speak Spanish. They did not know Columbus was taking their land from them. . . . The Taino seemed to like the Spaniards. They treated the Spaniards like friends. Columbus liked the Taino too. But he did not think of them as friends. He said he thought they would make good servants. (pp. 27-28)

Later, after discussing the fact that Columbus forcibly loaded 500 people onto ships bound for Spain ("away from their homes . . . away from their families"), Liestman continues:

> The Indians who where left behind were not any luckier. The Spaniards made them salves too. The Spaniards killed many of the slaves. The Spaniards killed some of the slaves because they could not work. And they killed some of them for no reason at all. (pp. 40-41)

Liestman then discusses Franklin Roosevelt's designation of October 12 as Columbus Day. "Every year," she notes:

> we remember the good things about Columbus and his exciting voyage. But there is something many people forgot. We forgot about the people Columbus called Indians . . . We forgot about the awful way the Native Americans were treated . . . We forget about the people who died. Maybe it's time to think of Columbus Day in a new way. . . . It can be a day to remember the Native Americans. (p. 52)

Liestman suggests that we carry the lessons of cataclysmic results of Columbus's meeting with the native peoples of the Western hemisphere with us as we explore the next frontier, outer space. She concludes by urging her young audience to consider how we will treat the living beings we meet on those voyages to come. "Maybe," she suggests in her penultimate sentence, "you can think about it on Columbus Day" (p. 56).

There is much wisdom in the questions posed by Liestman in her disarmingly simple book. By deftly reducing the complex issues developed in Meltzer's much longer book to what is perhaps their essence, Liestman provides a much needed example of a book that can engage young children in a conversation about one of the basic issues confronting our world today: whether the lives of certain groups of people are to be valued over those of others and whether human life is expendable in the name of "progress." In our increasingly interdependent global community, one that demands that people of all different nationalities, ethnic identities, and races, cooperate if our planet is to survive, this and similar questions must be asked. It would be fitting if we chose the commemoration of Columbus's momentous voyage as the occasion to begin helping our children to ask them.

SUMMARY

In this chapter, I have argued that the demand for multicultural books needs to be seen as part of an interpretive war, a long struggle to ensure that important narratives such as history and literature do not remain exclusively in the hands of "the people in charge." I have suggested that opposition to efforts to expand the literary canon, for example, are to a significant degree the result of resistance to the social changes ushered in by the civil rights and women's movements of the sixties and seventies. I have sought to show that because children's literature is an important part of this interpretive war, it must be considered to have important and neglected political dimensions. Recent books about Christopher Columbus were examined to show that, with several important exceptions, most authors continue to present a romantic and mythic conception of Columbus as a great adventurer and ignore the catastrophic impact his arrival had on the native people of the "New World." Native Americans are all but invisible from the pages of most books, part of their continued relegation to "the other side of history." The continued silencing of the Native American viewpoint, I argued, both reflects and serves to perpetuate their continued powerlessness.

I prefer to close, however, by pointing writers like Meltzer and

Liestman who demonstrate that there are authors and publishers who take seriously their social responsibility to provide young people with a variety of view points and perspectives.[16] Further, as I literally was making the final corrections on this manuscript, a box arrived containing Jane Yolen's *Encounter* (1992).[17] Sumptuously illustrated by David Shannon, this is the first fictionalized account I have come across that tries to imagine the arrival of Columbus from the viewpoint of the Taino, the native islanders who greeted Columbus and whose numbers dwindled from approximately 300,000 in 1492, to 500 fifty years later (Yolen, 1992). This book combines the sort of historical perspective I have been calling for, with the aesthetic sensibility found in a book like that of Peter Sis (1992). It is time for more writers, their editors and publishers, and the academic and critical establishment to take up the challenge and opportunity that 1992 affords us.

CHAPTER ENDNOTES

1. Noted historian Gary Wills (1992) made a similar point in relation to discussions of multiculturalism and Columbus. "Multiculturalism is not a plot of some left-wing professor in the U.S.; it is the most obvious of global facts . . ." (p. 61). Epstein (1992) points out, however, that while those in university and intellectual circles have considerable cultural influence, they have "virtually no political clout. This state of affairs can lead to frustration, cynicism about the possibility of political effectiveness and a temptation to focus on berating each other rather than finding grounds for unity" (p. 17). This tendency to berate then is transformed by individuals like D'Souze into a virtual conspiracy to take over the intellectual life of the nation.
2. A good bit has been written in recent years about how the political economy affects the nature of the books that get published. See, for example, Apple (1986) and Apple and Christian-Smith (1991).
3. The most recent of the books discussed by Bigelow was published in 1989, before the rush of books published in anticipation of the Columbus quincentennary began to appear. Although Meltzer's (1990) book is referenced, it is not discussed, an interesting omission in light of the fact that the book provides precisely the sort of discussion Bigelow rightly claims is missing from so many of the books.
4. The term "encountered" is being offered by those seeking a compromise between taking the traditional view of Columbus and those who take the view that "indigenous peoples were doomed by European arrogance, brutality, and infectious diseases. Columbus's gift was slavery to those who greeted him; his arrival set in motion the ruthless destruction of the natural world he entered" (Gray, 1991, p. 54). Auchincloss (1991) writing in *Newsweek* exemplifies the "encounter" view:

There is a danger, then, that this 500th anniversary of the East-West encounter will be just as distorted as the past ones — though in a different way. That will happen if it becomes an occasion for pursuing modern political agendas. Better [not to] look for heroes and villains, look for the vast changes that were wrought. Because of what happened in 1492, life in much of the world has never been quite the same. Not everyone will find this the occasion to celebrate. But it was indisputably one of the great divides in human history, an event to marvel at and to learn from. (p. 13)

5. I make no claims whatsoever that my sample is representative, in the "scientific" sense of the published books about Columbus. I have read, however, all of the books available to me.
6. Soule's book (1988), for example, devotes more space to the luminous palolo worms Columbus encountered at a critical stage of his first voyages than to issues relating to Native Americans. There is not even a heading in the index under Indians (or Native Americans). West and West's (1991) book also lacks an index heading under Indians (or Native Americans) and includes only the briefest discussion of the issue. Levinson (1990) and Pelta (1991) treatment of Native American issue, though better than the two previous books, also is inadequate, especially when compared to that of Meltzer (1990) to which they are comparable in terms of length and scope.
7. See, for example, Finkelstein's, *The Other 1492: Jewish Settlement in the New World* (1989).
8. "Columbus never had to convince any one the earth was a sphere. His task was rather to convince potential backers of a voyage that the earth's circumference was as small as he thought it to be" (Meltzer, 1990, p. 55).
9. Tragically, the practice of reducing peoples to "others" in order to justify the unjustifiable shows no sign of disappearing. It was the basis of Hitler's policy genocide against the Jews of Europe and clearly was central to the United State's policy in southeast Asia during the Vietnam War, a war waged against "godless communists" often referred to as "gooks." Because the Iraqis and their thoroughly demonized leader Sadam Hussein clearly were considered "others," the slaughter of well over 100,000 Iraqi soldiers in the recent war in the Persian gulf was carried out virtually without protest.
10. For an illuminating series of articles and suggestions for classroom activities pointing to the necessity to "rethink Columbus," see Rethinking Schools (1991). For a discussion of challenges and resistances to the dominant interpretation of the African-American experience, see Taxel (1992a).
11. Zinn (1980) states that "a report of the year 1650 shows none of the original Arawaks or their descendents left on the island" [of Haiti].
12. Speaking of Columbus's second voyage, an expedition that involved 17 ships and 1200 men, Zinn (1980) states: The aim was clear: slaves and gold" (p. 3.).
13. Maps of this sort provide the endpapers of the book.
14. It is impossible to really do justice to all that Sis packs into this book. On one-double paged spread, for example, Sis summarizes the main points of Columbus's log through words and pictures.
15. Morison is cited in virtually every book I read that includes a bibliography.

16. On the social responsibility of writers, see Meltzer (1989), Little (1990) and Taxel (1990).
17. I regret that the late arrival of this very important book makes impossible a fuller discussion of it.

REFERENCES

Adler, D. A. (1991a). *Christopher Columbus: A great explorer,* illustrated by L. Miller. New York: Holiday House.

Adler, D. A. (1991b). *A picture book of Christopher Columbus,* illustrated by J. and A. Wallner. New York: Holiday House.

Allis, S., Bonfante, J. and Booth, C. Whose America? *Time,* July 8, 1991, Vol. 138, No. 1, pp. 12-17.

Anderson, J. (1991) *Christopher Columbus: From vision to voyage,* photographs by G. Ancona, New York: Dial.

Apple. M. W. (1986). *Teachers and texts: A political economy of class and gender relations in education.* London: Routledge and Kegan Paul.

Apple, M. W. and Christian-Smith, L. (Eds.). (1991). *The politics of the textbook.* London: Routledge and Kegan Paul.

Auchincloss, K. (1992, Fall/Winter). Introduction to: When worlds collide: How Columbus's voyages transformed both east and west. *Newsweek* (special edition).

Belsey, C. (1980). *Critical practice.* London: Routledge, Chapman and Hall.

Bigelow, W. (1992). Once upon a genocide: Christopher Columbus in children's literature. *Language Arts, 69: 2,* 112-120.

Brink, C. R. (1935). *Caddie Woodlawn.* New York: Collier Books.

Broderick, D. (1973). *Image of the black in children's literature.* New York: Bowker.

Casey, K. (1992, July). Life history narratives of Afro-American activist teachers: An example of the collective subjective. Qualitative Research Conference, Athens, Georgia.

Cockburn, A. (1991, May 27). Bush & P. C. — A conspiracy so immense. *The Nation.* pp. 680, 690-91, 704.

Collier, C. and Collier, J. (1976). *My brother Sam is dead.* New York: Scholastic.

D'Aulaire, I. and D'Aulaire, E. P. (1955). *Columbus.* New York: Doubleday.

D'Souza, D. (1991). Illiberal education: The politics of race and sex on campus. New York: The Free Press.

Edmonds, Walter. (1941). *The matchlock gun.* New York: Putnam.

Epstein, B. (1992, Feb. 26/March 10). 'Political correctness' and identity politics. *In The Times, 16: 14,* 16-17.

Faludi, S. (1991). *Backlash: The undeclared war against women.* New York: Crown.

Finkelstein, N. (1989). *The other 1492: Jewish settlement in the new world.* New York: Beech Tree Books.

Fritz, J. (1980). *Where do you think you're going, Christopher Columbus?* New York: G. P. Putnam.

Fritz, J. (1992). *The great adventure of Christopher Columbus,* illustrated by T. de Paola. New York: The Putnam & Grosset Book Group.

Foner, E. and Weiner, J. (1991, July 29/August 5). Fighting for the West. *The Nation,* 163-166.

Forbes, E. (1943). *Johnny Tremain.* New York: Houghton Mifflin.

Goble, P. (1984). *Buffalo woman.* New York: Bradbury Press.

Goble, P. (1985). *The great race.* New York: Bradbury Press.

Gray, P. (1991, October 7). The Trouble With Columbus, *Time, 138: 4,* pp. 52-54.

Greenfield, E. (1985). Writing for children — A joy and responsibility. In D. MacCann and G. Woodard (Eds.), *The black American in books for children: Readings in racism,* (second edition). Metuchen, New Jersey: Scarecrow Press.

Haley, A. (1976). *Roots.* New York: Doubleday.

Hamilton, V. (1988). *Anthony Burns: The defeat and triumph of an escaped slave.* New York: Alfred A. Knopf.

Kelly, R. G. (1970). Mother was a lady: Strategy and order in selected American children's periodicals, 1865-189 pp. (Diss., University of Iowa).

Kelly, R. G. (1974). Literature and the historian. *American Quarterly, 26,* 141-159.

Kelly, R. G. (1984). Literary and cultural values in the evaluation of books for children. *Paper presented to the American Educational Research Association Annual Convention.* New Orleans.

Kopkind, A., (January 6/13, 1992). "The man the 'movement': Buchanan — we'd rather be right," (*The Nation,* Vol. 254, No. 1), pp. 1, 21-22.

Larrick, N. (1972). The all-white world of children's books. In *The black American in books for children: Readings in racism,* edited by D. MacCann and G. Woodard. Metuchen, New Jersey: Scarecrow Press.

Lasky, K. (1988). *The bone wars.* New York: Puffin Books.

Lasky, K. (1983). *Beyond the divide.* New York: Macmillan.

Lasky, K. (1990). The fiction of history: Or, what did Miss Kitty Really Do? *The New Advocate, 3: 3,* pp. 157-166.

Lester, J. (1968). *To be a slave.* New York: Dell.

Lester, J. (1972). *Long journey home.* New York: Scholastic.

Levinson, N. S. (1990). *Christopher Columbus.* New York: Lodestar Books.

Lieberman, M. (1972). "Some day my prince will come": Female acculturation through the fairy tale. *College English, 34: 3,* pp. 383-393.

Liestman, V. (1991). *Columbus Day,* illustrated by R. Hanson. Minneapolis: Carolrhoda.

Lowe, S. (1992). *The log of Christopher Columbus,* illustrated by R. Sabuda. New York: Philomel Books.

MacCann, D. and Woodard, G. (1972). *The black American in books for children: Readings in racism.* Metuchen, New Jersey: Scarecrow Press.

MacCann, D. and G. Woodard (Eds.). (1977). *Cultural conformity in books for children: Further readings in racism.* Metuchen, New Jersey: Scarecrow Press.

Marzollo, J. (1991). *In 1492,* illustrated by S. Björkman. New York: Scholastic.

Meltzer, M. (1989). The social responsibility of the writer. *The New Advocate, 2: 3,* 155-157.

Meltzer, M. (1990). *Columbus and the world around him.* New York: Franklin Watts.

Meltzer, M. (1992). Selective forgetfulness: Christopher Columbus reconsidered. *The New Advocate, 5: 1,* 1-9.

Mitchell, M. (1936). *Gone with the wind.* New York: Macmillan.

Monjo, F. N. (1968). *Indian summer.* New York: HarperCollins.

Pelta, K. (1991). *Discovering Christopher Columbus: How history is invented.* Minneapolis: Lerner.

Peterson, S. B. and Lach, M. A. (1990). Gender stereotypes in children's books: Their prevalence and influence on cognitive and affective development. *Gender and Education, 2: 2,* 185-197.

Rethinking Schools. (1991). *Rethinking Columbus: Teaching about the 500th anniversary of Columbus's arrival in America.* Milwaukee, WI: Rethinking Schools Ltd.

Rockwood, J. (1987). *To spoil the sun.* Athens, GA: University of Georgia Press. [Also 1976, Holt, Rinehart, & Winston].

Roman, L. and Christian-Smith, L. (1988). *Becoming feminine: The politics of popular culture.* London: Falmer Press.

Shor, I. (1986). *Culture wars: School and society in the conservative restoration 1969-1984.* London: Routledge, Chapman and Hall.

Sims, R. (1982). *Shadow and substance: Afro-American experience in contemporary children's books.* Urbana, IL: NCTE.

Sis, P. (1991). *Follow the dream: The story of Christopher Columbus.* New York: Alfred A. Knopf.

Soule, G. (1988). *Christopher Columbus on the green sea of darkness.* New York: Franklin Watts.

Tannenbaum, F. (1946). *Slave and citizen: The Negro in the Americas.* New York: Vintage Books.

Taxel, J. (1978). Justice and cultural conflict: Racism, sexism, and instructional materials. *Interchange, 9: 1,* 56-84.

Taxel, J. (1981). The outsiders of the American revolution: The selective tradition in children's fiction. *Interchange, 12: 2-3,* 206-228.

Taxel, J. (1983). The American revolution in children's fiction. *Research in the Teaching of English, 17: 1,* 61-83.

Taxel, J. (1986). The black experience in children's fiction: Controversies surrounding award winning books. *Curriculum Inquiry, 16: 3,* 245-281.

Taxel, J. (1988). Children's literature: Ideology and response. *Curriculum Inquiry, 18,* 217-229.

Taxel, J. (1990). Notes from the editor. *The New Advocate, 3: 2,* vii-xii.

Taxel, J. (1991a). Reclaiming the voice of resistance: The fiction of Mildred Taylor. In M. Apple and L. Christian-Smith (Eds.), *The politics of the textbook.* London: Routledge and Kegan Paul.

Taxel, J. (1991b). *Roll of thunder, hear my cry:* Reflections on the aesthetics and politics of children's literature. In W. Schubert and G. Willis (Eds.), *Reflections from the heart of educational inquiry: Understanding curriculum and teaching through the arts.* Albany, N.Y.: SUNY Press.

Townsend, J. R. (1969). Didacticism in new dress. In S. Egoff, G. T. Stubbs, and L. F. Ashley (Eds.), *Only correct: readings on children's literature.* New York: Oxford University Press.

Walker, M. (1975). *Jubilee.* New York: Doubleday.

Weitzman, L. J. et. al. (1973). Sex-role socialization in picture books for preschool children. *American Journal of Sociology, 77: 6,* pp. 1125-1149.

West, D. and West, J. (1991). *Christopher Columbus: The great adventure and how we know about it.* New York: Atheneum.

Wexler, P. (1982). Structure, text, and subject: A critical sociology of school knowledge. In M. Apple (Ed.), *Cultural and economic reproduction in education: Essays on class, ideology and the state.* London: Routledge and Kegan Paul.

Wills, G. (1992, October 7). 1492 vs. 1892 vs. 1992, *Time, 138: 14,* p. 61.

Yates, E. (1950). *Amos Fortune: Free man.* New York: E. P. Dutton.

Yolen, J. (1992). *Encounter,* illustrated by D. Shannon. San Diego: Harcourt Brace Jovanovich.

Zinn, H. (1980). *A people's history of the United States.* New York: HarperCollins.

2

Multicultural Literature for Children

Making Informed Choices

Rudine Sims Bishop

INTRODUCTION

Discussions of multicultural literature frequently lead to discussions of some of the issues relating to its selection and use in classrooms. By what criteria should such literature be judged? Aren't the usual literary criteria adequate? Does it matter whether the author is a member of the group being written about? If I don't know much about another cultural group, how can I make informed judgments?

These and other issues arise because, as the term is most frequently used in the United States, "multicultural literature" refers to literature by and about people who are members of groups considered to be outside the socio-political mainstream of the United States. In many cases, consequently, books featuring such groups have not been a part of the mainstream of children's literature in any significantly positive way. The percentage of books about people of color continues to hover between one and two percent, but as the numbers of children's books have increased, so has the quantity of multicultural literature, and with it the need to further clarify issues.

Most frequently the term multicultural literature refers to books about people of color in this country — African Americans, Asian Americans, Native Americans, Hispanics. Part of the reason such books are labeled "multicultural" is to avoid the use of the term "minority," which has come to carry connotations of low status and inferiority. In the case of children's literature, "minority" status has meant that, until quite recently, people of color have been either virtually excluded from literature for young people, or frequently portrayed in undesirable ways — as negative stereotypes or objects of ridicule. Thus, people who are members of so-called minority groups have become sensitive to the possibility of continued insults and slights.

Most lists of multicultural literature also include books about people of color outside the United States. Folktales from Africa and Asia, for example, constitute substantial portions of such lists. Fiction set in countries where people of color are in the majority and informational books about those countries are also considered part of the body of multicultural literature. Concerns have sometimes been raised about the accuracy of such books, and the representations they make of people and their culture. While there is general agreement that multicultural literature refers to literature about people of color in the United States and elsewhere, there is less agreement on whether the term also refers to Euro-American ethnic groups or others who claim some kind of minority status. Many discussions of multicultural books, include books about regional groups in the United States like in habitants of the Appalachians, or religious minorities like the Amish, groups which have also sometimes been misrepresented or portrayed inaccurately in children's books.

Given these histories, it is not surprising that many members of these groups and other sensitive people of good will, in order to effect change, have made known their concerns and tried to raise the level of awareness of people who write, publish, and select children's books. Educators and parents alike maintain a strong belief in the power of literature to affect the minds and hearts of its readers, particularly when those readers are children and youth. Multicultural literature is one of the most powerful components of a multicultural education curriculum, the underlying purpose of which is to help to make the society a more equitable one. In light of that purpose, the choice of books to be read and discussed in the nation's schools is of paramount importance. The purpose of this chapter is to provide information that will enable teachers to make careful, informed and sensitive choices from among the increasing numbers of books being published as multicultural literature. If most of the examples come from African-American sources, it is because, at this writing, they are the most readily available. The principles apply, however, to all multicultural literature.

THE NEED FOR CULTURAL AUTHENTICITY

One of the most sensitive current issues in the field of literature in general, and in children's literature as well, is the issue of cultural authenticity. Arguments usually are about individual books and their portrayals of people of color, as well as the representation of specific aspects of their cultures such as values, customs, and family relationships. Almost always the controversies are about books written by someone from a different cultural background, usually Euro-Americans. In children's literature, this is a significant issue because a substantial portion of children's books about people of color are created by Euro-American writers. For example, a survey and analysis of 150 fictional books published between 1965 and 1979 (Sims, 1982), revealed that a majority of the fiction about African-Americans was at that time being created by Euro-American writers. A substantial portion of books about people of color is still being written or illustrated by white writers. Many such books have merit and have been recognized for their positive contributions and artistic achievement. Other books have received mixed reviews; that is, even though their literary quality may be high, they have been found to contain both major and minor flaws. Still others have been denounced as lacking cultural authenticity; that is, the writers or artists have been accused of distorting or misrepresenting some aspects of the culture reflected in their books. In cases where books have been denounced, the assumption has been that as an outsider, the author was unaware of the nuances of day to day living in the culture portrayed in the book, or that the distortions and misrepresentations are reflections of an ethnocentric, biased, or at worst, racist point of view.

This concern with cultural authenticity reflects an assumption that the cultures of the major so-called minority groups are distinct and identifiably different from a more general American culture, and not casually understood by outsiders. In a *New York Times* article explaining why he insists on a Black director for the film of his play "Fences," August Wilson (1990), the award-winning African-American playwrite, articulates that position:

As Americans of various races, we share a broad cultural ground, a commonality of society that links its diverse elements into a cohesive whole that can be defined as "American."

We share certain mythologies. A history. We share political and economic systems and a rapidly developing, if suspect, ethos. Within these commonalities are specifics. Specific ideas and attitudes that are not shared on the common cultural ground. These remain the property and possession of the people who develop the . . .

The specifics of our [Black Americans'] cultural history are very much different. . . .

We have a different way of responding to the world. We have different ideas about religion, different manners of social intercourse. We have different ideas about style, about language. We have different aesthetics.

Someone who does not share the specifics of a culture remains an outsider, no matter how astute a student or how well-meaning their intentions.

Criticisms centering on cultural authenticity also reflect a political concern about who controls the way non-majority cultures are represented in books for children; and whether, when those outside the cultures are the creators and publishers of those books, as well as the gatekeepers who determine what gets published, they, in Wilson's words "seek to dilute and control it [Black culture] by setting themselves up as the assayers of its value and the custodians of its offspring." (p. A15)

Not all critics agree with the implication that persons outside one culture cannot write authentically about another. In another *New York Times* piece, noted African-American critic Henry Louis Gates, Jr. (1991) argues that membership in one cultural group does not, in and of itself, confer the ability to create "authentic" fiction; that writers are all influenced by various literary traditions, and that all writers are in some sense "cultural impersonators." While he also argues that a book is a "cultural event" and the identity of the author can be a part of that event, he rejects the idea that an "outsider" cannot create culturally authentic work:

The lesson of the literary blindfold test is not that our social identities don't matter. They do matter. And our histories, individual and collective, do affect what we wish to write and what we are able to write. But that relation is never one of fixed determinism. No human culture is inaccessible to someone who makes the effort to understand, to learn, to inhabit another world. (p. 30)

Those who criticize children's books for lacking cultural authenticity have argued that the writers of those books have failed to meet Gates's conditions; they have not "made the effort to understand, to learn, to inhabit" the world they write about, or if they have, they have been unsuccessful.

In school settings, concerns about cultural authenticity are related to the purposes that multicultural literature are expected to serve. All literature serves the purpose of offering insights into human experience. Multicultural literature also takes on the sociopolitical aims of the multicultural education movement of which it is a part. Within that context, multicultural literature becomes a vehicle for socialization and change. Elizabeth Fitzgerald Howard (1991), African-American children's book writer, expresses it this way:

> . . . We must also aim for that authentic body of literature for children which can lead us toward our goals: self-esteem for those previously not reflected in the mirror, and important enlightenment for those who, for too long, have seen only themselves in that mirror; all leading toward the celebration of living in the multicultural society." . . .
>
> If the purpose of literature is to liberate, the purpose of authentic multicultural literature is to help liberate us from all the preconceived stereotypical hang-ups that imprison us within narrow boundaries. (pp. 91-92)

From the perspective of educators, Howard's rationale is compelling because it implies that the book choices teachers and others make have potential consequences for children. If literature is a mirror that reflects human life, then all children who read or are read to need to see themselves reflected as part of humanity. If they are not, or if their reflections are distorted and ridiculous, there is the danger that they will absorb negative messages about themselves and people like them. Those who see only themselves or who exposed to errors and misrepresentations are mis-educated into a false sense of superiority, and the harm is doubly done.

BECOMING INFORMED

Many teachers who feel confident selecting literature on the basis of curricular goals or literary criteria lose that confidence when it comes to selecting multicultural literature. Aware of past controversies over specific books and general charges of stereotyping or racism, they fear being accused of insensitivity or worse. Feeling a lack of knowledge about cultural groups other than their own, they worry whether they can detect authenticity or its lack. Unfortunately, it is not possible to create a tidy checklist that can be applied to every book from a parallel culture. There are however, at least two general strategies that, if adopted, can raise levels of awareness and make teachers better informed selectors and evaluators of multicultural literature.

Be Aware of Various Types of Multicultural Literature

One of the complicating factors in evaluating multicultural children's literature is that the label is an umbrella term that covers great diversity, not only in the groups included under the umbrella, and in the literary genres represented, but in underlying purposes and points of view. Teachers who would make informed selections should be aware of these differences, so that they can apply appropriate criteria. Multicultural literature includes informational books, folktales, biographies, poetry, fantasy, fiction, and picture books. While general selection guidelines (see below) will apply to all genres, it is useful to think further about fiction and picture books. As creative products, books resist placement in neat categories, and it is not necessary to spend time trying to put individual books into figurative cubbyholes. The point is that different types of books may serve different purposes, and that in order to evaluate cultural authenticity, one should consider those differences.

Recent children's fiction and picture books published in the United States (and England) about people of color can be placed in three general categories based on their approach to the cultures of the people they portray. They might be labeled *specific, generic,* and *neutral.*

A culturally-specific children's book illuminates the experience of growing up a member of a particular, non-white cultural group. Such a book often delineates character, setting, and theme, in part by detailing the specifics of daily living that will be recognizable to members of the group. Such specifics might include language styles and patterns, religious beliefs and practices, musical preferences, family configurations and relationships, social mores, and numerous other behaviors, attitudes and values shared by the members of a cultural group. In the hands of a skilled writer, these details do not preclude other readers from understanding, appreciating and enjoying the book; in fact, they add texture and increase readers' appreciation for the many different designs for living that humans create. The specific details also increase the likelihood that readers will find the characters convincing, and their problems, concerns and resolutions plausible for any humans caught in the same or similar circumstances.

Given the history of so-called minorities in the United States and elsewhere, it should be expected that some books of this type will focus on the ways people cope with discrimination, racism and oppression, and still manage to survive with dignity. Mildred Taylor's books about the Logan family (*Roll of Thunder, Hear My Cry* (1976), *Let the Circle Be Unbroken*

(1981), *The Road to Memphis* (1990)), and their struggles in Mississippi in the 1930s are examples of such books. Most current culturally-specific children's books about people of color, however, focus on other common literary themes played out within the cultural context of one of the so-called minority groups in this or similar societies. Picture books like Elizabeth Fitzgerald Howard's *Aunt Flossie's Hats (And Crab Cakes Later)* (1991), and Arthur Dorros' *Abuela* (1991) both of which feature relationships between young children and elderly relatives, fit this category. So do novels such as Laurence Yep's *Child of the Owl* (1977) and Walter Dean Myers's *The Mouse Rap* (1990). These are books that a critic, particularly an "insider," would expect to find culturally authentic.

In picture books, where texts are often not long enough to include many details of any kind, sometimes what might be considered culturally specific details are in the artwork. Tom Feelings (1991), African-American artist, points out, for example, subtle differences in style, sensibility, and point of view that distinguish the work of Black artists working with Black subjects in picture books. Other cultural markers in seemingly generic picture books may be in such subtleties as the names of the characters, the form of address for a parent, the values or attitudes of the characters, the description of skin color. Such picture books as Eloise Greenfield's *Grandpa's Face* (1988), for example, fit in this category.

A second type of fiction book might be called generically American (or Canadian or English). Books of this type feature characters who are members of so-called minority groups, but they contain few, if any, specific details that might serve to define those characters culturally. The characters, plots and themes reflect what August Wilson referred to as American "common cultural ground." Such books are sometimes called "universal" as if the experiences and themes are common world wide. (Some themes and situations are indeed universal. For example, cycles of birth and death are part of all living. On the other hand, to use a simplistic example, playing in snow is not universal though it may be commonplace in temperate and colder climates.) Many such books are picture books, and it is the pictures that identify the characters racially, if not culturally. Since specific cultural details are absent from the texts in these books, they may be judged primarily on other criteria, such as literary and visual artistry. Illustrations can be judged, for instance, on whether the characters resemble real people and are not stereotypes. Although many books of this type are excellent picture books, some have been criticized for their very lack of cultural specificity. One of the best known examples is Ezra Jack Keats's Caldecott Medal winner *The Snowy Day* (1962). Another example of this type of

book is Ann Herbert Scott's *Sam* (1967). A more recent, example is
Catherine Stock's *Secret Valentine* (1991), which is unsatisfactory in its
depiction of the hair style of the little African-American girl who is the main
character.

A third type of book considered under the multicultural label could be
called culturally neutral. These are generally picture books that feature
people of color, but are fundamentally about something else. Included in
this category would be informational books that show people from diverse
backgrounds engaged in activities related to the topic of the book, or in
certain occupations or professions. In a book intended to provide
information about medical examinations, for example, a Japanese-American
child might be shown visiting the doctor, who might be an African-
American female. These are often books that feature photographs, such as
Bruce McMillan's *Mary Had a Little Lamb* (Hale, 1990). In choosing to
include or feature various people of many races and cultures, the writers
and illustrators of such books make a strong statement about valuing
diversity. Like the generic books, these books, too, can be evaluated on the
basis of their accuracy, their literary and visual artistry, and possible
omissions, but cultural authenticity is not likely to be a major consideration.

Read Extensively in Literature
Written by "Insiders"

Teachers who seek to gain confidence in their ability to select
culturally authentic children's literature need to become familiar with
the literary traditions of the various cultural groups. Once one accepts the
existence of cultural groups that both share in general American culture
and have developed unique cultures of their own, it becomes logical to
assume that the authentic literature of those cultures will come from
members of those groups. In regards to other settings, no controversies
exist over such questions. It would not be considered absurd, for
example, to expect that French-Candian literature would be written by
French Canadians. Nor would it be controversial to claim that authentic
Jewish literature is not likely to be written by Irish Catholic priests or
Palestinian Arabs. My claim here is not that an author from one group
cannot write worthwhile books about another group, but that the
resulting literature is likely not to be claimed by members of the featured
group as *their* literature. Reading the literature of insiders will help
teachers learn to recognize recurring themes, topics, values, attitudes,
language features, social mores — those elements that characterize the

body of literature the group claims as its own. It will also acquaint them with the variety and diversity to be found *within* the culture. No one book can represent the literature of an entire cultural group. In some cases, teachers may need to read books produced for an adult audience, since few children's book authors from some groups (e.g. Native Americans, Hispanics) have been published by the major publishing companies. As an artistic endeavor, each book will be unique, but it is still likely to have some aspects in common with other literature coming out of the same cultural experience. Even when the cultural or racial identity of an author is unknown, teachers who have read widely in the literature by members of the group will be able to recognize differences between "typical" insider and outsider perspectives. Armed with that background, teachers will find it easier to trust their own judgments about the authenticity of new books.

SELECTION GUIDELINES

Literary Criteria

In their introductory chapter of *The Multicolored Mirror,* Kruse and Horning (1991) state: "High standards must be applied to the evaluation of all books, as always. Evaluation criteria must always make room for any book to be valued for what it is, for the way in which it is unique, and for what it contributes..." (p. 9) In children's books, as in all literature, form and content are equally important. Children's literature textbooks (e.g. Huck, Hepler and Hickman, 1987; Lukens, 1990) almost always include discussions of or guidelines for evaluating children's literature. The authors of such texts assert that a book of fiction should, among other things, be well-written, tell a good story, have strong characterization, and offer a worthwhile theme or themes children could be expected to understand. Good nonfiction, at the least, should be accurate and well-presented.

Although an argument for judging children's books by literary criteria may appear to belabor the obvious, at least two factors make it important to mention such criteria in discussions of multicultural literature. In their eagerness to include multicultural literature in the curriculum, many well-intentioned professionals, finding a very limited selection of books available, become indiscriminate in their choices. If a book features people of color, it may be selected simply for that reason, in spite of its being mediocre — or worse — as a piece of literature. Of course, other literature of poor quality is to be found in many classrooms and libraries as well. The point is, however, that because of the limited quantity of multicultural literature available, there may be a greater tendency to accept poor literary quality just to have *something* in the classroom or library.

A related concern is that, mindful of the underlying rationale for including multicultural literature in the curriculum — the creation of a more equitable society — some teachers select fiction with the intention of using it to teach lessons about tolerance or to provide specific information about various cultural groups. Some children's fiction *is* written with didactic intent, but often the writer of such a book neglects important aspects of literary quality, such as plot and characterization in order to emphasize the moral or lesson of the story. Fictional books are not social studies texts, and when they are written, selected, and used as such, inadequate attention may be given to their literary quality, and neither children nor children's books are well served.

As the body of multicultural literature grows, it will also become necessary to develop an awareness of the cultural traditions out of which it comes. Traditional criteria derive from Euro-American aesthetic standards. Other cultures will have different aesthetic values, resulting in forms and styles potentially unfamiliar to Euro-Americans. In a brief discussion of the Black Aesthetic, for example, Darwin Turner (1985) pointed out that African-American writers often base their writing styles on other elements of African-American culture. For instance, he argues that Langston Hughes cannot be faulted for not writing poetry in iambic pentameter when he was intentionally imitating jazz forms, which come out of an entirely different tradition. Nor should an African-American novelist be denounced because his language reflects African-American rhetorical styles rather than those of highly respected Euro-American male writers:

> Until recently, few individuals questioned the validity of European-American literary standards as a basis for judging the quality of works by black writers . . . However, since contemporary Black Arts writers are consciously modeling their work upon styles derived from Afro-American culture, a conscientious teacher must consider the need to examine Afro-American culture to understand the bases of some styles and language patterns. . . . Rather than judging a black writer as necessarily inferior because he does not use a European model, the teacher must acquire sufficient cultural breadth to be able to judge whether the black

has created beauty according to a non-European model. . . . Literary work cannot be evaluated outside its own tradition. Certainly, one does not condemn an apple for not being a good orange. (p. 305)

Other Criteria

A number of resources (Council on Interracial Books for Children, 1974; Klein, 1985; Rudman, 1984; Slapin, Seale, and Gonzales, 1989; Norton, 1987) offer criteria for analyzing and evaluating multicultural literature. While many of today's books avoid the pitfalls of the past, a few "problem books" still surface from time to time, and many of the books of the past are still in circulation. The need for critical examination of books for classrooms still exists. The following compilation reflects many of the recommendations of the sources cited above.

Select a Balanced Collection

Have available a variety of books that show the diversity within and across human cultures. All kinds of people should be shown in many occupations, lifestyles, roles, economic situations, and so forth, both in the United States and the rest of the world. Children need to be helped to develop a world view.

In books set in the United States, select a variety that helps to counter subtle stereotyping. For example, be certain that the collection does not, by virtue of the choices available, imply that all African-Americans are living in poverty, or that Asians are the "model minority," or that Mexican-Americans are all migrant workers. Including only historical fiction about Native Americans feeds into the "vanishing Indian" myth. The idea is not to avoid a book because it features a poor African-American family, for instance, but to be sure to include books that feature African-Americans in other more fortunate economic circumstances as well.

Have available enough books to present different perspectives on issues and events. For example, try to find books that present Native American points of view on the European settlement of North America.

Search for books that correct distortions or omissions of significant information. For example, if some books about the U.S. in World War II do not mention the internment of Japanese-Americans, other books that tell that story should be a part of the collection.

Along with biographies of people who are known by and appealing to the dominant society, include books that present heroes who are revered by their own people. These may include people, like Paul Robeson, who took positions unpopular in the dominant society.

Select Individual Books Carefully

Look for the point of view the author takes toward his or her subject. Are non-white or non-Western peoples and societies shown as primitive or quaint? Does the author assume a paternalistic attitude? Are contributions of non-Western peoples made to seem insignificant?

Examine relationships between characters from different cultures. Do people of color lead as well as follow? Do they solve their own problems or depend on white benefactors? Are people of color the only ones expected to exercise forgivenes? What standards for success apply to people of color?

Analyze the way people of color are characterized. Are they presented as unique individuals, rather than as representatives of a group? Are main characters well-rounded and fully developed? Are stereotypes avoided? Even though blatant stereotypes such as the eye-rolling, head-scratching, shuffling, Black or the Mexican-American macho bandito are not prevalent in today's literature, more subtle stereotypes may still exist.

Examine the language, both of the narrator or author, and the fictional characters. In light of the history of racism, offensive terms such as *brutal, conniving, primitive, savage,* and *backward* should be avoided as descriptors of people of color. Writers should also avoid terms, such as *shacks, superstitions,* and *costumes,* that would be offensive were they applied to their own homes, religious beliefs, or everyday wearing apparel.

Examine the language of the characters. It should be accurate, authentic, and appropriate to the characters' historical time, educational and social background, and the social situation in which they are operating. Carefully written colloquial speech or dialect may be used to enrich characterization, but should not be used to mark the character as intellectually inferior or as an object of ridicule.

Look carefully at the pictures. Do they present accurate, authentic, nonstereotypical presentations of people of color? Do they show variety in physical features among the people of any one group, or do they all look alike? Do they avoid stereotypes such as the whooping Indian in feathers and a loincloth? Do pictures show the diversity of people who would naturally be present in certain settings such as urban centers?

Look for accuracy. Information should be factual and up-to-date. For example, the changed and changing roles of females in many social groups should be reflected in modern books. Significant omissions should be as much cause for concern as inaccuracies and misstatements.

Consider the background of the author. In nonfiction, what credentials or background qualify him or her to write about the topic? What resources or authorities have been consulted? In fiction, look for the author's perspective and themes. Consider whether an insider or outsider's perspective has informed the book, and the success with which it fulfills its apparent purpose or is likely to reach its presumed audience.

Consider the possible effect on a child's self-esteem. Put yourself in the place of the child reader. Is there anything in the book that would embarrass or offend you if it were written about you or the group you identify with? If so, choose a different book. Would you be willing to share this book with a group of mixed-race children? An all-black or all-white group? If not, choose a different book.

CONCLUSION

Following the guidelines above will help teachers make informed selections of new and recent multicultural literature for their classrooms. A well-balanced collection of unbiased books should be essential in classrooms filled with young people who will live most of their lives in the twenty-first century. The late James Baldwin (cited in Watkins, 1979) asserted that "Literature is indispensable to the world . . . The world changes according to the way people see it, and if you alter, even by a millimeter, the way a person looks at reality, then you can change it." That is the underlying purpose of multicultural education, to change the world by making it a more equitable one. Multicultural literature can be a powerful vehicle for accomplishing that task.

REFERENCES

Council on Interracial Books for Children. (1974). *10 quick ways to analyze children's books for racism and sexism.* 1974.

Feelings, T. (1991). Transcending the form. In Lindgren, M. (Ed.), *The multicolored mirror: Cultural substance in literature for children and young adults.* Fort Atkinson, Wisconsin, 1991.

Gates, H. L., Jr. (1991, November 24). "Authenticity," or the lesson of Little Tree. *The New York Times,* pp. 1, 26-30).

Howard, E. F. (1991). Authentic multicultural literature for children: An author's perspective. In Lindgren, M. (Ed.), *The multicolored mirror: Cultural substance in literature for children and young adults.* Fort Atkinson, Wisconsin.

Huck, C., Hepler, S. & Hickman, J. (1987). *Children's literature in the elementary school.* (4th ed.). New York: Holt, Rinehart and Winston.

Kruse, G. M. & Horning, K. T. (1991). Looking into the mirror: Considerations behind the reflections. In Lindgren, M. (Ed.), *The multicolored mirror: Cultural substance in literature for children and young adults.* Fort Atkinson, Wisconsin.

Klein, G. (1985). *Reading into racism: Bias in children's literature and learning materials.* London: Routledge & Kegan Paul.

Lukens, R. (1990). *A critical handbook of children's literature.* (4th ed.). Glenview, IL: Scott, Foresman/Little, Brown.

Norton, D. (1987). *Through the eyes of a child: An introduction to children's literature.* Columbus, OH: Charles Merrill.

Rudman, M. (1984). *Children's literature: An issues approach.* (2nd ed.). New York: Longman.

Sims, R. (1982). *Shadow and substance: Afro-american experience in contemporary children's fiction.* Urbana, IL: National Council of Teachers of English.

Slapin, B. Seale, D. & Gonzales, R. (1989). *How to tell the difference: A checklist for evaluating Native American children's books.* Berkeley, CA: Oyate.

Turner, D. (1985). Black experience, black literature, black students, and the English classroom. In Brooks, C. K. (Ed.). *Tapping potential: English and language arts for the black learner.* Urbana, IL: National Council of Teachers of English.

Watkins, M. (1979, September 23). James Baldwin writing and talking. *New York Times Book Review,* pp. 3, 36-37.

Wilson, A. (1990, September 26) I want a black director. *New York Times,* p. A15.

CHILDREN'S BOOKS

Dorros, A. (1991). Illustrated by E. Kleven. *Abuela.* New York: E. P. Dutton.

Greenfield, E. (1988). Illustrated by F. Cooper. *Grandpa's face.* New York: Philomel.

Howard, E. F. (1991). Illustrated by J. Ransome. *Aunt Flossie's hats (and crab cakes later).* New York: Clarion.

Hale, S. J. (1990). Photo-illustrated by B. McMillan. *Mary had a little lamb.* New York: Scholastic.

Keats, E. J. (1962). *The snowy day.* New York: Viking.

Myers, W. D. (1990). *The mouse rap.* New York: Harper & Row.

Scott, A. H. (1967). *Sam.* New York: McGraw-Hill.

Stock. C. (1990). *Secret valentine.* New York: Bradbury.

Taylor, M. (1976). *Roll of thunder, hear my cry.* New York: Dial.

Taylor, M. (1981). *Let the circle be unbroken.* New York: Dial.

Taylor, M. (1990). *The road to Memphis.* New York: Dial.

3

Contemporary Griots

African-American Writers of Children's Literature

Violet J. Harris

INTRODUCTION

Two persons, among others, valued in African communities were the storyteller and the *griot* or historian. The storyteller fascinated fellow villagers with his ability to weave stories that entertained, taught a lesson, or apprised the group of its heritage. Sometimes the stories were humorous, other times ironic or satiric, and occasionally somber. His facile and inventive use of language was perceived of as possessing power beyond the ability to communicate. The storyteller gives life force or *Nommo* (Jahn, 1961). He brought objects, people, and ideas to life. The griot, in contrast, was a storyteller of sorts as well. He was responsible for retaining and sharing knowledge about the group's history and the role of individual families in its development. He functioned as a human encyclopedia.

The storyteller and the griot, captured in Africa and sold in North and South America and the Caribbean, brought their roles to these new lands. Because of them, we have Brer Rabbit and Anancy, two figures prominent in African-American folklore. Today's African-American authors inherited the spiritual legacies and creative powers associated with village storytellers and griots and continue the life-giving tradition of "the word." Oral storytelling still exists, but books assume many of its functions in some communities such as entertainment, education, inspiration, and socialization.

Faith Ringgold and Leontyne Price, artists who achieved fame and success in art and opera, are storytellers and griots. Both wrote children's books that received immediate notice and critical recognition. For example, imagine the sense of exhilaration, freedom, and power that eight-year-old Cassie Louise Lightfoot experiences at "tar beach" in the book of the same name, *Tar Beach* (Ringgold, 1991). She possesses an imagination unrestricted by race or gender stereotypes. She is free and the reader can sense that her freedom will continue through adulthood:

> Sleeping on Tar Beach was magical. Lying on the roof in the night, with stars and skyscraper buildings all around me, made me feel rich, like I owned all that I could see. (unnumbered pages)

Ringgold's illustrations exhibit a sense of freedom, joy, and unfettered creativity. She combined quilting, painting, and various folkloric and narrative motifs to create an artistic vision unusual in children's literature. *Tar Beach* appeals to children and adults; children can envision comparable adventures at beaches or other places and adults can reminiscence about the pleasures of their childhoods. *Tar Beach* earned a well-deserved 1992 Caldecott Honor Medal.

Aida (Price, 1990) is a retelling of the Giuseppe Verdi opera by diva Leontyne Price. Price uses the familiar opening lines of fairy tales to begin her tale of love, betrayal, sacrifice, and war: "Long ago, in the faraway land of Ethiopia, there lived a Royal Princess who was gentle as moonlight and beautiful as the morning star. Her name was Aida" (unnumbered pages). Once again, the reader enters a world that promises excitement, adventure, intrigue, and passion. Leo and Diane Dillon's illustrations enhance the text through their choice of color, symbols, and the decorative borders that surround each page. Further, their depictions of Ethiopians and Egyptians as unmistakably brown-skinned people, belie the attempt to depict them as light or white-skinned Arabs. Price supports this observation in her storyteller's notes:

> Aida as a heroine — and Aida as an opera — has been meaningful, poignant and personal for me. In many ways, I believe Aida is a portrait of my innerself. She was my best friend operatically and was a natural for me because my skin was my costume. This fact was a positive and strong feeling and allowed me a freedom of expression, of movement, and of interpretation that other operatic heroines I performed did not. (unnumbered pages)

Notice the themes Price emphasizes — freedom, affirmation of self, and identification. Both *Aida* and *Tar Beach* celebrate similar values and encourage the reader to share in the liberating effects of imagination, empowerment, and creativity. Few children or adults could resist that invitation.

Tar Beach and *Aida* are just two of the many extraordinary books that signal the dawning of another golden age in African-American children's literature. Unprecedented artistic and literary excellence are the hallmarks of the literature created in the 1980s and 1990s. Well-respected and established authors Virginia Hamilton, Walter Dean Myers, Eloise Greenfield, and Mildred Taylor produced works that demonstrated the expansiveness of their artistic visions and their abilities to create word magic. Talented authors Camille Yarbrough, Eleanora Tate, Emily Moore, Angela Johnson, and others reaffirmed the promise evident in previously published works. The future of African-American children's literature seems unlimited and no longer does it appear necessary to ask as one author did in 1896, "Is Juvenile Literature Demanded on the Part of Colored Children?" (Elliot, 1991). The answer is a resounding **yes** but for all children because of the excellence of the literature and the ability of the authors and illustrators to generate intellectual, aesthetic, and emotional responses. The joy offered by these books, however, becomes a reality only when they are purchased, read, and shared. History suggests that some Herculean efforts combined with some persistent, everyday actions are necessary to ensure a permanent audience for African-American children's literature.

In this chapter, I examine the history of African-American children's literature and detail some of the milestones in its 100-year history. Examination of the historical development of the literature provides essential knowledge for understanding the struggles that were waged to bring it to fruition. The chapter also includes a discussion of major trends, themes, and an examination of the works of some of the authors. The authors selected are those who write "culturally conscious" fiction or fiction written from the experiences and perspectives of African Americans. They are divided into three groups: the vanguard, individuals who began publishing in the mid-to-late 1960s and early 1970s; the reinforcers, individuals who acquired prominence in the 1970s; and the reinterpreters, an emerging group of authors who show exceptional promise and whose writings appeared in the 1980s. The remaining segments of the chapter consist of strategies for incorporating African-American children's literature in the elementary school and a recommended listing of books. Readers should note that the recommended list is not exhaustive nor is it intended as the final arbiter for selections of books by and about African Americans; it is merely a starting point.

A PERNICIOUS TRADITION

Many would prefer to think of literature as a cultural artifact that remains unaffected by historical and cultural processes. Or at least, literature is supposed to reflect Truth, Beauty, and Values (Daiches, 1938). Our examinations of literature, therefore, should only involve determining how the writer develops the various literary elements in order to produce a work of art. We are encouraged to leave questions of political significance out of literary judgments (Taxel, 1991). Literature cannot stand apart from the cultural and historical milieus that nurtured it, the individuals who created it, or the views they hold.

This non-critical view is refuted when one examines the portrayal of African Americans in cultural artifacts including literature. The images of African Americans in literature were decidedly negative or paternalistic. Critic William Braithwaite (1924) was one of the first to document the depictions of African Americans in literature in a systematic fashion. He examined literature published between 1860 and 1900 and found two extreme but incomplete patterns, pathos and humor. Braithwaite argued that racial inequalities and the refusal of many Whites to view African Americans as equals resulted in these inaccurate portrayals. He stated that the same patterns existed in children's literature. Braithwaite urged writers to demonstrate moral and artistic courage and create more diverse, authentic stories.

Similarly, W. E. B. Du Bois expressed concern about the images of African Americans in literature and popular culture. As editor of *The Crisis,* the official publication of the NAACP, he instituted a symposium titled "The Negro in Art: How Should He Be Portrayed?" in the April 1926 through September 1926 issues. The responses, written by publishers, authors, editors, and critics diverged considerably. White respondents emphasized freedom of expression, especially for their portrayals of African Americans even though they were stereotyped, and the commercial aspects of publishing. In contrast, African-American respondents tended to view literature as an artistic endeavor shaped and circumscribed by socio-political conditions. They also indicated that a "New Negro" had begun to write. Scholar Alain Locke had written of this "New Negro," one who exhibited a new, transforming psychological stance (Locke, 1925). New Negroes were less accepting of their low-caste status. They were brash, intelligent, creative, and political. They would not wait for their equality; they would demand it. These New Negroes created a literary, musical, and artistic movement known as the Harlem Renaissance. Their presence was especially felt in the literary realm because of the work of poets and novelists such as Langston Hughes, Countee Cullen, Arna Bontemps, Nella Larsen, Jessie Fauset, and Zora Neale Hurston in the 1920s and 1930s. They created works that emanated from African American experiences, culture, and universal values. The Harlem Renaissance authors could not eradicate the pernicious stereotypes of African Americans even though many of their books exhibited exceptional literary merit. What were those stereotypes and why were they so entrenched in popular culture, religion, politics, and schooling?

Stereotypes of African Americans

Sterling A. Brown argued that the portrayals of African Americans in literature were decidedly negative and stereotyped. He developed seven categories to describe the stereotypes in literature that were prevalent (Brown, 1927). The stereotypes included the contented slave, the wretched freedman, the comic Negro, the brute Negro, the tragic mulatto, the local color Negro, and the exotic primitive. Broderick (1973) applied Brown's categories to children's literature and found that the same stereotypes existed. The contented slave was an especially popular stereotype in books such as the Elsie Dinsmore series and *Two Little Confederates* (Page, 1932). These books portrayed slavery as a civilizing, paternalistic institution and not a brutal, dehumanizing economic, political, and social system.

Perkins (1979) delineated the functions of stereotypes. According to Perkins, stereotypes are examples of hegemonic cultural power; that is, they are used as instruments of power by individuals and groups and they help legitimize established order. They are cognitive concepts that are not neutral. They may or may not be negative. They are abstractions that are reduced and generalized to a deceptive level of simplicity. Stereotypes are shared cultural meanings. They are part of the reality of culture that all members have access to but in a differentiated manner. That is, some groups create them about other groups; they become part of society's knowledge and the maligned groups generally lack the power to challenge them. Stereotypes also refer to both role and status. African Americans had been and remain a "pariah" group because of their color, structural position in society, and their relative lack of power.

Perkins argued that stereotypes are related to the group's structural position in society. Further, Perkins asserted that stereotypes are supported by laws, traditions, and institutions. Because stereotypes are supported in this manner, Perkins argued that they "are stable and central in socialization, widely and consistently believed in and highly effective" (p. 147). Stereotypes of pariah groups are structurally supported and reinforced, but ". . . belief in them is inconsistent, but very subject to manipulation at particular times. They are, by definition, highly pejorative" (p. 148).

Perhaps no children's book entrenched and perpetuated stereotypes of African Americans as *The Story of Little Black Sambo* (Bannerman, 1899; 1923). *The Story of Little Black Sambo* contains several stereotypes: the comic Negro, the local color Negro, and the exotic primitive. Support for this contention rests upon the following facts: the book remains in publication today, albeit without the gross, caricatured illustrations; dozens of companies published versions of the book; other cultural artifacts such as playing cards, cookie jars, toys, towels, postcards, and so forth featured Sambos; and the very name has come to symbolize African Americans (Yuill, 1976; Harris, 1990). Many well-regarded magazines such as *Lippincotts* featured plantation and "Sambo-like" stories. The book proved so popular that Bannerman produced other books of that ilk — *The Story of Little Black Bobtail* (1909), *The Story of Little Black Mingo* (n. d.); *Sambo and the Twins* (1936), *The Story of Little Black Quibba* (1903), *The Story of Little Black Quasha* (1908), *The Story of Little Kettle-Head* (1904), and *The Story of The Teasing Monkey* (1907).

The popularity of *The Story of Little Black Sambo* resulted in numerous imitations, for example, *New Nigger Nursery Rhymes* (n.d.), *Little Pickaninnies* (Chubb, 1929), seven Nicodemus books written by Inez Hogan, and scores of other books. One of these, *Pinky Marie* (Graham, 1939), illustrates the deprecating nature of the stories. Pinky Marie and her parents, Mr. and Mrs. Washington Jefferson Jackson, prepare for Mr. Jackson's trip to town to purchase seeds for planting. Mr. and Mrs. Jackson are described as "Black as Ink!;" they also have large, thick, red lips. Pinky Marie is described as "brown like a chocolate bar;" her hair has scores of braids with yarn in each. Undoubtedly, she and her parents are comic Negroes and the antics of the family are suggestive of the minstrel tradition; and excerpt supports this view:

> One day Mrs. Washington Jefferson Jackson called, "Pinky Marie-e-e-e! Pinky Marie-e-e-e-e!" And Pinky Marie, who was making mud pies out by the old rain barrel, said, "Yes Mammy." Then Mrs. Washington Jefferson Jackson said, "Pinky Marie, this is goin'-to-town-day. Yo' Pappy is goin' to town to buy some seeds for us to plant. Would you like to go along?" And Pinky Marie said, "Oh, yes, yes, yessum, Mammy. Is you goin' too?" "Oh,

no," said Mrs. Washington Jefferson Jackson. "I'se goin' to stay home and bake-bake pies and bread and cake for us to eat. But I'll dress you up and you can go. Only be good. Be good as gold, Pinky Marie." And Pinky Marie said, "Yes Mammy, I will. I sho' will (unnumbered pages).

This is an unacceptable story because the author included subtle and not so subtle stereotypes. For example, some Whites denigrated the names selected by African Americans as being too pompous, especially the appropriation of presidential surnames; this view is echoed here. Also, the gross illustrations perpetuate the view that African American physical features are not regarded as beautiful.

It would be misleading to suggest that all White authors created stereotyped literature, although most did. A few, during and immediately after slavery, attempted to create literature that would encourage abolitionist sentiments or notions of interracial tolerance and equality. For example, the authors of books such as *Cousin Ann's Stories for Children* (1849), *The Young Abolitionists; or Conversations on Slavery* (1848), *Juvenile Poems, for the Use of Free American Children, of Every Complexion* (1835), and *The Anti-Slavery Alphabet* (1847) attempted to imbue children with noble sentiments. Authors such as Mary White Ovington wrote books during the early twentieth century that provided a range of images about African Americans. Her novels, *Hazel* (1903) and *Zeke* (1931) were praised because of their sensitivity and veracity. Despite these periodic examples of authenticity, stereotypes about African Americans abounded in children's literature.

A parallel body of children's literature created by African Americans for African-American children existed contemporaneously with the stereotyped literature. However, these authors lacked the power needed to usurp the authority of the images presented in *The Story of Little Black Sambo* and other books of that ilk. Research indicates that this parallel literature appeared in the late 19th century (Muse, 1975; Fraser, 1973). Many of the books were published by small presses owned by African-American religious groups or commercial publishers. Several reasons account for the creation of this unheralded and marginalized literature. An educated, African-American middle class increased after the Civil War and demanded more affirmative literature. The status of children's literature, in general, improved as a golden age evolved. African Americans concerned about the education of their children considered children's literature an appropriate medium for informing their children of their heritage, instilling race pride, and inculcating values such as racial uplift. African Americans demanded texts for their children that would challenge the power of textbooks that depicted them as inferior. The 1880s saw the creation of a few texts that served as harbingers of a body of literature that trickled out one or two books at a time, but would eventually become a constant flow by the last decades of the twentieth century. Some of these first attempts remain in publication today as reprints of historical series; others remain "undiscovered."

IN THE BEGINNING: CLARENCE AND CORINNE AND LITTLE BROWN BABY

Mrs. A. E. Johnson authored two novels titled *Clarence And Corinne* (1890) and *The Hazelby Family* (1894) and one periodical, *The Joy* that circulated for two years in the 1880s (Muse, 1975). Some researchers regard these books and Mrs. Johnson's periodical as the first examples of African-American children's literature (Fraser, 1973; Muse 1975). The novels, although written by an African American, featured Whites. This suggests that Mrs. Johnson felt her stories would acquire an audience if the characters were White or their race was obscured. The fact that she did so indicates that publishing opportunities were limited or she simply chose not to write as a representative of the race. The central characters in each are stalwart children who overcome various vicissitudes to triumph by acquiring education, middle-class morality, and the appropriate social values. Thus, far, no extant copies of *The Joy* have been found and researchers have depended upon the comments provided by Mrs. Johnson's contemporaries about the short-lived periodical. It is quite conceivable that some literature written by and for African-American children existed prior to the publication of Mrs. Johnson's works, but these no longer exist or go unnoticed in attics, archives, or other respositories.

A stronger case exists for labelling Paul Laurence Dunbar's *Little Brown Baby* (1895) as one of the first books written and focused on African Americans (Muse, 1975; Harris, 1990). Whether Dunbar sought to create a book of poetry specifically for children seems not the case based on an examination of some of the available biographies and critical studies (Gayle, 1971). What seems likely is that Dunbar's publisher sought to capitalize upon his growing popularity. More than likely, an editor selected from Dunbar's canon that poetry suitable children. Most of the poems are written in dialect and convey images of African Americans that supported some of the prevailing attitudes and stereotypes. They contain lots of singing, dancing, picnics, and fun times. Given that the book was for children, this would likely be the case. The poems, as a whole, compare favorably to other collections of poetry for children. Nevertheless, the book garners attention because of its historical significance.

According to Muse (1975) other historic examples of African-American children's literature will have to be recovered from the archives of churches, particularly the African Methodist Episcopal, Colored Methodist Episcopal, and Baptist Sunday School press. These religious denominations were primarily responsible for most of the literature produced during the next 40 years. If one expands the definition of literature to include biographies, speeches, essays, and readers, then the number of books expands somewhat in the early 1900s. For instance, Silas X. Floyd wrote *Floyd's Flowers or Duty and Beauty for Colored Children* in 1905. The book underwent at least three reprints with different titles through 1925. If one adheres strictly to a definition of children's literature as poetry, fiction, and drama, then significant numbers of books do not appear until the 1920s and 1930s. Two intellectuals and social/political activists, W. E. B. Du Bois and Carter G. Woodson, founded publishing companies, Du Bois & Dill Publishing Company and the Associated Publishers, respectively, that were responsible for the advancement of African-American children's literature.

Both publishers, dismayed and angered by the effects upon children of reading stereotyped literature, decided to publish children's literature that depicted a range of perspectives, beliefs, and values held by African Americans. The publishers sought to inform, entertain, and inculcate specific ideologies within readers. Racial pride and uplift were basic tenets in their publications. Equally important, the illustrations found in the books and periodicals reflected the immense variety among African Americans in terms of skin color, hair textures, and physical features. Du Bois and Woodson set for themselves the tasks of battling centuries of denigration and racism by presenting literature that challenged stereotypes and authentic images.

Du Bois, along with partner and business manager Augustus G. Dill and literary editor, Jessie Fauset, were responsible for *The Brownies' Book,* presumably, the second periodical for children created by African Americans (Sinnette, 1965; Saul, 1984; Harris, 1986, 1990; Vaughn-Roberson, & Hill, 1989; Johnson, 1991). *The Brownies' Book* featured the philosophies of Du Bois and Fauset, philosophies that championed race pride, intellectual excellence, and commitment to racial uplift among others. In addition, they tried to entertain and inform children through a combination of monthly columns, poetry, playlets, stories, biographies, and news selections. The Du Bois & Dill company also published a collective biography, *Unsung Heroes* (Haynes, 1921) and a biography of Paul Laurence Dunbar titled *A Child's Story of Dunbar* (Henderson, 1921).

Carter G. Woodson and his associates strengthened and advanced the new tradition inaugurated by Du Bois and Dill. Woodson argued that African Americans were "miseducated;" they were provided schooling that only prepared them to assume a low caste status. He argued that African Americans needed an education that would promote lifelong learning and achievement as well as group advancement. Woodson decided to publish literature and school texts that would achieve these goals. Woodson had an exceptional ability to recognize talent. For instance, many of the books his company published were illustrated by Lois Mailou Jones, an artist of considerable talent and acclaim. In addition, many of the writers of the biographies, rhyme books, and stories were teachers who were, presumably, aware of the types of literature that appealed to children. Among the books published were *The Picture Poetry Book* (McBrown, 1935), *The Child's Story of the Negro* (Shackelford, 1938), *Negro Art Music and Rhyme, Book II* (Whiting, 1928), *Negro Folk Tales, Book I* (Whiting, 1938), and *African Heroes and Heroines* (Woodson, 1939). Woodson published several books in the 1940s and 1950s among them *Gladiola Garden* (Newsome, 1944) and *Pioneers of Long Ago* (Roy & Turner, 1951). Some of these books were adopted by school districts and a few were placed in libraries throughout the country. The Associated Publishers remains in existence today and many of the works exhibit qualities that keep them timely generations later.

Most of the literature produced by African Americans for children emanated from small, independent publishers. These publishers managed to garner an audience but they lacked the marketing power of "mainstream" children's book publishers. One African-American author who succeeded in breaking publishing barriers and gaining wide acceptance in the 1930s was Arna Bontemps. Bontemps, along with poet Langston Hughes, wrote a novel, *Popo and Fifina* (1932) that remained in publication for more than 20 years and was translated into several languages (Nicholas, 1980). Bontemps also created a substantial body of literature — 16 novels, biographies, poetry anthologies, histories, and folk tales well into the late 1970s. The books were popular with African-American children and children of other races/ethnicities. Bontemps propelled African-American children's literature into the mainstream. Although less overtly racial in tone, the fiction conveyed a subtle sense of race. Generally, the books depicted the universal activities in which most people engage.

Other authors followed Bontemps into the mainstream in the 1940s, 1950s, and 1960s although they struggled such as Jessie Jackson and Lorenzo Graham. Sims (1982) characterized the literature produced during these decades as social conscience and melting pot books. Social conscience books were deliberate attempts to imbue a "social conscience — mainly in non-Afro-American readers, to encourage them to develop empathy, sympathy, and tolerance for Afro-American children and their problems" (p. 17). In contrast, Sims argued that melting pot books "ignore all differences except physical ones: skin color and other racial related features. The result is that the majority of them are picture books" (p. 33). These books, however, served a useful function; they allowed glimpses into African-American life for those whose primary images and information resulted from stereotyped materials. A major shift occurred in children's literature during the mid-to-late 1960s, a move to create literature categorized by Sims as "culturally conscious." Arguably, this significant shift resulted from the historical efforts of African Americans and some progressive Whites. Many cite an article written by Nancy Larrick as pivotal.

Nancy Larrick did not initiate concern about the dearth of African Americans in children's literature, but her article "The All-White World of Children's Books (1965) succeeded within the mainstream in a manner that eclipsed the efforts of individuals such as Virginia Lacy, Charlemae Rollins, and Augusta Baker. In a scenario undoubtedly repeated in classrooms around the country, a young African-American girl inquired of Larrick why the characters in books were always white. Larrick could not provide an acceptable answer. She sought to determine the reasons why the situation existed. She surveyed publishers about the depiction of African Americans in books published from 1962 through 1964. Larrick found that of the 5,206 books published, only 6.7% included African Americans in plots or illustrations. Publishers offered many excuses and rationales: their customers, i.e., White, customers, were not interested in books about African Americans; a market for the literature did not exist; publishers would offend Southern White sensibilities and consequently, lose long-standing customers; and few African-American authors and illustrators created works for children. The efforts of Du Bois and Woodson to publish children's literature contradicted these excuses.

Changing socio-political conditions, the advances of the modern civil rights movement, a burgeoning Black Arts movement, the end of colonialism in Africa and elsewhere, the contradictions evident in U. S. foreign policy regarding the espousal of freedom around the world and the existence of racism at home, an infusion of federal dollars into literacy programs, increasing numbers of authors and illustrators who created for children, and the demands of African Americans for literature relevant to their children, combined to result in more books depicting African Americans. By the late 1970s, 14.4% of children's books published included illustrations of African Americans or featured them in plots (Chall, et al., 1979).

The boom, however, did not last. By the early 1980s the inclusion of African Americans in children's literature dropped drastically; fewer than 2% of the total number of books published included them (Sims, 1985). The reasons given for the sharp decline were comparable to those given Larrick in the 1960s. The end of the 1980s provided some hope that the percentages would improve.

THE CURRENT STATUS OF AFRICAN-AMERICAN CHILDREN'S LITERATURE

Over 5000 children's books were published in 1990; only 51 of these were written and/or illustrated by African Americans (Cooperative Children's Book Center, 1991). That figure amounts to less than 2% of all children's books. Other data illustrate the precarious status of African-American literature. Only one book written by an African American for children was a best-seller in 1990 (Roback, 1991). That book was *Roll of Thunder, Hear My Cry* (Taylor, 1976). A book has to post minimal sales of 100,000 in paperback or 75,000 in hardback to garner designation as a best-seller. Further, in a survey of booksellers, fewer than 5% indicated a possible increase in requests for multicultural literature (Roback, 1990). Coupled with perennial problems and excuses such as perceptions among some that the books are only for African-American children, or the belief that customers do not want to purchase the books, or the limited availability of the books in local, regional, and chain bookstores, and the limited publication life of books, the problems seem insurmountable.

Anecdotal information and sales data offer support for the contention that an unserved market for African-American children's literature exists. For example, at a recent speaking engagement in New Jersey, an attendant related the success she and her colleagues had with a book fair featuring African-American children's literature (personal communication, January

15, 1992). They planned a book fair in conjunction with a specialty bookstore, an organization that supported African-American families, and local school officials. The book fair posted sales in excess of $2500. Another example illustrates the need for the literature. After I made an announcement at a local church about the third annual African-American Read-In Chain sponsored by the National Council of Teachers of English, several congregants approached me for information about books and places to purchase the books. There are examples involving publishing companies as well. Wade and Cheryl Hudson founded Just Us Books because they could not locate children's books that provided positive portrayals of African-American children. In just three years, their company has sold over 350,000 copies of seven titles including *Bright Eyes, Brown Skin* (Hudson & Ford, 1990). Janus Adams was swamped with membership applications for the Harambee Bookclub whose purpose is to make available literature by and about African Americans (Ihejirika, 1990). Numerous bookstores, The Hue-Man Experience in Denver, Colorado, Nkiru Books in Brooklyn, New York, and the African-American Book Center in Chicago, Illinois serve patrons in their local markets as well as throughout the country.

Clearly, a need for literature by and about African Americans exists, but the need remains unmet for many. Despite the precarious market conditions, the authors and illustrators labor at their craft to create books that readers desire; again, these fit under the rubric of culturally conscious literature.

Culturally conscious books nearly constitute a body of Afro-American literature for children according to Sims (1982). These books were written by and for African-American children. They have certain characteristics: characters who are African American, set in African-American homes or communities, they contain the variety of language patterns found among African Americans, and they include African-American customs, rituals, and history. The literature began appearing in the late 1960s. Perhaps, the one book that signalled the emergence of culturally conscious literature is Virginia Hamilton's *Zeely* (1967). Hamilton, an extraordinarily gifted writer succeeded in conveying new perspectives about African and African-American families. Geeder, the protagonist, and her brother Toeboy (names they assume as they vacation at their uncle's farm) are loved, nurtured, and guided by their parents and extended family. While poking around in her uncle's attic, Geeder discovers a treasure trove of old magazines. As she peruses through them she encounters a photograph of a Watutsi woman that leaves her awestruck. The woman's extraordinary beauty entrances Geeder. Later, she receives a shock when she discovers that a local woman, Zeely, bears an eerie resemblance to the woman featured in the magazine. They form a friendship, tentative at first, but more comfortable later. *Zeely* contains no images of Africa as the dark continent peopled by uncivilized hordes unlike the popular Tarzan series. Instead, the Watutsi are depicted as regal, proud people with a complex culture. Hamilton's book helped insure that children would have alternative portrayals of Africa and African-American families.

Many other writers emerged along with Hamilton to create a body of literature notable for its literary and artistic excellence and its ability to, in the words of Eloise Greenfield (1975), "take effect." Some recurring trends and themes as well as new ones began appearing in this culturally conscious literature. A discussion of those trends and themes follows.

Recurring and New Trends and Themes

Several new changes are apparent in today's African-American children's literature. Two trends relate to authors and illustrators and publishers, the rest to the content found in the literature (Harris, 1991; Bishop, 1990). Picture books flourish. They detail a variety of experiences in a many settings. For example Elizabeth Howard's (1991) *Aunt Flossie's Hats (And Crabcakes Later), The Train to Lulu's* (1988), and *Chita's Christmas Tree* (1989) depict the intergenerational experiences of a middle class family. Angela Johnson's books, *Tell Me a Story Mama* (1989), *Do Like Kyla* (1990), *When I Am Old With You* (1990), and *One of Three* (1991), focus on the everyday experiences of siblings, their parents, and grandparents. Many of the illustrators utilize a variety of artistic styles from representational to impressionistic to expressionistic. The late John Steptoe's books suggest this range. The father and son duo, Jerry and Brian Pinkney, also use divergent, though recognizable styles. Notable in most of the illustrations is the individuality evident in the character's physical features.

A second trend involves the push by small presses to fulfill the unmet needs of readers. Just Us Books, founded by Cheryl and Wade Hudson is one of the more successful. The Hudsons created their publishing company because they could not find literature that positively reflected their children's cultural heritage (Hudson & Hudson, 1991). They carved a niche in publishing through a particular marketing strategy. They created a network of regional distributors and independent sales personnel and sell their books in non-traditional venues such as beauty and barber shops, bakeries, and beauty supply stores. In addition, in a recent venture with

Scott Foresman, one of their books, *Bright Eyes, Brown Skin* (Hudson & Ford, 1990), will appear in the company's new reading program. Other presses, for instance, Derek-Winston have also made some inroads (Igus, 1990).

A hallmark of culturally conscious literature is the inclusion and celebration of African-American cultural traditions. These are not attempts to explain the cultural traditions, but rather a sharing of information the reader is thought to possess, or at least, recognize. Some of the rituals celebrated include church attendance, Sunday suppers, beautification rituals, double dutch jump rope rhymes, commentaries about slavery and segregation, and interactions with social and political organizations. Granted, these activities are found in many cultures but they are rendered as central to the lives of African-American families and reflect their interpretation of them. Consider *Irene's Big Fine Nickel* (Smalls, 1991), a book in which the author states explicitly her intention to celebrate a time in African-American history when modern ills did not have such a devastating effect on communities. Other indications that diversity is acknowledged stems from the use of varied language patterns ranging from regional and invented dialects to Standard English and Black Vernacular English.

The extended family, a crucial feature of African-American culture, receives extensive coverage, especially the relationships between grandparent or elderly relative or friend and child. These elders serve as family griots or persons responsible for the transmission of family memories as well as African-American history; *The Patchwork Quilt* (Flournoy, 1985) is an excellent example of this. A certain amount of humor is evident in some of the books. For instance, *What Kind of Babysitter Are You?* (Shelby, 1991) features a spunky, elderly woman who wins over her young charge through unorthodox behavior; or at least, behavior considered unusual by the boy she baby-sits. She knows quite a bit about the history of baseball and wears the baseball hat and waves the pennant of her favorite team as they watch a televised game.

Contemporary realistic fiction tended to be the most popular genre in the past but a resurgence in the popularity of other genres is evident. Single folk tales and collections of folk tales appeared with greater regularity. For example, the folk tales *Mufaro's Beautiful Daughter* (Steptoe, 1987) and *Mirandy and Brother Wind* (McKissack, 1988) highlight African and African-American cultures respectively. Each won a Caldecott Honor Medal for distinguished illustrations. Examples of folk tale collections include three volumes of Uncle Remus tales retold by Julius Lester and Virginia Hamilton's collections — *The People Could Fly* (1985), *In the Beginning*

(1988), *The Dark Way* (1990), and *The All-Jahdu Storybook* (1991) — represent a virtual cottage industry.

Historical fiction, for example *Taking Care of Yoki* (Campbell, 1982), *Fallen Angels* (Myers, 1988), and *Anthony Burns* (Hamilton, 1988), demonstrate the renewed interest in documenting the accomplishments and history of African Americans. Many more biographies appeared in traditional formats and non-traditional formats, for example, *Don't Explain* (De Veaux, 1984) and as picture books, for instance, *Rosa Parks* (Greenfield, 1973). Information books on topics as diverse as the pullman car porters, dance, scientists, and the underground railroad provided historical information generally omitted or given limited exposure in textbooks. James Haskins' books and Patricia and Frederick McKissack's *A Long Hard Journey* (1990) are exemplars.

A welcome addition children's literature was the creation of books for early childhood featuring African-American children. Two popular books, *Afro-Bets ABC* (Hudson, 1987) and *Afro-Bets 123* (Hudson, 1987) led the way. The contributions of Donald Crews are also important because his illustrations feature children from a range of ethnicities and races. Eloise Greenfield's greatest contribution in the 1990s is, arguably, the four board books with charming titles such as *My Doll Keisha* (1991), *Daddy and I* (1991), *Big Friend, Little Friend (1991)*, and *I Make Music* (1991). Poetry has not experienced a resurgence although Greenfield was responsible for two major offerings, *Nathaniel Talking* (1988) and *Night On Neighborhood Street* (1991). Also, Sharon Bell Mathis, author of *The Hundred Penny Box* (1975) and other books, returned to children's literature in 1991 with an illustrated volume off poetry entitled *Red Dog, Blue Fly*.

One area of neglect is series books. A series book features one or more characters who appear in at least three books. Some series do exist, for example, Lorenzo Graham's four "town" books, Lucille Clifton's six *Everett Anderson books,* Mildred Taylor's six books of historical fiction that chronicle the Logan family, and Virginia Hamilton's three books of science fiction-fantasy, the Justice trilogy. What has been missing are the light-hearted series books that focus on the everyday fun and foibles that children face or mystery series. The Baby-sitters Club series fills the void somewhat for girls. One of the major characters, Jessi, is African American; she is intelligent, talented and confident. She does not live in an African-American community; her father received a job promotion and they relocated from a predominantly African-American community. Her family integrated into a community, that on the whole, has accepted them after some initial problems. True to fashion, those individuals who resented the family are given scant attention. In some ways, Jessi represents the fulfillment of the goals of integrationists. Two books that featured Jessi, *Jessi and the Superbrat* (Martin, 1989) and *Jessi's Baby-sitter* (Martin, 1990) were paperback best-sellers in 1990.

Two independent publishers have plans for series featuring African-American girls. The William Ruth Company, a marketing firm, published an historical fiction series titled *Willie Pearl* (King, 1992). Willie Pearl's family are hard-working individuals who believe in values such as love for family, the work ethic, and lessened emphasis on materialistic goals. Thus far, one book *Willie Pearl* (Green, 1990) in a planned series of six has been published. A second book, *Under the Mountain,* is in development. In addition to the books, the company has ancillary materials such as a doll version of Willie Pearl; they plan to produce a doll of her best friend and her brother as well as other items. The series has achieved some success (King, 1992). The company published a total of 2500 books as a part of the first edition and increased the second edition to 10,000. School districts in California, Georgia, and the Washington, D.C. area have adopted the series.

The Pleasant Company, publisher of the *American Girls* series, plans to publish a set of six books with an African-American character named Addie (Johnson, 1991). The stories will be set in the periods during and after the Civil War. The Pleasant Company also plans to introduce a doll and other ancillaries.

Several themes and topics are explored by the authors. Among the themes woven within the various plots are:

- Questions of identity. What does it mean to be a person of African descent in the United States or a hyphenated American?
- The effects of racism and legal discrimination
- Information about slavery as an institution and its impact
- Struggles for equality
- Interracial relationships
- Families and their loyalties and obligations to each other
- Love and its meanings and manifestations
- The effects of beauty standards that oppress
- Friendships
- Everyday rituals and events in life
- Extraordinary events that create unlikely heroes and heroines

- Intragroup color differences
- Struggles for and the value of education
- Commitment to racial uplift and progress
- Consequences of drug and alcohol abuse, unemployment, under-education, single parenthood, and poverty
- Strength and resilience of African-American people and culture
- Contributions of African Americans to United States history and culture
- Knowing, valuing, and preserving African-American history and culture
- Strength of African-American families, especially the extended family.

These changes in publishing and genres and the examination of universal and culturally specific themes and topics insure that African-American children's literature will remain a viable force in literature. The exceptional talent of the authors and illustrators should help eradicate the notion that African-American children's literature is without literary merit.

Other Considerations

Several authors who write books that fit under the rubric of culturally conscious literature are not discussed, in particular, non-African-American authors. Some authors create texts that present African Americans in a non-stereotyped fashion, for instance, Ezra J. Keats, Milton Meltzer, Arnold Adoff, Vera Williams, Crescent Dragonwagon, and others. Many of their works are included on the recommended reading list. This "exclusion" was not meant to suggest that these authors cannot or should not write about African Americans, but rather to discuss authors who must fight for exposure. As discussed in a previous section, Du Bois initiated a debate about who could portray African Americans most authentically. The discussion continues today. For example, Sims (1984) engaged in a written debate with author Belinda Hurmence about Hurmence's *A Girl Called Boy* (1982). Sims conceded that Hurmence had literary license to write about a culture outside her experience but wondered why. Sims argued that Hurmence lacked the insider's perspective that would have enabled a more authentic presentation. Had Hurmence possessed this perspective, she would not have written a scene, among other unauthentic ones, that strongly suggested that African Americans did not care about their families.

Author Patricia Howard addressed the issue as well (April, 1990). She contended that authentic books result from those who are a part of the culture. She stated that it was possible for others to write about African Americans, but that certain pre-conditions had to be met such as an awareness of the infinite variety that exists among African Americans, acknowledgment of the bonding that occurs in African-American families and communities, an understanding of the influence of African Americans on American culture, and some perception of the loyalty of African Americans to America. I agree with Sims and Howard.

In some cases, an insider's perspective is not necessary. For example, many of the board books created to teach ABCs, counting, and object identification skills are not dependent on cultural specificity. These usually require photographs or illustrations of children that can be of any race/ethnicity. However, publishers and authors can recognize the diversity that exists within the country and work to insure that children of all races/ethnicities appear in the books.

More than likely, the question will not be resolved especially when the resulting books result in the perpetuation of stereotypes as depicted in *Jake and Honeybunch Go To Heaven* (Zemach, 1982) and *Big Sixteen* (Calhoun, 1983). Censoring these books is not the answer; promoting and sharing authentic literature is the just action. Furthermore, why select these books when other examples exist that can offer the reader so much more?

CONTEMPORARY GRIOTS AND WORD SORCERERS

Writing children's literature centered on the experiences, history, and culture of African Americans transformed many of the authors. A few, for example, John Steptoe and Mildred Taylor, deliberately set out to challenge racist images in textbooks and fiction that bombarded them as children. Others, for instance Hamilton, shared the sacred "Knowledge" received from family members and elders with children because they did not want to lose this valued part of history. All use language to express their creativity, entertain, educate, and socialize. I examine a representative sampling of those who are in the vanguard — Virginia Hamilton, Lucille Clifton, Eloise Greenfield, Mildred Taylor, the late John Steptoe, and Walter D. Myers; the reinforcements — Ashley Bryan, Jeanette Caines, and Patricia McKissack; and the reinterpreters — Angela Johnson, Emily Moore, and Patricia Fitzgerald. Without a doubt, these authors create culturally conscious literature.

Virginia Hamilton

As mentioned previously, *Zeely* (1967) helped recast the image of Africa in children's literature. Her literary muse unleashed, Hamilton proceeded to produce six more books by 1974. These books varied in terms of genre — folk tales, contemporary realistic fiction, biography, science fiction, and mystery. Each book received highly favorable reviews and awards. Unquestionably, she is one the best writers today; for example, she is the United States' 1992 nominee for the Hans Christian Andersen Award which recognizes lifetime achievement in children's literature. Critics hailed Hamilton's works, especially *M. C. Higgins, the Great* (1974). This book succeeded in a manner unequalled in children's literature. The book received numerous awards including the Newbery Medal (the first book written by an African American to do so), the Boston Globe-Horn Book Award, and the National Book Award. *M. C. Higgins, the Great* chronicles the coming of age of Mayo Cornelius Higgins as he confronts the environmental threat to his family's home and his dreams for helping his family leave the mountain in search of upward mobility elsewhere. It is also a book about love, family heritage, bequeathing historical memories, the centrality of music in the lives of individuals, and the duties and obligations to one's family.

Hamilton's talent grows with each book. She manages to include a range of emotions from the bemused to the sweet anguish of first love. Another earlier book, *Willie Bea and the Time the Martians Landed* (1983) conveys Hamilton's sense of humor, her belief in the importance of family, and her familiarity and ease with African-American culture and language. The following excerpt illustrates these qualities:

> "Commere, baby girl!" said Grand, wiping her hands on a dish towel. Willie Bea was in her grandmother's arms. Letting herself be petted, pampered, her hair smoothed around her face. The ruffles of her bodice were pulled up through the fingers that were long, dark and tough, testing the amount of starch in the pinafore. Those sure hands knew their business of soothing and raising grandchildren. Next Mattie Wing came forward. She had been rolling dough out with the rolling pin on the counter beneath the cabinets. She kept her floured hands away from Willie Bea's pretty dress. "Uh-huh," she said. "You gettin' just too beautiful chile. Marva, where she get her looks?" "Me, who else?" said her mama. "Sweet, mercy me!" And the women laughed. (p. 22).

Even Willie Bea's name bespeaks of African-American culture as well as phrases such as baby girl and chile.

Writing is an art form for Hamilton that is gilded by her personal political philosophy: "I write from a love of creating and fabricating. It is also very important to me that I speak to the history, culture, and traditions that I grew up with (Hamilton, 1986, pp. 16-17). Unmistakably, Hamilton grew up in a home that valued African-American heroes and her-oes (her term), culture, and history. She refers to this as the "Knowledge" (Hamilton, 1975). Hamilton induces her reader into the realms of the remembered, the known, and the imaged (Hamilton, 1987) in a non-didactic manner. In more than 28 books, Hamilton creates fictive and real worlds that expand the creative boundaries of children's literature. Other authors, to a great extent, must measure up to her creative standards.

Young readers possess distinct preferences in literature (Arbuthnot & Sutherland, 1991). They prefer literature that contains families, animals, children similar to themselves, and satisfying endings. They find these qualities and more in the 17 books created by Lucille Clifton.

Lucille Clifton

Although she has not written for children in several years, Clifton's books possess timeless qualities that make them fresh and appealing to today's young readers. Clifton, too, celebrates and champions African-American people and culture. Her role as mother enabled her to observe children in all their moods and stages. Many of those observations are found, though transformed, in her works. Clifton is particularly notable because of her defense and use of Black Vernacular English.

> I do not write out of weakness. That is to say, I do not write the language I write because I don't know any other. I often say I write "Everett Anderson" to prove I know about iambic pentameter and standard written speech. But I have a certain integrity about my art, and in my *art* you have to be hones and you have to have people talking the way they really talk. So all of my books are not in the same language. (Senich, 1983, p. 52)

In the six Everett Anderson books, *All Us Come Cross the Water* (1973), *My Brother Fine With Me* (1975) and *Amifika* (1977), urban children can see themselves and hear their voices. Their fears, dreams, and needs are given full expression. For instance, the reader grows with Everett Anderson as he plays, goes to school, experiences the death of his father, his mother's remarriage, and the birth of a new sister.

Clifton's poetic forms in some of the stories and her poetic language in others lend a special tone to her works. One of her best works is *The Times*

They Used to Be (1974), an example of historical fiction that captures the spirit of a segregated African-American community after World War II. The narrator, Sookie, and her friend Tassie are on the verge of adolescence and cannot wait to try its adventures, as illustrated in this excerpt:

> Me and Tassie, Tassie and me. We was best friends; going to the show together, and hitching on the iceman's truck, and going on long walks over to the white folk's section to look in their windows. One time we walked all the way uptown to see Johnny Ray come out of the radio station. He touched Tassie's hand, and she swore she wasn't never going to write with it anymore or nothing. Her whole name was Tallahassie May Scott and she lived next door to us with her granny. And she wasn't saved. (unnumbered pages)

Clifton writes poetic narratives. She uses Black Vernacular language and slips in aspects of African-American history such as Sookie's family boarding members of the Elk convention because the hotels did not allow "coloreds" to rent accommodations, or references to "colored" divisions in World War II, or getting one's hair done. The reader sense instantly Clifton's intimate connections with the culture she recreates.

Few African-American authors create books in which all the characters are European Americans. Clifton did in her novella, *Sonora Beautiful* (1981). She also did not shy away from including characters of many ethnicities in her books, for example *My Friend Jacob* (1980) and *The Boy Who Didn't Believe in Spring* (1973). Another experiment that proved successful was her foray into fantasy in which a character is placed in the historical past, *The Lucky Stone* (1979). The book recounts the story of a stone passed from generation to generation that enabled its possessor to persevere through many obstacles including slavery. Clifton concentrates now on writing poetry for adults but her contributions to children's literature endure.

Eloise Greenfield

Like Lucille Clifton, Eloise Greenfield creates poetry, picture books, biographies, and now, board books for younger readers with some occasional works for intermediate readers. She has also written two book with her mother. Perhaps best known for *Me and Neesie* (1975) and *Honey, I Love* (1978), Greenfield's latest offerings, four board books, two volumes of poetry, and a picture book, will guarantee legions of new fans.

She, too, extols African-American culture through everyday acts, for example, children playing in the neighborhood, chanting the words to handclap games and jump-rope rhymes. She believes that writing serves aesthetic and political functions:

Writing is my work. It is work that is in harmony with me; it sustains me. I want, through my work, to help sustain children. My attempts and those of other writers to offer sustenance will necessarily be largely ineffectual. Not only do we as human beings have limitations — so does the written word. It cannot be eaten or worn; it cannot cure disease; it cannot dissipate pollution, defang a racist, cause a spoonful of heroin to disintegrate. But, at the right time, in the right circumstances, falling on the right mind, a word may take effect. (1975, p. 624)

The goals she hoped to achieve with her writing ranged from "[to] give children a love for the arts," "to give children a true knowledge of Black heritage," and "to help children celebrate language" (pp. 624-626).

A certain sassiness permeates Greenfield's poetry. Her poems evoke images of children who like themselves and feel comfortable venturing into the world. The poem "Honey, I Love" (1978) calls forth knowing smiles and pleasant memories.

The poetry conveys a sense of orality that is enhanced more if readers read the poems aloud and images how a child would sound doing so. Greenfield's other books of poetry expand the usual topics found in children's books. *Nathaniel Talking* (1988) featured an African-American boy and *Night on Neighborhood Street* (1991) presents the scenarios children face in an urban neighborhood — the good, evil, and in-between. *Under the Sunday Tree* (1988) pairs Greenfield with artist Mr. John Ames whose bold colors and folk images give the poems a new dimension.

Her other works explore many themes such as the love between grandchild and grandparent, sibling conflict and support, divorce and its effects on children, play and its rewards, and dreams. In each, she retains the feelings and voices of children. Greenfield has also made a concerted effort to publish with African-American companies. Many of the books published in the late 1980s and 1990s were illustrated by Jan Gilchrist Spivey and published by Black Butterfly Children's Books.

Unlike Hamilton, Clifton, and Greenfield, Mildred Taylor focuses solely on historical fiction as she chronicles the Logan family in Mississippi. The saga of the Logan family, in many ways, symbolizes the trials and triumphs of all African Americans prior to the advent of the modern civil rights movement.

Mildred Taylor

Storytelling was crucial to Mildred Taylor's development as a writer; she is indeed a modern day griot. Her father and other relatives told stories about the family's experiences in the South. These family stories left an indelible impression upon Taylor. Family lore contradicted the official versions of history presented by teachers and in textbooks. According to Taylor, these depicted African Americans as happy-go-lucky, hapless people who benefitted from a paternalistic, benign system of slavery (Taylor, 1990). In contrast, the stories she heard at home detailed her family's proud heritage, their struggle to maintain and retain ownership and control of their land in Mississippi at a time when many African Americans were chained to an exploitative sharecropping system.

The stories shared in the home became the catalyst for an extraordinary series that rivets the reader through honesty, poignancy, humor, tragedy, strong characterization, bold action, and its sense of hope. It began with *Song of the Trees* (1975), a short novella told from the perspective of Cassie Logan, a young girl. Cassie, her parents David and Mary, grandmother Big Ma, and brothers Stacy, Little Man, and Christopher John are a close-knit, religious, educated, and proud family. The family is also the envy of most Whites and some African Americans. They are unbowed by racism; their land is coveted by a vindictive White landowner who does everything, legal and illegal, to wrest control of the land. David Logan and his family quell all attempts to do so. The novella won a contest sponsored by the Council on Interracial Books for Children in 1973.

The sequel, *Roll of Thunder, Hear My Cry* (1976) had the distinction of being the second book written by an African American to receive the Newbery Medal. It, too, has an unrelenting tone of honesty, drama, and emotional ups and down. The characterization rings true: Cassie is a child who possesses none of the obnoxious precociousness that affects many youthful characters. She is intelligent, temperamental, occasionally perplexed and frightened but never broken in spirit. Cassie possesses the sensibilities of a child. Consider the following excerpt in which Cassie has been allowed to accompany Big Ma and Stacy to the larger town of Strawberry to sell foodstuffs. Cassie and Stacy accompany a neighbor friend, T. J., to a store where he purchases foodstuffs and household items. Cassie does not understand why they must wait until White customers, including children, are served first:

> After waiting several minutes for Mr. Barnett's return, Stacy said, "Come on, Cassie, let's go." He started toward the door and I followed. But as we

passed one of the counters, I spied Mr. Barnett wrapping an order of pork chops for a white girl. Adults were one thing; I could almost understand that. They ruled things and there was nothing that could be done about them. But some kid who was no bigger than me was something else again. Certainly Mr. Barnett had simply forgotten about T. J.'s order. I decided to remind him and, without saying anything to Stacey, I turned around and marched over to Mr. Barnett. (p. 110)

Cassie had not been informed of the "proper" protocol for venturing into a White-owned store. She commits an unforgivable breach of conduct when she interrupts Mr. Barnett and tugs on his sleeve:

He recoiled as if I had struck him.

"Y-you was helping us," I said, backing to the front of the counter again. "Well, you just get your little black self back over there and wait some more," he said in a low, tight voice. I was hot. I had been as nice as I could be to him and here he was talking like this. "We been waiting on you for near an hour," I hissed, "while you 'round here waiting on everybody else. And it ain't fair. You got no right." "Whose little nigger is this!" bellowed Mr. Barnett. Everyone in the store turned and stared at me. "I ain't nobody's little nigger!" I screamed, angry and humiliated. "And you ought not be waiting on everybody 'fore you wait on us." (p. 111)

Other African Americans in the store attempt to quiet Cassie to no avail. Stacy tries to get her to leave and she continues to talk. Finally he forces her to leave before something awful occurs. Cassie does not escape unscathed. On the sidewalk, she bumps into her nemesis, Lillian Jean Simms. She demands an apology and Cassie refuses. Lillian's father grabs Cassie and forces her to do so; she is hurt and humiliated. These feelings are compounded by Big Ma's reaction; Cassie had expected her to defend her but Big Ma makes her apologize. Later, Cassie tells her family what happened. Uncle Hammer rushes out of the house to confront the Simms. He is calmed by Mr. Morris, the family's farm helper and protector. Something drastic could have occurred, for example, a lynching, had Uncle Hammer succeeded in finding the Simms. Cassie learns a bitter lesson: Racism limits the extent to which one can have an innocent childhood.

The adult members of Cassie's family exhibit a great many virtues, too. They are politically astute and involved; they voice their convictions, and they love themselves, each other, and their community. Yet, they must sometimes acknowledge that racism forces them to tread lightly.

In some sense, each new volume in the Taylor family saga mirrors the experiences of African Americans throughout the nation. There are no happily-ever-after endings, only the realities of the conditions of the time. Happy endings await fundamental changes in interracial relationships and equality for African Americans in all institutions.

Most of Taylor's books — *Let the Circle Be Unbroken (1981)*, *The Gold Cadillac* (1987), *The Friendship* (1987), *The Road to Memphis* (1990) and *Mississippi Bridge* (1990) have won awards such as the Newbery Honor Medal, Boston Globe-Horn Book Magazine honor book designation, National Book Award finalist, Coretta Scott King Award, and Notable Children's Book in the field of Social Studies designation. Taylor's popularity with children is exceptional. *Roll of Thunder, Hear My Cry* remains a paperback best-seller (more than 100,000 copies were sold in 1990) after 14 years. Undoubtedly, Taylor's books help correct serious historical omissions and distortions. Her family's stories, because of their historical parallels, symbolize and become the history of all African Americans in much the same way that Alex Haley's *Roots: The Saga of an American Family* did.

Like the griots of the past Taylor bequeaths historical memories to her readers. Some of it will make them proud. Other aspects will make them cringe. Still others will cause laughter or tears. None will be forgotten. Taylor renders components of African-American experiences visible in an emotionally wrenching and thoughtful manner.

Few fairy tales feature a hero who is literally tall, dark, and handsome; a heroine who is beautiful, dark-skinned, intelligent, and kind, and a setting in southern Africa. *Mufaro's Beautiful Daughters* (Steptoe, 1987) did and it earned the accolades showered on it by critics, children, and adults. *Mufaro's Beautiful Daughters* is a variant of Cinderella that required nearly three years to research, write, and illustrate (Natov & De Luca, 1987). The late John Steptoe, in completing the book, underwent creative, spiritual, and psychological rejuvenation. His works are examined next.

John Steptoe

His first book, *Stevie* (1969), caused critics and readers to take note of a promising new talent in children's literature. It was the first children's book published in its entirety in *Life* magazine. Steptoe's last book, *Baby Says* (1988) was the culmination of a brilliant career. Between the first and last books were *Uptown* (1970), *Train Ride* (1971), *My Special Best Words* (1974), *Daddy is a Monster . . . Sometimes* (1980), *The Story of Jumping*

Mouse (1984), and *Mufaro's Beautiful Daughters* (1987). He illustrated books for others as well.

Steptoe, like everyone else, received negative images about Africa, Africans, and African Americans from the electronic and print media. He, too, believed many of them: ". . . because there are a lot of talented black people who could do what I do and most people don't believe that. In America, people say, of course white folks are talented and they have the right and the privilege to go ahead and achieve. But black people are told they're not talented. We're not supposed to read or produce art; we're supposed to play a little basketball" (Natov & DeLuca, 1987, pp. 124-125). He purposefully attempted to give voice to the hopes, dreams, and aspirations of the working class in general, and African Americans in particular (Natov & De Luca, 1987). He stated that their lives were excluded from literature and art. Consequently, his books give life to the sounds, sights, and smells of urban areas. Boys riding the subway, boys hanging out in the neighborhood, a boy and girl on an outing with their single parent, and simple celebrations were the heart of Steptoe's books. He wrote using Black Vernacular English, for which he received criticism, and Standard English. Nonetheless, the books permit an intimate glimpse into the lives of youth as suggested by this excerpt from *Stevie:*

> This morning I got up out of bed real fast Mamma only had to call me twice. Today is gonna be the best day of my life, and I'm gonna have the most fun I ever had. Today is special and I'm special too because I was the firstborn in our new place, the first child of a whole new thing. My name is Javaka, and today is my eighth birthday. (unnumbered pages)

Steptoe paid a significant price for his desire to write and create art. He also detailed the burden of race placed upon his shoulders. In some sense, he felt as if he were a token who was admitted to art circles provisionally, always subject to exclusion.

Mufaro's Beautiful Daughters was a labor of love for Steptoe that healed him and changed his perceptions about Africa. His mother was the model for the elderly woman in the tale, his daughter for the twins, and another relative for the Prince. This Cinderella variant does not include a wicked stepmother or stepsisters or a disinterested father. Nor is beauty the central quality necessary for females. There is a happy ending but it is one that emphasizes forgiveness and harmonious relationships among family and community members. The illustrations are simply stunning. Steptoe abandoned his experimentations with the expressionism of earlier works and turned to a more representational style. The illustrations evoke feelings of love and tenderness as well as a sense of lushness. The book received a Caldecott Honor Medal. *Mufaro's Beautiful Daughters* and *Baby Says,* the simple story of two brothers interacting, are precious swan songs.

Walter Dean Myers

Walter Dean Myers has created more than a score of books in a variety of genre — historical, contemporary, and fantasy fiction, history, and short stories in magazines such as *Boy's Life.* His most recent book is, *Now Is Your Time!* (1991), a history of African Americans in the United States. Myers, too, gives voice to urban youth, often with a deft humorous tone. Consider, for example, *The Mouse Rap* (1990). Each chapters begins with a "rap" created by the title character. Myers' penchant for basketball finds expression in several novels, especially *Hoops* (1981) and *The Outside Shot* (1984). The central character in these two books, Lonnie, faced many obstacles that confront some youth today such as the temptation of drugs, fast money, underemployment, and inadequate education. Many of Myers' novels are "coming of age" explorations. For example, the teens in *Fast Sam, Cool Clyde and Stuff* (1975), and *The Young Landlords* (1979) confront the aforementioned dilemmas but survive them with grace and their minds and bodies intact.

Harlem, once the mecca for African American art, literature, music, and politics, is the setting for many of Myers' books. Myers does not romanticize Harlem; he notes its poverty and drug problems. Neither does he present so harsh a portrait of the community that the vibrancy and power that pulsate throughout or the individuals who lead productive lives are ignored. His Harlem is a study in contrasts — intimate glimpses of someone who has lived there or frequents the many neighborhoods. Myers gives life to the brownstones and high-rise apartments, the playground pick-up games of basketball, the barbecue joints, and the camaraderie of teens sitting on the front stoop of an apartment building.

Myers takes many critical risks. Although his command of teenage humor is impressive, Myers wrote other books that showcased his ability to handle other stylistic features. One of his most intriguing books is *The Legend of Tarik* (1981). Myers combined elements of historical fiction and fantasy. The novel is set in North Africa and the Spain in the years of the Moorish conquest. Tarik's quest is to avenge the deaths of his family and fellow countrymen and women. Before he embarks on his quest, he must first acquire proficiency in handling horses and weapons and undergo a spiritual transformation. The spiritual transformation must result in his understanding the consequences of his actions and the decisions that he must make throughout life.

Two other books demonstrate successful creative risks. *Scorpions* (1988), which won the Newbery Honor Medal and *Fallen Angels* (1988), are remarkable in their explorations of friendship and bonding among males. The males in both books face warfare of one kind or another. Jamal and Tito, the major characters in *Scorpions,* have some basic dreams: they want to own a boat; Jamal wants the freedom to draw and paint; and, they both want uneventful, safe and secure childhoods. Neither can have his dream fulfilled. Circumstances beyond their control merge to force them into interactions with the gang that Jamal's imprisoned brother once led. They resist efforts to force them into the gang unwillingly, but do not have the inner resources or adult support that would enable them to resist the snares of the gang ultimately. The book has a decidedly somber tone; there is no happy ending. Like the lives of its two major characters, the book is unsettled. Jamal's and Tito's futures are uncertain as many of the boys in urban areas whom Myers attempted to give voice and bring to literary life.

The teens in *Fallen Angels* find themselves in Vietnam as draftees or volunteers. None will survive the experience unscathed. During the period of their deployment, the men — Perry, Peewee, Johnson, Brunner, and others — undergo crises that result in fundamental doubts about their identities, the values they believe and hold dear, and the consequences to heart and soul that result from killing. *Fallen Angels,* just as somber as *Scorpions,* leaves the reader a bit more hopeful. At least, the military action in Vietnam is over, but the battles in the streets of Harlem continue unabated. Myers (April, 1990) spoke of the factors that caused the more serious novels. He worked with a group of urban students in something akin to a writer's workshop. He was struck by the abilities of the children and teens to weather some harsh environments. Myers also recognized that the lives of these youngsters was not a part of children's literature. Myers, in a manner reminiscent of Steptoe, wanted to inform the world of these youngsters. *Scorpions* and *Fallen Angels* are two of his best works to date. His latest, *Now is the Time!* (1991), promises to continue that tradition and challenges readers to take up the struggle.

Hamilton, Clifton, Greenfield, Taylor, Steptoe, and Myers fulfilled the promise evident in African-American children's literature prior to the 1960s. They refused to become creatively complacent. They continue to explore universal truths and questions that are particular to African Americans. None has resorted to formulaic writing or copied previous literary success. As many of their statements suggest, they are artists who need to express their creative energy and offer something hopeful to their readers. Their books have found an audience and their words are taking effect as they blaze new literary trails that other writers follow and expand. The works of those who followed, the reinforcements, are examined next.

THE SECOND WAVE: THE REINFORCEMENTS

The second wave of culturally conscious writers gushed forth in the mid-to late 1970s and early 1980s. Among these literary griots are Muriel Feelings, Camille Yarbrough, Ashley Bryan, Jeanette Caines, Mildred Pitts Walter, Candy Dawson Boyd, and others. The emergence of these writers insured that African-American children's literature would remain viable despite the problems faced in the marketplace. Three of these authors, Ashley Bryan, Jeanette Caines, and Patricia McKissack brought new visions of folk tales, contemporary issues, and historical truths to literature. Their contributions are discussed next.

Ashley Bryan

Ashley Bryan illustrates, retells folk tales, and compiles African-American spirituals and folk songs. His artistic style is both unique and recognizable. Bryan functions as a modern-day griot. His illustrations and compilations help ensure that African-American folk music does not die out or remain confined to musical archives. Du Bois characterized these musical offerings as "sorrow songs." He thought of them as "the most beautiful expression of human experience born this side of the sea" (Du Bois, 1986; p. 537). He also argued that they were a neglected and despised art form. But the sorrow songs embodied universal, primal yearnings:

> Through all the sorrow of the Sorrow Songs there breathes a hope — a faith in the ultimate justice of things. The minor cadences of despair change often to triumph and calm confidence. Sometimes it is faith in life, sometimes a faith in death, sometimes assurance of boundless justice in some fair world beyond. But whichever it is, the meaning is always clear: that sometime, somewhere, men will judge men by their souls and not by their skins. Is such a hope justified? Do the Sorrow Songs sing true? (Du Bois, 1986; p. 544)

Bryan answered Du Bois' plaintive question with a resounding yes. He, too, shared Du Bois' love and respect for African-American spirituals and believes they are African-American gifts to the world. The illustrations that accompany the songs compiled by Bryan give full glory to the sorrow songs. In his hands, the nobility of the songs comes to the fore and they possess an aura of grandeur that belies their humble origins and that magnifies the deep yearnings contained within them. Bryan compiled three books of spirituals and folk songs, *Walk Together Children* (1974), *I'm Going to Sing* (1982), and *All Night All Day* (1991). In speaking engagements at conferences sponsored by the NCTE and IRA, Bryan detailed the reasons why he dedicated himself to immortalizing African-American musical forms. Among the reasons were his belief that the music possesses special qualities that touch the hearts of those who hear them the world over and because they are unique contributions.

The books are a visual delight. Bryan uses a variety of techniques and meshes a number of artistic styles. There is a sense of movement within the illustrations. Note, for example, the manner in which the Granny dances in *The Dancing Granny* (1977). The colors are intense but not overly stimulating or harsh. There are no jagged or sharp lines, only smooth ones delineating patterns, individuals, or objects. The colors selected by Bryan remind one of the Caribbean: azure, cerulean, and turquoise seas and sky, oranges, pinks, and yellows of tropical flowers, and occasion darker hues such as brown or red. His power as an artist reaches a peak in *What a Morning,* the Christmas story told through African-American spirituals.

Some of the folk tales retold by Bryan draw upon his Caribbean heritage or his fascination with African folk tales. Among the books in this genre are *Beat the Story Drum, Pum, Pum* (1980), *Lion and Ostrich Chicks* (1986), and *The Dancing Granny* (1977). As typical of many folk tales, these offer a valuable lesson as well as humor. Additionally, Bryan conveys a sense of orality in his versions. This excerpt from *The Dancing Granny* demonstrates Bryan's skill in conveying a spoken texture to the written text. Granny boasts to Spider Ananse that she is prepared to take him on and stop his antics:

> "See what you see and see what you like and have a fit too," said Granny,
> "cause that see and that fit is all you're going to get. You can sing for beans
> and sing for peas for all I care. It's going to take two to dance to your tune
> today." Granny shuffled her feet lightly. Yeah! Take a good look. You'll see
> that your Mama lives right here, and she don't plan to go nowhere. Uh-uh,
> no wheres away. Not this here day." (unnumbered pages)

Bryan succeeds in his efforts to preserve African-American folk literature and songs as viable cultural gifts. Critics and awards committee agree; he has won the Coretta Scott King Award and the ALA Notable Children's Books among others. Bryan's gentle crusade should continue because there are hundreds more songs that need a child (and adult) audience.

Jeanette Caines

Today's children face many issues — some major, others seemingly insignificant — from child abuse to the selection of a lunch box. Author Jeanette Caines covers these same topics and more in her picture books. Categorizing her books as simply problem or issue books would be unfair. She tells stories and creates a sense of adventure and occasional conflict within the limitations of length. There is nothing essentially African American about these topics, nor does Caines artificially inject African Americans into her stories. She demonstrates universal truths, questions, and values through the perspective of characters who happen to be African American. She accentuates the universal aspects of African-American culture.

Caines' first book was *Abby* (1973). A little girl is depicted involved in everyday day activities such as dressing, playing with her brother, and interacting with her parents. Only later does the reader come to the recognition that Abby is an adopted child. In a similar gentle manner, Caines portrays the roller-coaster emotions of a little girl as she awaits a weekly visit from her father in *Daddy* (1977). Although divorce is often traumatic for children, Caines depicts a father's attempts to support and nurture his daughter. The love both feel for each other is perceptible to young readers.

Caines forte seems to be her ability to capture complicated human relationships and present them to children in a manner that is not "dummied down." For example, in *Window Wishing* (1980) two children acquire a zest for everyday experiences when they visit their spunky grandmother. This grandmother exercises, window wishes, dreams, and picnics. Caines forgoes the temptation to present a fragile senior citizen in a rocking chair. Sibling rivalry, though harmless in this case, is the subject of *I Need a Lunch Box* (1988). A little boy wants a lunch box because his sister has one as she begins first grade. He bugs his parents and they relent cheerfully. *Just Us Women* (1982) is another example of the warm, loving family relationships in which Caine excels. This one is filled with fun and adventure as the women, a young girl and her aunt, hit the highway journeying from New York to North Carolina. The book conveys a sense of exhilaration, adventure, and fun.

In contrast to these loving, positive relationships is *Chilly Stomach* (1986). Two little girls are friends; one's family is loving and supportive. The other has a relative who abuses her. Her stomach reacts and she feels "chilly" each time the relative visits. She tells her friend who encourages her to talk with her parents. The book ends with the little girl relating her abuse. Caines handles the topic of child abuse in a sensitive manner, but the reader is caught unaware that child abuse is the topic and the unresolved ending requires discussion. In the hands of a sensitive adult, however, the book can prove invaluable.

Again, Caines' forte is the family in many of its possible configurations. She writes in a lively manner and creates characters that possess appeal for readers and occasionally depicts major social problems. She also portrays the seemingly mundane in new ways.

Patricia McKissack

Like many women, Patricia McKissack juggles several roles: author, teacher, editor, educational consultant, wife, and mother. Occasionally, she co-authors books with her husband Frederick McKissack. Her literary output is prodigious; 30 books in less than 20 years. She writes about an assortment of topics within a variety of genres. Among the genres are folk tales, biographies, information books, and picture books. Many of the folk tales are based on stories she heard as a child growing up in the South such as *Flossie and the Fox* (1986), *Mirandy and Brother Wind* (1988), *Nettie Jo's Friends* (1989), and *A Million Fish . . . More or Less* (1992).

The first three folk tales capture the lilting language of the rural South and showcase heroines who are lovable, likeable, and spunky. Each girl, Flossie, Mirandy, and Nettie Jo, seems familiar; they could be your sister, cousin, or best friend. Their personas come to life with the dialogue McKissack gives to each. Consider an excerpt from *Flossie and the Fox:*

Flo-o-o-ossie!"

The sound of Big Mama's voice floated past the cabins in Sophie's Quarters, round the smokehouse, beyond the chicken coop, all the way down to Flossie Finley. Flossie tucked away her straw doll in a hollow log, then hurried to answer her grandmother's call. "Here I am, Big Mama," Flossie said after catching her breath. It was hot, hotter than a usual Tennessee August day. Big Mama stopped sortin' peaches and wiped her hands and face with her apron. "Take these to Miz Viola over at the McCutchin Place," she say reaching behind her and handing Flossie a basket of fresh eggs. "Seem like they been troubled by a fox. Miz Viola's chickens be so scared, they can't even now lay a stone." Big Mama clicked her teeth and shook her head. "Why come Mr. J. W. can't catch the fox with his dogs?" Flossie asked, putting a peach in her apron pocket to eat later. "Ever-time they corner that ol' slickster, he gets away. I tell you, that fox is one sly critter."

Children can revel in the playful language and share Flossie's sense of confidence.

McKissack also writes books intended for "emergent readers," or readers who have not made the leap to total independence in reading. These books feature controlled vocabulary, simple sentence structures, short text, and illustrations that reinforce the textual content. McKissack and her husband retold several folk tales, *Cinderella, Country Mouse and City Mouse,* and *The Little Red Hen,* using this format. Some criticized these books because of their lack of literary vitality.

McKissack has greater success with the biographies and information books she has written. The biographies profile historic and contemporary figures such as abolitionist Frederick Douglass, educator Mary McLeod Bethune, poet Paul L. Dunbar, civil rights leaders Martin L. King, Jr. and Jesse Jackson, and pop star Michael Jackson. McKissack does not produce idealized biographies; she discusses the highlights and troublesome issues. For example, the biography of Jesse Jackson includes commentary about the perceptions that he is anti-Semitic or guilty of financial improprieties. The books are balanced in that she acknowledges the diversity of opinions that exist among African Americans.

She also documents the struggles of individuals and groups to gain acceptance in mainstream institutions. Many of these stories are omitted or given limited scrutiny in textbooks, but they are significant. For instance, *The Long Hard Journey* (1990), written with her husband, chronicles the importance of labor movements and labor history in the fight for equality. The gentlemen profiled were responsible for the creation of the Brotherhood of Sleeping Car Porters union. These unheralded heroes are just one example of the many individuals whose efforts helped spark the modern civil rights movement. McKissack's nonfiction helps fill important gaps in United States history books. Critics praise the even-handed manner in which she goes about the task of revising history. That will require many more books and arguably, McKissack is committed to doing so.

Bryan, Caines, and McKissack share many things in common. They feel a need to document and share African-American history and culture with children. They balance aesthetic concerns with their personal political views, and continue to create and challenge the assumption that work of this type is not necessary or will not sell.

The third group, the reinterpreters, came to the fore at an opportune time. They do not labor alone and the work they create links them to their literary predecessors. The reinterpreters tackle a number of themes in a variety of locales using a range of voices. All in all, the stories they weave demonstrate the multifaceted nature of African-American life and culture. Angela Johnson, Emily Moore, and Patricia Howard are notable members of this group and their work is assessed next.

THE REINTERPRETERS: NO LONGER WAITING IN THE WINGS

Angela Johnson

The nightly storybook ritual is a common feature in many homes. Educators and public service announcements trumpet the benefits of family storybook reading. Angela Johnson transformed this ritual with an elegant picture book, *Tell Me a Story Mama* (1989). In the picture book, a little girl goes to bed each night with this request, "Tell me a story, Mama" as indicated in this excerpt:

> Tell me a story, Mama, about when you were little.
>
> What kind of story, baby?
>
> Just any old story. How 'bout the time you lived in a little white house across the field from that mean old lady?

Notice that she did not say read me a story. The mother knows that this is her cue to tell her daughter about her life at a similar age and the ways she coped with uncertainties. The little girl knows most of the details and pipes in at the appropriate moments, their voices becoming a duet as both enjoy the nightly ritual. The soft watercolor illustrations enhance the feeling of love that permeates the story.

Angela Johnson is a new voice who has produced four books in two years. Johnson's voice is soft and poetic; the positioning of the text in her picture books reflects this poetic quality. Each book focuses on some aspect of family life: siblings in *Do Like Kyla* (1990), a grandson and grandfather in

When I Am Old With You (Johnson, 1990), and sisters in *One of Three* (1991). She is currently working on a fourth, tentatively titled *The Leaving Morning.* The illustrations by David Soman and paintings by James E. Ransome enhance the gentle, loving feelings evoked by the text. Each book garnered excellent reviews; two, *Tell Me a Story, Mama* and *When I Am Old With You* received starred reviews or special designations from reviewers for journals such as *School Library Journal* and *Kirkus Reviews.*

Storytelling was a part of Johnson's childhood: "I am amazed that my father and grandfather could tell my brothers and me a story thousands of times. After a while we knew them so well that with a bit of encouragement we could recite them by heart, leaving out only the unique comments of the original story-tellers. They'd fill these in for us" (1989, book jacket). Johnson was an active participant in oral storytelling and has brought that same interest to written texts. Her stories possess an oral quality that invites read-alouds.

Her second book, *Do Like Kyla,* speaks volumes through its simplicity. A little girl adores her older sister Kyla. She imitates every action from combing and braiding her hair in the same style to wearing similar clothes and eating the same food. Again, Johnson portrays loving familial relationships that are reminiscent of everyone's childhood. Similarly, *When I Am Old With You* pairs a grandfather and grandson who sit on the porch and while away the time, cook breakfasts of bacon, fish in a small stream, explore attic treasures and family history, and share in a neighborhood corn roast. The tone of the book, too, is gentle love and caring. The artist, David Soman, lends an unexpected surprise, the grandson sports dreadlocks, a hairstyle associated with Rastafarians.

Johnson's books present important aspects of African-American families that underscore their humanity and the similarities they share with other families. The lyrical language makes the books excellent read-aloud choices.

Emily Moore

She wrote book reviews for journals such as the *Interracial Books for Children Bulletin.* Now others review her literary efforts. Emily Moore, a public school teacher, has written three books for children: *Just My Luck* (1982), *Something to Count On* (1980), and *Whose Side Are You On?* (1988). Her works appeal most likely to intermediate aged students. The characters in these books are likable and encounter situations that run the gamut from wanting a puppy, to flunking math and needing a tutor, to facing the divorce of parents. The families are nuclear, extended, and sometimes fractured, but they are loving.

Moore's stories are set against the back drop of Harlem. The Harlem she spotlights is a working and middle-class community of co-op apartments and brownstones. Adults work, often in professions. For example, Barbra's mother, Mrs. Conway, in *Whose Side Are You On?* receives a promotion to vice-president at work; her late father was a reporter. Barbra and her brother Billy cope with their father's death by keeping some of his belongings and talking about him. Moore introduces elements of African-American culture in subtle ways. For McLeod, the family participates in many church activities such as singing in the choir; Mrs. Conway picks up an *Essence* magazine (a periodical aimed at African-American women), one of Barbra's favorite authors is Virginia Hamilton; and there are comments about the boycotts initiated during the civil rights movement.

Moore is adept at capturing pre-teen and teen culture. For example, she presents a credible version of teen language without resorting to obvious slang terms to indicate a teen is speaking. Other insertions of teen culture, such as references to popular musical groups and discussions about boys, sleep-overs, and clothes help convey the sense that Moore is familiar with teens. Moore knows their insecurities and their need to belong to popular groups, their need to achieve, and their need to act childish one moment and impossibly grown-up the next. For instance, Barbra teases her friend T. J. and he does the same to her, yet she comes to his defense when he has to go to a youth center temporarily. The reader can sense the Moore cares about this age group.

Like the other authors, Moore depicts the diversity that exists among African Americans and she focuses on the neglected middle class. Although her largely middle-class characters have achieved economic stability and upward mobility, they maintain their ties to African-American culture and are still subject to discrimination. For instance, Barbra and T. J. go to a local bookstore to browse and purchase books. A clerk in the store follows them in a surreptitious manner wherever they go. Barbra is aware of the clerk but T. J. is not. Barbra, too, thinks that T. J. cannot afford to pay for the books and just wants to leave. However, he has earned money with which to pay for the books and even buys Barbra one. Moore does not present sentimental or idealized books. On the whole, however, her characters have pleasant lives that are sometimes touched by universal life challenges.

Patricia Fitzgerald Howard

Many of the current group of writers are teachers. Howard is one also, a college professor of library science. Although she has written only three books, her talents came into full bloom with the third one. A few authors state emphatically that their personal lives are not the source of their stories. Howard, in contrast, noted the impact of her family upon her art (Howard, 1991). She had many happy memories of times with her extended family who were achievers. The stories they told are transformed in Howard's books.

Howard (1991) listed the effects she hoped to achieve with her books — to: share and tell the truth, help create an authentic body of literature reflecting all genres; help children celebrate life and build self-esteem and promote enlightenment; describe the universality that is evident in the particularities of the African-American experience; liberate the majority from stereotyped hang-ups, and liberate from invisibility those about whom she writes. She especially seeks to portray the range of beliefs and experiences found among African Americans. She summed up her comments by stating that being African American meant having stories as a way of feeling in the gaps. The gaps are those components of African-American life omitted from print and electronic media.

Indeed, Howard fills in gaps, shares historical memories, and entertains in *The Train to Lulu's* (1988), *Chita's Christmas Tree* (1989), and *Aunt Flossie's Hats* (1991). The African-American middle class is the subject for Howard's books. Again, the veil is lifted from this historically significant group. The setting for the books is Baltimore, Maryland. *Chita's Christmas Tree* takes place at the turn of the century. Chita is the daughter of one of Baltimore's first African-American physicians — the story is based on Howard's cousin. Chita's family prepares to celebrate Christmas and she and her father make an outing of selecting a tree. There is a large gathering of the extended family on Christmas Eve; they eat, talk, play music, and dance. The book ends with Chita coming downstairs on Christmas Day and searching for her name carved in the trunk of the tree; to her delight, she finds it.

The Train to Lulu's has a contemporary setting. Two nieces, Beppy and Babs, visit their beloved, elegant great aunt. The girls anticipate the train ride as much as the visit with their aunt. The expect lots of action and adventure and they get it in the form of watching the changing landscape and experiencing a train ride without adults. The book culminates with a mini family reunion at the train station. *Aunt Flossie's Hats* is Howard's best work to date. Susan and Sarah visit their great aunt, who like many African-American women, has a passion and flair for hats. Each of Aunt Flossie's hats, however, carries a particular story. The nieces have heard and know these stories, but they delight in hearing them told over and over as they wear them. Each visit ends with a dinner of crabcakes at a restaurant where the girls are joined by their parents.

James Ransome's illustrations fill in the gaps Howard identified as well. The community he portrays is a well-kept, middle-class one with African-American businesses. In addition, the firemen are African American, veterans returning from one of the world wars are part of African-American regiments,, and the restaurant features an African-American clientele and staff. These touches enable Ransome to recreate a vibrant community.

Indeed, Howard has fulfilled some of her goals with these books. She presents the African-American as an American without denying or diluting the experiences that are peculiar to them.

Johnson, Moore, and Howard uphold a proud and exemplary tradition. Never more will African-American authors of children's literature create their works in isolation or produce books that languish in publisher's warehouses. An enormous demand exists for their books and the books of the earlier and contemporaneous writers. They all have a bold attitude and an entrepreneurial spirit to some extent. Many more of these authors appear at major conferences such as those sponsored by the American Booksellers Association, the International Reading Association, and the National Council of Teachers of English. They engage in many more book-signings and readings. Their articles appear in *Children's Literature in Education* and *The Lion and the Unicorn.* They are visible to some and they are being read.

Unfortunately, they remain invisible to a number of teachers. That invisibility, however, can be lessened. Three typical questions arise when teachers are informed about the existence of African-American children's literature: Why haven't I known about these books? Where can I purchase the books? How can I use the literature in my classroom? The answer to the first involves at the very least a discussion of knowledge, what constitutes important knowledge, and how knowledge becomes a part of curricula and tradition. A partial discussion is found in previous sections. It also concerns a discussion of racism, intentional and otherwise. The second question is simply a matter of locating resources. The third is addressed in the next section.

STRATEGIES FOR CLASSROOM USE

Literature selected for use in the classroom should include both fiction and nonfiction. In addition, books that reflect students' interests deserve inclusion. Teachers can conduct surveys, informal interviews, or observe children as they browse in order to determine interests. Award-winning works and classics should be available along with books that are more contemporary.

One simple way to include African-American children's literature is to make the literature available for students through read-alouds, recreational reading periods, and classroom assignments. For example, the child interested in reading a book similar to the Baby-sitters Club series might have some interest in reading *Mariah Keeps Cool* (Walter, 1990) or *Mariah Loves Rock* (Walter, 1988). Those who are interested in biographies have a wide selection available such as *Anthony Burns* (Hamilton, 1988). Another way to select books is based on the ideas explored within them. For instance, children who want books about the effects of war can read *Charlie Pippin* (Boyd, 1987) or *Fallen Angels* (Myers, 1988).

Pre-school and Primary Ages

Children at this age level prefer books that contain families, animals, and children like themselves. Scores of picture books exist that include these elements. For instance, the teacher might read *The Patchwork Quilt* (Flournoy, 1985). A teacher can follow this procedure to crate a unit that encourages participation and involves writing, listening, reading, and art activities.

- Talk with children and discuss whether they had a favorite blanket or quilt when they were younger or now.
- Allow children to look at a quilt or pictures of quilts. Discuss how quilts are made (briefly) and that people tend to associate certain memories with them.
- Read *The Patchwork Quilt*. Before reading discuss what special significance grandma's quilt may hold.
- Encourage children to respond to the story and the illustrations. Connect the story with their lives whenever possible. For example, determine how they spend time with grandma or the things grandma has made for them.

- Suggest that the children create a classroom quilt that captures major events in their lives as a group. Each child can create a square for the quilt.

- Write a class book about the creation of the quilt or videotape periodically and children can create a narrative to accompany the filmed segments.

- Gather additional information about quilts such as their existence and significance in other countries and the types of textiles used to create them. Children might interview family members, visit the library, or contact a local museum for additional information. Discuss the similarities and differences.

This activity allows children to perceive that African Americans share many things in common with other groups. Other picture books convey similar sentiments such as *What Mary Jo Shared* (Udry, 1966), *Clean Your Room Harvey Moon* (Cummings, 1991), *Children of Long Ago* (Little, 1988), and *Spin a Soft Black Song* (Giovanni, 1987).

Intermediate Grades

Students in this age group are less dependent on parents, are attuned more and more to their peer group, exhibit some flexibility in their moral judgements, and they can understand the viewpoints or others. Folk tales present excellent opportunities to explore African-American children's literature.

Most children will have some familiarity with fairy tales. Teachers can augment this knowledge with a number of contemporary and retold variants. For example, students can read *Mufaro's Beautiful Daughters* and compare it with other variants and discuss how the country of origin shapes the way in which a tale is created. Or, consider dividing a class into small groups and give each group a sample of tales from books such as *The All-Jahdu Storybook* (Hamilton, 1991), the three volumes of Uncle Remus Tales retold by Julius Lester, *The Talking Eggs* (San Souci, 1989), *The Ballad of Belle Dorcas* (Hooks, 1990), *A Million Fish . . . More or Less* (McKissack, 1991), and *The Magical Adventures of Pretty Pearl* (Hamilton, 1983). Adapt the following procedure for classroom use:

- Read a sample tale aloud so that children can hear how the language is interpreted. Allow the children to read aloud and silently in their small groups.

- Discuss and list the motifs that appear, for example, the use of magic or enchantment, transformation, flying, and so forth.

- Determine the values, beliefs, or behaviors that are promoted by the tales. Are these universal or particularly African American?

- Discuss whether the tales include references to African-American culture and history. Identify those elements that do.

- Note the use of humor.

- Discuss the variation in language styles in each book and the effects the variation produces.

- Create tales in the tradition of Anancy, High John the Conqueror, Uncle Remus, or other folk tale characters.

Upper Elementary

Upper elementary students have many concerns. They must prepare to make the transition from junior high to high school. Questions of identity come to the fore. Relationships with parents and peers change and develop in new and different ways. They want information about a variety of topics. Children at this stage might enjoy reading books that explore some of these issues.

A thematic idea that lends itself to extensive exploration is a "coming of age" unit. Select a number of books by Hamilton, Myers, Clifton, Greenfield, Candy Dawson Boyd, Joyce Hansen, Joyce Carol Thomas, and others that feature students in this age group.

- Ask students to discuss, in small groups, the issues that concern them as they go from pre-teen to teen. Share ideas as a whole class.

- Encourage students to think about the factors, historical and otherwise, that determine how one becomes of age in a particular community, religious or social group, or ethnic/racial group. Do individuals in these groups celebrate a "rites of passage" ceremony or some other ritual?

- Share the books with students and encourage them to select a book that interests them.

- Prompt students to write journal entries that speculate on what it means to be an African-American teenager in the United States. What are some of the achievements and pleasures, for example, the influence they have on popular culture, and the problems, for instance, violence?

- As students read the books, encourage them to note the various ways in which the authors portray teens. Are there any recurring motifs?
- Share magazines such as *YSB*, a magazine directed at African-American youth and compare with other teen magazines such as *Sassy*. What are the similarities and differences?

Historical Information

The amount of information about African-American history included in textbooks has increased. Whether the increased information goes beyond the "great man or woman" syndrome, the Civil War, or the Civil Rights movement is debatable. Teachers and students need information that extends beyond these important events and that include other, equally pivotal topics. For example, slavery and its impact as an economic institution, its effects on the creation and interpretation of the Constitution, and the lasting effects on contemporary society are not addressed. Teachers and students can read the autobiographies of Frederick Douglass or some of his speeches such as "What Does the Fourth of July Mean to Me" for an introduction to one of America's greatest activists. Slavery from the perspective of former slaves is rarely addressed. Teachers and students might read *To Be A Slave* (Lester, 1968), or *The Classic Slave Narratives* (Gates, 1987). These provide some sense of the horror, uncertainty, and day-to-day manner in which the system was interpreted. Biographies such as *Paul Robeson: The Life and Times of a Free Black Man* (Hamilton, 1975), *W. E. B. Du Bois* (Hamilton, 1972), and *Anthony Burns* (Hamilton, 1988). A broad overview may be obtained from reading *Now Is Your Time!* (Myers, 1991). These and other books broaden the scope of traditional history and make it less biased towards a particular group.

SOME FINAL WORDS

"Knowledge is like a garden: if it is not cultivated, it cannot be harvested."

Guinean proverb

The literary gardens planted by African-American authors of children's literature bloom each publishing season. The earliest seedlings took root and inspired generation and generation. Mrs. A. E. Johnson and Paul L.

Dunbar were lonely blooms, but others stopped, read their works, and became inspired. The tradition they started in the 1890s has shown remarkable resilience to the pests — limited publishing support, book-sellers who refused to stock their works, adults who could not recognize the beauty contained within the pages because they depicted the vibrancy and value of African-American people and culture, and the cultural guardians who decreed that the works lacked literary merit — that sought to make it wither. The authors who followed these pioneers flourish now and then. Somehow, that precarious status must end. The authors should no longer have to validate their works. Publishers and booksellers must understand that the books deserve recognition every day of the year and not just during Black History Month.

We who teach must take a more proactive stance and apprise ourselves of the literature and share it with our students. We must recognize and convince others that the literature offers endless aesthetic, literary, and cognitive benefits and has earned a place in our classrooms. We can all become griots, of a sort, and follow in the footsteps of Walter Dean Myers who wrote that:

> I claim the joy and the light and the musica and the genius and the muscle and the glory of those I write about, of those many more I know about, and of the legions who have passed this way without yet having their stories told . . . I bring as much truth as I know. (Myers, 1991; pp. x-xi)

We, too, can do no less.

RECOMMENDED READINGS

Where can teachers begin? Which books represent a core listing that children should read? The list that follows is not prescriptive or written in stone. Nor is it meant to function as a canon. Teachers can start by reading and reviewing some of the books listed and then select others written by the authors. An asterisk that appears before a listing indicates that the book is appropriate for young readers. Publisher information may be found in *Books in Print.*

Adler, David. *Jackie Robinson*
Adoff, Arnold. *In For Winter, Out for Spring; *Malcolm X*
Albert, Burton. *Where Does the Trail End*
Barrett, Joyce. *Willie's Not the Hugging Kind*
Boyd, Candy. *Breadsticks and Blessing Places; Circle of Gold; Forever Friends*

Cameron, Ann. *The Stories Julian Tells

Chocolate, Deborah. *Kwanzaa*

Crews, Donald. *Big Mama's

Daly, Nikki. *Something on my Mind

Davis, Ossie. *Escape to Freedom: A Play About Young Frederick Douglass*

De Veaux, Alexis. *Enchanted Hair Tale

Dragonwagon, Crescent. *Half a Moon and One Whole Star

Fields, Julia. *The Green Lion of Zion Street

Feelings, Muriel. *Jambo Means Hello: Swahili Alphabet Book; Mojo Means One: Swahili Counting Book

Haskins, James. *Black Theatre in America*

Havill, Juanita. *Jamaica's Find; Jamaica Tag-Along

Hoffman, Mary. *Amazing Grace

Hudson, W. *Jamal's Busy Day

Johnson, Dolores. *What Kind of Baby-sitter is This?; What Will Mommy Do When I'm at School

Jordan, June. *Kimako's Story

Mathis, Sharon. *Hundred Penny Box; Sidewalk Story; Teacup Full of Roses

Mattox, Cheryl. *Shake It to the One That You Love Best

Mendez, Phil. *The Black Snowman

Meltzer, Milton. *Mary McLeod Bethune: Voice of Black Hope; Winnie Mandela; Underground Man*

Petry, Ann. *Harriet Tubman; Tituba of Salem*

Shelby, Anne. *We Keep a Store

Stolz, Mary. *Go Fish

Sullivan, Charles. *Children of Promise: African-American Literature and Art for Young People*

Tate, Eleanora. *Thank You! Dr. Martin Luther King, Jr.; The Secret of Gumbo Grove*

Thomas, Joyce. *Golden Pasture; Journey*

Wahl, Jan. *Tailypo*

Walker, Alice. *Finding the Green Stone; To Hell With Dying*

Yarbrough, Camille. *Cornrows; The Shimmershine Queens

WORKS CITED

Arbuthnot, M. & Sutherland, Z. (1991). *Children and books,* 8th ed. Glenview, IL: HarperCollins.

Bishop, R. (1990). Walk tall in the world: African-American literature for today's children. *Journal of Negro Education, 59,* 556-565.

Braithwaite, W. (1924). The Negro in literature. *Crisis, 28,* 204-210.

Broderick, D. (1973). *Image of the Black in children's literature.* New York: R. R. Bowker.

Brown, S. (1933). Negro character as seen by white authors. *The Journal of Negro Education, 2,* 179-203.

Chall, J., Rashburn, E., French, V., & Hall, C. (1979). Blacks in the world of children's books. *The Reading Teacher, 32,* 527-533.

Cooperative Children's Book Center. (April 5-6, 1991). The multicolored mirror: Cultural substance in literature for children and young adults. Annual meeting of the Cooperative Children's Book Center, Madison, WI.

Cullinan, B. (ed.). (1987). *Children's literature in the reading program.* Newark, DE: International Reading Association.

Clifton, L. (1981). Writing for Black children. *The Advocate, 1,* 32-37.

Daiches, D. (1983). *Literature and society.* London: Victor Gollancz Ltd.

Elliot, R. (Fall, 1991). A literature whose time has come. *Children's Advocate,* 4-5.

Fraser, J. (1973). Black publishing for Black children. *School Library Journal, 20,* 19-24.

Gates, Jr., H. (Ed.). (1987). *The classic slave narratives.* New York: Mentor Books.

Gayle, A. (1971). *Oak and ivy: A biography of Paul Laurence Dunbar.* New York: Doubleday & Company, Inc.

Goodard, C. (1992, Jan. 20). Aiming for the mainstream. *Publishers Weekly, 239,* 28-34.

Greenfield, E. (1975). Something to shout about. *The Horn Book Magazine, 51,* 624-626.

Haley, A. (1976). *Roots.* New York: Doubleday.

Hamilton, V. (1986). On being a Black writer in America. *The Lion and the Unicorn, 10,* 15-17.

Hamilton, V. (1987). The known, the remembered, and the imagined: Celebrating Afro-American folk tales. *Children's Literature in Education, 18,* 67-76.

Harris, V. (1987). Jessie Fauset's transference of the "New Negro" philosophy to children's literature. *Langston Hughes Review, 6,* 36-43.

Harris. V. (1990). African-American children's literature: The first one hundred years. *Journal of Negro Education, 59,* 540-555.

Heath, S. B. (1983). *Way With Words.* New York: Cambridge University Press.

Howard, P. (1991). Authenticity in children's books: The author's perspective. Presented at the Multicolored Mirror: Cultural substance in literature for children and young adults. Annual meeting of the Cooperative Children's Book Center, University of Wisconsin-Madison, April 5-6, 1991.

Hurmence, B. (1984). A question of perspective. *The Advocate, 3,* 20, 23.

Hudson, C. & Hudson, W. (1991). Authenticity in children's books: The publisher's perspective. The Multicolored mirror: Cultural substance in literature for children and young adults. Annual meeting of the Cooperative Children's Book Center, University of Wisconsin-Madison, April 5-6, 1991.

Jahn, J. (1961). *Muntu.* New York: Grove Press.

Igus, T. (1990). Publishing books for Black kids. *ABBWA Journal, 4,* 13-18.

Ihejirika, M. (1990, March 11). African-American book club fills a marketing void. *Chicago Sun-Times,* Section 2, 33.

Johnson, D. (1991). Telling tales: The pedagogy and promise of African American literature for youth. Westport, CT: Greenwood Press.

Johnson, R. (December, 1991). Personal communication about the Addy series.

King, M. (February 10, 1992). Personal communication about the Willie Pearl series.

Larrick, N. (1965). The all-white world of children's books. *Saturday Review, 48,* 63-65, 84-85.

Locke, A. (1925; 1968). *The new Negro.* Salem, NH: Ayer Co. Publishers.

Muse, D. (1975). Black children's literature: Rebirth of a neglected genre. *Black Scholar, 7,* 11-15.

Myers, W. (1991). Speech at The Ohio State University children's literature conference. Columbus, Ohio.

Natov, R. & De Luca, G. (1987). An interview with John Steptoe. *The Lion and the Unicorn 11,* 123-129.

Nicholas, C. (ed.). (1980). *Arna Bontemps-Langston Hughes letters, 1925-67.* New York: Dodd, Mead.

Roback, D. (1990, Nov. 30). Bookstore survey: Zeroing in. *Publishers Weekly, 237,* 36-38. 42-44.

Roback, D. (1991, March 8). Commercial books scored big with kids. *Publishers Weekly, 238,* 30-35.

Saul, E. (1984). *The Brownies' Book.* In R. Kelly (ed.). *Children's Periodicals of the United States,* pp. 62-68. Westport, CT: Greenwood Press.

Senich, G. (1983). Lucille Clifton. *Children's Literature Review, 5,* 51-60.

Sinnette, E. (1965). The Brownies' Book: A pioneer publication for children. *Freedomways, 5,* 133-142.

Sims, R. (1982). *Shadow and substance.* Urbana, IL: National Council of Teachers of English.

Sims, R. (1984). A question of perspective. *The Advocate, 3,* 145-155.

Sims, R. (1985). Children's books about Blacks: A mid-eighties status report. *Children's Literature Review, 8,* 9-13.

Taylor, M. (1990). Growing up with stories. *Booklist, 87,* 740-741.

Taxel, J. (1991). On the politics of children's literature. *The New Advocate, 4,* vii-xii.

Vaughn-Roberson, C. & Hill, B. (1989). The Brownies' Book and Ebony Jr.!: Literature as a mirror of the Black experience. *Journal of Negro Education, 58,* 494-510.

Yuill, P. (1976). *Little Black Sambo:* The continuing controversy. *School Library Journal, 23,* 71-75.

CHILDREN'S BOOKS CITED

Bannerman, H.
(1899; 1905). *The story of little black Sambo. New York:* Stokes.
(1903). *The story of little black Quibba.* New York: Stokes.
(1904). *The story of little Kettle-head.* New York: Stokes.
(1907). *The story of the teasing monkey.* New York: Stokes.
(1908). *The story of little black Quasha.* New York: Stokes.
(1909). *The story of little black Bobtail.* New York: Stokes.
(n. d.). *The story of little black Mingo.* New York: Stokes.
(1936). *Sambo and the twins.* New York: J. B. Linppincott.

Bontemps, A. & Hughes, L. (1932). *Popo and Fifina.* New York: Macmillan.

Boyd, C.
(1987). *Charlie Pippin.* New York: Macmillan.
(1985). *Breadsticks and blessing places.* New York: Macmillan.
(1984). *Circle of gold.* New York: Apple Paperbacks.

Bryan, A.
(1974). *Walk together children: Black American spirituals.* New York: Atheneum.
(1977). *The dancing granny.* New York: Atheneum.
(1980). *Beat the story drum, pum-pum.* New York: Atheneum.
(1982). *I'm going to sing. Black American spirituals, Vol. Two.* New York: Atheneum.
(1986). *Lion and the Ostrich Chicks and other African folk tales.* New York: Atheneum.
(1991). *All night, all day: A child's first book of African-American spirituals.* New York: Atheneum.

Caines, J.
(1973). *Abby.* New York: Harper & Row.
(1977). *Daddy.* New York: Harper & Row.
(1980). *Window wishing.* New York: Harper & Row.
(1982). *Just us women.* New York: Harper & Row.
(1986). *Chilly stomach.* New York: Harper & Row.
(1988). *I need a lunchbox.* New York: Harper & Row.

Calhoun, M. (1983). *Big sixteen.* New York: William Morrow & Company.

Campbell, B. (1982). *Taking care of Yoki.* New York: Harper & Row.

Chubb, I. (1929). *Little Pickaninnies.* Racine, WI: Whitman Publishing Company.

Clifton, L.
(1970). *Some of the days of Everett Anderson.* New York: Holt, Rinehart & Winston.

(1973). *All us come cross the water.* New York: Holt, Rinehart & Winston.

(1973). *The boy who didn't believe in spring.* New York: Dutton.

(1974). *The times they used to be.* New York: Holt, Rinehart & Winston.

(1975). *My brother fine with me.* New York: Holt, Rinehart & Winston.

(1977). *Amifika.* New York: Dutton.

(1979). *The lucky stone.* New York: Delacorte.

(1980). *My friend Jacob.* New York: Dutton.

(1981). *Sonora beautiful.* New York: Dutton.

"Cousin Ann." (1849). *Cousin Ann's stories for children.* Philadelphia: J. M. M'Kim.

Cumming, P. (1991). *Clean your room Harvey Moon.* New York: Bradbury Press.

Dunbar, P. (1895; 1968). *Little brown baby.* New York: Dodd, Mead & Company.

Floyd, S. (1905). *Floyd's flowers or duty and beauty for Colored children.* Atlanta: Hertel Jenkins.

Flournoy, V. (1985). *The patchwork quilt.* New York: Dial Books.

Giovanni, N. (1971; 1987). *Spin a soft black song.* New York: Farrar, Straus & Giroux.

Graham, L. (1939). *Pinky Marie: The story of her adventure with the seven bluebirds.* Akron, OH: The Saalfield Publishing Company.

Green, M. (1990). *Willie Pearl.* Oxon Hill, MD: William Ruth Comp.

Greenfield, E.
(1975). *Me and Neesie.* New York:
(1973). *Rosa Parks.* New York: Crowell.
(1978). *Honey, I love.* New York: Harper & Row.
(1991). *First pink light.* New York: Henry Holt.
(1988). *Grandpa's face.* New York: Philomel.
(1988). *Under the Sunday tree.* New York: Harper & Row.
(1988). *Nathaniel talking.* New York: Black Butterfly Children's Books.
(1991). *Big, Friend, Little Friend.* New York: Black Butterfly Children's Books.
(1991). *Daddy and I . . .* New York: Black Butterfly Children's Books.
(1991). *I make music.* New York: Black Butterfly Children's Books.
(1991). *My doll, Keisha.* New York: Black Butterfly Children's Books.
(1991). *Night on neighborhood street.* New York: Black Butterfly Children's Books.

Greenfield, E. & Little, L. (1979). *Childtimes: A three generation memoir.* New York: Crowell.

Hamilton, V.
(1967). *Zeely.* New York: Macmillan.
(1968). *The house of Dies Drear.* New York: Macmillan.
(1974). *M. C. Higgins, the great.* New York: Macmillan.
(1983). *Willie Bea and the time the Martians landed.* New York:
(1983). *The magical adventures of Pretty Pearl.* New York: Harper & Row.
(1985). *The people could fly.* New York: Knopf.
(1988). *In the beginning.* New York: Harcourt Brace Jovanovich.
(1988). *Anthony Burns.* New York: Knopf.

(1990). *The dark way.* New York: Harcourt Brace Jovanovich.

(1991). *The all-Jahdu story book.* New York: Harcourt Brace Jovanovich.

Haskins, J. (1990). *Black dance in America.* New York: Crowell.

Haynes, E. (1921). *Unsung heroes.* New York: Du Bois & Dill Publishing Company.

Henderson, J. (1921). *A child's story of Dunbar.* New York: Du Bois & Dill Publishing Company.

Hooks, W. (1990). *The ballad of Belle Dorcas.* New York: Knopf.

Howard, E.

(1988). *The train to Lulu's.* New York: Bradbury Press.

(1989). *Chita's Christmas tree.* New York: Bradbury Press.

(1991). *Aunt Flossie's hats.* New York: Clarion Books.

Hudson, C.

(1987). *Afro-bets ABC.* Orange, NJ: Just Us Books.

(1987). *Afro-bets 123.* Orange, NJ: Just Us Books.

Hudson, C. & Ford, B. (1990). *Bright eyes, brown skin.* New Jersey: Just Us Books.

Johnson, A.

(1989). *Tell me a story, Mama.* New York: Orchard Books.

(1990). *Do like Kyla.* New York: Orchard Books.

(1990). *When I am old with you.* New York: Orchard Books.

(1991). *One of three.* New York Orchard Books.

Johnson, A. E.

(1890; 1988). *Clarence and Corinne.* New York: Oxford University Press.

(1894; 1988). *The Hazeley family.* New York: Oxford University Press.

Johnson, D. (1991). *What kind of baby-sitter are you?* New York:

Jones, J. (1848). *The young abolitionists; or conversations on slavery.* Boston: The Antislavery Office.

Langstaff, J. (1987). *What a morning! The Christmas story in Black spirituals.* New York: Margaret K. McElderry Books.

Lester, J. (1968). *To be a slave.* New York: Dial.

Martin, A.

(1989). *Jessi and the superbrat.* New York: Scholastic.

(1990). *Jessi's Baby-sitter.* New York: Scholastic.

Mathis, S.

(1975). *The hundred penny box.* New York: Viking.

(1991). *Red dog, blue fly.* New York: Viking.

McBrown, G. (1935). *The picture poetry book.* Washington, D.C.: The Associated Publishers, Inc.

McKissack, P.

(1983). *Who is who?* Chicago: Children's Press.

(1985). *Cinderella.* Chicago: Children's Press.

(1985). *Country mouse and city mouse.* Chicago: Children's Press.

(1985). *The little red hen.* Chicago: Children's Press.

(1986). *Flossie and the fox.* New York: Dial.

(1988). *Mirandy and Brother Wind*. New York: Knopf.

(1989). *Nettie Jo's friends*. New York: Knopf.

(1989). *The long hard journey*. New York:

(1991). *A million fish . . . more or less*. New York:

Myers, W. (1975). *Fast Sam, Cool Clyde, and Stuff*. New York: Viking.

(1979). *The young landlords*. New York: Viking.

(1981). *Hoops*. New York: Delacorte.

(1981). *The legend of Tarik*. New York: Viking.

(1984). *The outside shot*. New York: Delacorte.

(1988). *Fallen angels*. New York: Scholastic.

(1988). *Scorpions*. New York: Harper & Row.

(1990). *The mouse rap*. New York: HarperCollins.

(1991). *Now is your time!*. New York: HarperCollins.

Ned, N. & Toby. (n. d.). *New Nigger Rhymes*. (n.p.). Found in the collection of the Schomburg Center for Research in Black Culture.

Newsome, E. (1944). *Gladiola garden*. Washington, D.C. The Associated Publishers, Inc.

Ovington, M.

(1903). *Hazel*. Freeport, NJ: Books for Libraries.

(1931). *Zeke*. New York: Harcourt Brace.

Page, T. (1932). *Two little confederates*. New York: Charles Scribner's Sons.

Price, L. (1990). *Aida*. New York: Harcourt Brace Jovanovich.

Ringgold, F. (1991). *Tar beach*. New York: Crown Publishers, Inc.

Roy, J. & Turner, G. (1951). *Pioneers of long ago*. Washington, D.C.: The Associated Publishers, Inc.

San Souci, R. (1989). *The talking eggs*. New York: Dial.

Shackelford, J. (1938). *The child's story of the Negro*. Washington, D.C.: The Associated Publishers, Inc.

Smalls-Hector, I. (1991). *Irene's big fine nickel*. New York: Little, Brown & Co.

Steptoe, J.

(1969). *Stevie*. New York: Harper & Row.

(1970). *Uptown*. New York: Harper & Row.

(1971). *Train ride*. New York: Harper & Row.

(1974). *My special best words*. New York: Viking.

(1980). *Daddy is a monster . . . sometimes*. New York: Viking.

(1984). *The story of jumping mouse*. New York: Lothrop Lee & Shepard.

(1987). *Mufaro's beautiful daughters*. New York: Lothrop Lee & Shepard.

(1988). *Baby says*. New York: Lothrop Lee & Shepard.

Taylor, M.

(1973). *Song of the trees*. New York: Dial.

(1975). *Roll of thunder, hear my cry*. New York: Dial.

(1981). *Let the circle be unbroken*. New York: Dial.

(1987). *The friendship*. New York: Dial.

(1987). *The gold cadillac*. New York: Dial.

(1990). *Mississippi bridge.* New York: Dial.

(1990). *The road to Memphis.* New York: Dial.

Udry, J. (1966). *What Mary Jo shared.* New York: Scholastic.

Walter, M. P.

(1988). *Mariah loves rock.* New York: Bradbury.

(1990). *Mariah keeps cool.* New York: Bradbury.

Whiting, H.

(1938). *Negro folk tales, Book I.* Washington, D.C.: The Associated Publishers, Inc.

(1938). *Negro art, music and rhyme, Book II.* Washington, D.C.: The Associated Publishers, Inc.

Woodson, C. (1939). *African heroes and heroines.* Washington, D.C.: The Associated Publishers, Inc.

Zemach, M. (1982). *Jake and Honeybunch go to heaven.* New York: Farrar, Straus & Giroux.

(n. a.). (1847). *The antislavery alphabet.* Philadelphia: Merrihew & Thompson, Printers.

(n. a.). (1835). *Juvenile poems for the use of free American children of every complexion.* Boston: Garrison & Knapp.

4

Turning the Page

Asian Pacific American Children's Literature

Elaine Aoki

INTRODUCTION

When I was a child, children chanted, "Are you Chinese? Are you Japanese? Or are you just a mixed-up kid?"

When I was a child, the teacher read, "Once upon a time there were five Chinese brothers and they all looked exactly alike." (Bishop and Wiese, 1938)

Cautiously the pairs of eyes stole a quick glance back. I, the child, sank in my seat and looked down to the floor.

The teacher turned the book our way: bilious yellow skin, slanted slit eyes. Not only were the brothers look-alikes, but so were all the other village characters!

I, the teacher, talk with my students on their choice of books. Bruce brings *The Five Chinese Brothers*.

"Tell me about the story, Bruce."

"Well, it's about these five Chinese brothers. You know, kinda like you. . .!"

"What do you mean, 'kinda like me?'"

"Well, your family is kinda Chinese or something." Bruce pauses and stares at me and then again at his book. He quickly adds. "But maybe you're different. Aren't your eyes supposed to slant up or down?"

I, the teacher, sit up. We have work to do.

So I wrote 12 years ago in a review of Asian Pacific American children's literature. Today I meet with teachers, parents, publishers' representatives and in retrospect, I turn the pages, book after book, and ask where are we? I

111

rarely run across a book that evokes an emotional or personal reader response from an Asian Pacific American child. As I share the few Asian Pacific American books with Asian Pacific American children, their identification is so spontaneous that they immediately develop a linkage with the characters. In the picture book illustrations of Allen Say's book, *The Lost Lake* (1989), Asian Pacific American children respond: "He looks just like my dad with that ol' hat" or "My dad doesn't talk much either." In contrast, older Asian Pacific American students reflect on their identification of Casey's evolution as a Chinese American in *Child of the Owl* (Yep, 1977):

> And I knew I talked back to Paw-Paw (maternal grandmother) more than some of the other Chinese kids . . . And if I pretended I was an owl I suddenly had a way of talking about my feelings because I felt like someone who'd been trapped inside the wrong body and among the wrong people. (p. 87)

When questioned about the importance of Asian Pacific American literature, young Asian Pacific American students usually reply that it's nice to have the book, but don't question the lack of such Asian Pacific American books because they just think "that's the way things are. We do what the teachers tell us. Teachers just give us books about non-Asian Pacific Americans."

Recently, I listened to a presentation by an Asian author. The teachers and librarians attending the session were enamored with the author/illustrator's works. They felt he had fulfilled the literature needs of their recent Asian immigrants and now encouraged him to translate the books bilingually to meet the needs of the Asian population. Listening to well-meaning educators, I again sank in my chair, shook my head and muttered, "Yes, we do need books for the bilingual reader, but we also need books reflecting contemporary situations for our Asian Pacific American students who now span over five generations! We need to expose non-Asian Pacific American students to read about others, as well."

ASIAN PACIFIC AMERICAN LITERATURE

Asian Pacific American people have been separated from Asia and the Pacific by geography, culture, and history for more than seven generations. We have more than 150 years of history in America, yet where are we in the literature? Are we still the foreigners in this white person's society? Are we still perceived as whining and apologetic? Are we still seen as the look-alikes of Bishop and Wiese's *The Five Chinese Brothers?*

What do we know about Asian Pacific American children's literature? In 1976 a committee of Asian American book reviewers formed the Asian American Children's Book Project under the Council for Interracial Books for Children. Their objectives were to evaluate books and identify those that could be used effectively in education programs.

The committee evaluated children's books in which one or more central characters were Asian Pacific Americans. They found a total of 66 books that fit this requirement. (Compare this number with the more than 3000-5000 children's books that are published each year in the U.S. alone.) The committee accepted the definition of Asian Americans to include Americans of all Far Eastern, East Indian, Southeast Asian, and Pacific countries, but were unable to locate books in all the categories.

Of the 66 titles, most were about Chinese Americans and Japanese Americans. Two each were about Korean Americans and Vietnamese Americans. Most of the books were published between 1945 and 1975, with the greatest number published in the 1970s.

The committee concluded that, with the exception of one or two, the 66 books were "racist, sexist, and elitist and that the image of Asian Americans they present is grossly misleading." The stereotyped image presented was that "Asian Americans are foreigners who all look alike and choose to live together in quaint communities in the midst of larger cities and cling to outworn alien customs."

Since the publication of the Asian American Children's Book project where have we been? The authors reviewed in this project included writers such as Laurence Yep and Yoshiko Uchida. They are still contributing quality literature. Yet over the past 15 years, Asian Pacific American authors have been largely nonexistent. Notably missing is the children's literature representing Korean American, Pacific Islander American, and the many Southeast Asian American groups. Some of their old culture folktales have been appearing in translations and retellings but not in the Asian American children's literature representing these groups in this country.

With so few books accurately portraying Asian Pacific Americans, it is likely that children like Bruce will continue to stereotype and hold misconceptions about Asian Pacific Americans. Likewise more Asian Pacific American students will needlessly continue to sink in their seats.

Asian Pacific American authors have indicated that publishers look at a limited audience for their works. The publishing houses are looking for major sales and when sales do not materialize, the books are no longer published. With so few books, Asian Pacific American children's literature can find itself stumbling through a revolving door, going nowhere. Being an Asian Pacific American author under these circumstances requires extraordinary forbearance especially when economics prevail and educators see Asian Pacific American literature books useful for only a small population of students. Three Asian Pacific American authors, in particular, exemplify the tenacity as well as creativity needed to become successful in such a demanding and restrictive market. Let us briefly look at how they have charted new options for others to follow.

THE EVOLUTION OF ASIAN PACIFIC AMERICAN AUTHORS AND ILLUSTRATORS

If one looks at the writing career of Yoshiko Uchida, one can see that she has developed a sense of public awareness and reader acceptability of her works. At the start of her writing career, folktales were the only acceptable Asian Pacific American literature.

Yoshiko Uchida, a Nisei (second generation Japanese American) uses the following metaphor to illustrate the plight of Asian Pacific Americans and other minorities during her youth in California.

> A young boy was confronted by his mother, who compelled him to sit in the corner. His father walked by and asked what he was doing. The son replied, "I am sitting down on the outside, but on the inside I am standing up."

She said at that time, most did not "dare to stand up" and speak out. Many young Asian Pacific Americans, treated as inferior felt they were in fact, inferior with feelings "bordering on self-contempt." This situation, according to Uchida, "caused us to diminish ourselves by rejecting our heritage, ashamed of who we were and of those traditions and values that made us seem so different from our white classmates." Wanting to stand up for Asian Pacific American children, Uchida departed from her translations of Japanese folk and fairy tales and delved into historical events and issues of Japanese Americans as depicted in such books as *Samurai of Gold Hill* (1972), *Journey to Topaz* (1971), and *Journey Home* (1978).

Laurence Yep began his writing career as a science fiction author before producing his successful Caldecott Honor Book *Dragonwings* (1975). Yep did exactly what most successful authors will advise: Write about what you know and about your experiences. Yep wrote about alienated people and aliens. In doing so he was writing about himself as a Chinese American. In his biography, *The Lost Garden,* (1981), Yep discusses his evolution from "being a puzzle to a puzzle solver." At one point Yep says he felt like the old Chinese puzzle box with interlocking pieces of wood whose instructions were locked up inside. Later, Yep said he could become the puzzle solver and could:

> reach into the box of rags that was my soul and begin stitching them together. Moreover, I could try out different combinations to see which one pleased me the most. I could take these different elements, each of which belonged to something else, and dip them into my imagination where they were melted down and cast into new shapes so that they became uniquely mine. (p. 91)

The works of José Aruego, Filipino American author/illustrator, are certainly not to be overlooked. Aruego, born and raised in Manila, came from a family of prominent lawyers who specialized in constitutional law. Following in this tradition, Aruego completed his law studies and passed the bar. However, after a relatively short practice, he was dissatisfied with the profession and subsequently left for New York City. There he studied graphic arts and advertising at Parsons School of Design. After a few years of freelancing as a cartoonist for publications like the *Saturday Evening Post* and *The New Yorker,* Aruego decided to illustrate children's books.

He confesses that, as a child, instead of doodling he drew animals busily engaged in funny antics and that he thrived on comic books. His evident love for animals shows clearly in the books he has writtten and illustrated. This internationally known author/illustrator presents colorful, comic animals in fantasy stories. While the content of his works are not specifically focused upon Asian American characters, Aruego draws upon his cultural heritage and the folklore of the Philippines (e.g., *Crocodile's Tale* (1972) focuses on the theme of gratitude and helping). Aruego, at once an ambassador of friendship and goodwill, says that his work has also been influenced by places and people in the Middle East and Orient. With over 40 books to his credit, José Aruego is an exemplary role model for young authors and illustrators, as he strives to present whimsical characters in universal themes.

WHAT IS BEING PROMOTED IN THE LITERATURE?

Standards for Asian Pacific American literature have been established by authors such as José Aruego, Yoshiko Uchida, and Laurence Yep. Why then do we continue to use *The Five Chinese Brothers?*

In a study conducted by Smith, Greenlaw and Scott (1987), 254 Texas and Kansas teachers in grades K-6 listed their favorite books for reading aloud to children. The intent of the study was to demonstrate how reading aloud affects children's acquisition of attitudes. They found that teachers' read aloud preferences included twice as many books with male protagonists as female protagonists. Upon further analysis, images of minorities, the elderly, and the mentally or physically challenged were, in general, omitted. An important conclusion made by Smith, et al. was that teachers are probably unaware of the degree of bias in their read-aloud preferences. Their choices were contributing to the perpetuation of materials which do not reflect the rich diversity of American culture.

Smith's study along with the research by Grant and Sleeter (1986) support the notion that schools and teachers at the present time do little to teach from a multicultural approach. Despite mandated coursework at the university level in human relations and multicultural education, evidence exists that once college students become teachers, they do little to support a multicultural approach in their schools. Further, tenured and other faculty members are not required to learn about multicultural studies and to apply these concepts to their own classes. Yet, failure to address the cultures of ethnic minority groups found in this nation clearly gives the message that these groups are insignificant and less worthy than certain other groups (Gollnick and Chinn, 1990).

What is even more frightening is covert censorship: the unconscious presentation of just one side of an issue that distorts reality by making it seem that the one position is all there is worth considering about the issue (Shannon, 1989). While conducting a study concerning the genre types among children's favorites books (Abrahamson and Shannon, 1983), Shannon related that "regardless of the genre type — whether it was about an individual or a group, about animals or people about the city or the country, about males or females — the authors of children's books promoted concern for self-development, personal emotions, self-reliance, privacy, and competition rather than concern for social development, service to community, cooperation toward shared goals, community, and mutual prosperity or even a balance among these social attributes" (p. 101).

In his investigation, Shannon and two other adults looked at a random sample of the International Reading Association's Children's Choice books from 1978, 1980, and 1982. The Children's Choice Award recipients were selected because:

1. all books published by major houses are submitted to the program

2. over 10,000 opinions on the books are solicited from school children around the United States concerning which among them are their favorites.

3. the Children's Choice lists, published annually in *The Reading Teacher,* often serve as a primary source concerning decisions about books purchased by schools and public librarians.

After randomly selecting 30 books the group concluded that 29 of these books presented an individualistic message and only one offered a balanced perspective, in which a boy pursued self-development but not at the expense of his responsibilities to his family and his immediate community. According to Shannon, "the unconscious censorship, then, is hidden in the consensus of opinion that holds, in this case, that individualism provides a better social arrangement than either of the other perspectives" (p. 103).

People may not make a conscious decision to exclude alternative views. Rather, Shannon contends that "it is more likely that belief in individualism may be so deeply rooted in the American psyche that most participants value personal concerns more highly than social concerns, and their choices in children's literature reflect their viewpoint. That is, few balanced books are written, fewer are published, fewer still are selected for 'choice lists' and so forth" (p. 102).

Shannon continues that he:

believes it is the covert nondebate of such issues as the individual versus community, the lives of women, minority cultures, the environment, and social organizations that presents a greater danger — not because it is any more insidious but simply because it is even more difficult to combat. To remain silent on covert censorship in children's and adolescent literature is to rob American youth of their rightful place in the debate about the future (p. 103).

If this is the dominant type of literature that is being published and utilized, it is a wonder that any books reflecting Asian Pacific American viewpoints are published at all.

Editors, publishers, and educators groomed in Western literary standards may fail to grasp the essence of literature grounded in Eastern thought. According to the analysis of Richie (1983), Austin and Jenkins (1987), and Matsuyama (1983), the narrative structure of Asian Pacific literature is different. Briefly, the plot structures are non-linear and do not necessarily have a beginning, a middle, and an end.

Richie (1983) contends that Western critics who complain of the plotlessness of Japanese narratives are quite correct in noticing its absence. Common Japanese structural forms have a narrative that merely places one event after another, a narrative that proceeds entirely through parallels and continually stresses sameness rather than differences, or a narrative that turns conflict into accord (1983, p. 5). Richie further delineates that Western narratives are based on conflict and resolution while Japanese narratives are based upon continuity and resolution. Other notable differences are that the West presumes segmentation, difference, and specialization while Japan presumes wholeness, accord, and sameness. The Western narrative then is about overcoming, changing, hope, and promise while the Japanese narrative is about conforming, renewing, and continuing.

Matsuyama (1983) writes, "Do story grammars speak Japanese?" Her analysis indicated that 80% of the Japanese folk tales used for her study had no goal structure for the main character and could not follow the story grammar model developed by Thorndyke (1977) and others.

An example of a well-known Japanese folk tale which has no goal structure is "Urashima Taro". In this tale, Urashima Taro, a young fisherman, rescues a tortoise from a group of children. The tortoise thanks Taro for saving his life and takes him to the Palace of the Sea Princess. After a few days, Taro wishes to return home. In remembrance of his visit, the Sea Princess gives him a beautiful jewelled box. Upon his return home, Taro cannot recognize the place. His family and friends are gone. He opens the gift box and a puff of white smoke changes him into the old man he really is.

A second major pattern that emerged in 25% of the stories is the combining of combining an episode without a goal and an episode with a goal. The stories contrasted a good person and a bad person. This pattern is highlighted in the tale "The Rice Cake that Rolled Away."

This tale begins with a kind old man and woman who sat down to make rice cakes. Suddenly one rolled off the plate and rolled down the village into a tiny hole in front of a shrine. The kind old man rescues the rice cake and gives half of the cake as a shrine offering. Suddenly the statue speaks and asks him to help frighten away a group of ogres. The kind old man assists and is given the gold coins left in haste by the ogres.

The next door neighbors hear about the gold coins and the next morning the greedy old man and woman repeat the actions of the kind couple. The old man does not make an offering to the statue nor does the statue request his assistance. Instead, the greedy old man automatically invades the shrine and scares away the ogres, only to laugh at their flight. At that instance, the ogres realize it is human laughter and pounce on the greedy man.

Traditional Japanese culture, deeply rooted in Buddhism, emphasizes the importance of having no desire. It denies aggressiveness, and usually does not encourage goal-oriented behavior. Matsuyama states that "this is an example of how cultural values affect story structure."

Matsuyama warns us that there is a " danger in assuming that all well-structured stories from different cultures have the same common structural elements (1983, p. 5)." Again, if we covertly censor works based upon Western literary guidelines, then it is a wonder that our students are not exposed to different points of views.

Asian Pacific American children's literature is also grounded in symbols and creatures of folklore and myth. Dragons, demons, and "Asuangs" (spirits from the Philippines) are so central to much of the Asian Pacific literature that Asian Pacific American authors run the risk of "overt censorship," due to the efforts of groups like the Educational Research Analysts. Here the Texas-based Gablers appeal to parents and educators to carefully identify materials that they consider anti-family, anti-Christian, or anti-American.

According to Banks (1991) the demographic data indicates that "five out of six people in the world are non-White. The vast majority of the world's population is non-Christian. Because the birthrate of non-Whites greatly exceeds that of Whites, White Christians will be an even smaller world minority by the year 2000." The schools have a responsibility to "present students from all racial, ethnic, and social class groups with cultural and ethnic alternatives and teach them to live in a world society that is ethnically and racially diverse. Students should be helped to develop the vision and commitment needed to make our world more humane" (p. 32).

EFFECTS OF LITERATURE

In *What Reading Does to People,* Waples, Berelson, and Bradshaw (1958) state that "reading is a social process. It relates the reader to his/her environment and it conditions that relationship." Sometimes that relationship is primary. That is, the reader has direct physical contact with the environment. In other instances, he/she has a secondary relationship. That is, he/she establishes contact only through symbols as in reading or listening. This secondary relationship affects primary or direct interactions later. Both types of interactions help to develop the individual's experiences and attitudes.

The importance of books as socializing agents continues to be attested to by numerous researchers (Kummel, 1970; Weitzman, et al., 1972; Zimet, 1973 and so forth). Social scientists tell us that socialization helps develop a set of values and attitudes, likes and dislikes, goals and purposes, patterns of response, and concept of self. According to Child, Potter, and Levine (1946):

> It is assumed that in reading a story, a child goes through symbolically, or rehearses the episode that is being described. The same principles, then are expected to govern the effect of the reading on the child as would govern the effect of actually going through such an incident in real life. (p. 3)

Milton Meltzer quotes E. B. White (1989, p. 156) in confirming the social responsibility of authors, "Writers do not merely reflect and interpret life, they inform and shape life."

RATIONALE AND GOALS FOR ASIAN PACIFIC AMERICAN CHILDREN'S LITERATURE

Educators should provide a wide array of Asian Pacific American literary experiences in literature and language arts. These experiences will bring children into the magnificent cultural mosaic that is our society. Some of these literary experiences will match their own cultural backgrounds; others will widen their horizons. Both will enhance their abilities to actively engage in literary experiences.

While much quality Asian Pacific American literature is based upon folk tales, historical issues, and struggles with identity, educators and publishers must not forget the contemporary stories that are common to all students. An example of this might be Allen Say's *Lost Lake* (1989). Here Mr. Say tells the gentle story of a young boy and his father who become closer during a camping trip. This story could have been told through the eyes of any child. But in *Lost Lake,* the author chose to focus on an Asian American child and his father. By doing so, both Asian Pacific American children and those from other ethnic backgrounds can see that children of color can and do live in contemporary stories.

In America, we are working to achieve a society in which all our peoples are truly equal. Differences in physical features should be judged as merely normal variations of a common humanity. If this is our yet unrealized dream, then protagonists in children's literature should be of different hues and different featural types. There is no reason that characters such as Ramona the pest cannot be portrayed also as an Asian Pacific American.

Such stereotypical representation has been noted in other artistic areas. For example in response to the casting of actors roles, Mako, an Asian American actor, commented:

> In an ideal situation, I would not care who was cast in the part, whether a white man or a black man or a yellow man. But we're not in an ideal situation. We are still categorized. White actors can do white roles or Asian roles or whatever. Asian actors get Asian roles only. Unless we can expand and get away from that situation, this is not a two-way street. This is a one-way street, and it offends me. (Frymer, 1991)

Likewise, Asian Pacific American book characters should be offended. They should not just be reserved for Asian Pacific American folk tales and/or specific Asian Pacific American character roles. Asian Pacific American characters need to be part of the literature mainstream.

The goals of an Asian Pacific American children's literature curriculum (Office of Superintendent of Public Instruction, 1988) should help all our students to:

1. read to understand the diverse perspectives in a multicultural society;

2. read to accept and affirm the uniqueness of self and others;

3. read materials written and illustrated by authors and artists from diverse groups

4. learn about diverse groups (ethnic, cultural, handicapped, age, and gender);

5. appreciate and empathize with other points of view about material being read;

6. respond to text written from diverse social, economic and political perspectives.

Teachers can achieve these goals by using literature that depicts Asian Pacific Americans in multivaried themes, settings, situations, and literary genres. They must further provide instructional settings for individual responses and identification with the characters and/or situations.

CRITERIA FOR SELECTING QUALITY ASIAN PACIFIC AMERICAN LITERATURE

Knowing that literature can affect attitudes, concepts, and achievements of individuals, we must select books and stories with care. To assist us in the evaluation of quality Asian Pacific American literature, the Asian American Children's Book Project Committee (Bulletin, 1976, p. 4) has established the following guidelines:

1. A children's book about Asian Pacific Americans should reflect the realities and ways of an Asian Pacific American People.

2. A children's book about Asian Pacific Americans should transcend stereotypes.

3. A children's book about Asian Pacific Americans should seek to rectify historical distortions and omissions.

4. A children's book about Asian Pacific Americans should avoid the "model" minority and "super" minority syndromes.

5. A children's book about Asian Pacific Americans should reflect an awareness of the changing status of women in society.

6. A children's book about Asian Pacific Americans should contain art and photos which accurately reflect the racial diversity of Asian Pacific Americans.

The committee has also suggested that authors should avoid certain loaded words and images which reinforce offensive stereotypes. Avoid words which suggest that many, most, or all Asian Pacific Americans are:

- smiling, calm, serene, quiet, shy, reserved, peaceful
- short, stocky, small, buck-toothed, myopic, delicate, stunted
- excessively obedient, passive, stolid, docile, unquestioning, overly accommodating
- menial (the waiter-houseboy-cook syndrome), servile (as shown through repeated bows), subservient, submissive
- artistic, mystical, inscrutable, philosophical, sagacious
- quick, dextrous, expert in martial arts
- exotic "foreigners" (even unto the second, third or later generations), faceless hordes, or a "Yellow Peril"
- sinister, sly, evil, cunning, crafty, cruel or a people who place little value on human life.

Such considerations also extend to artwork. Illustrators must note facial structures, especially the eyes, and ensure that they are definitely not slanted and without pupils (slits). Skin color should vary from white to black and include shades of brown or tan. Asian Pacific Americans are not bright yellow! Dress should be appropriate and settings should not be confused scenes of pagoda roofs or ancient emperors' courts. Illustrators can portray the past or how Asian countries look today, not mix them with little regard to fact. Authors, illustrators, publishers, and educators must choose a variety of Asian Pacific American realities

In evaluating and using these books, we must consider that each of the books is an experience or viewpoint of a person. It is realistic from the author's perspective and it is his/her right as an author to share that view. Publishers and educators need to present a multitude of viewpoints of Asian Pacific American experiences, to be shared by Asian Pacific American children as well as by others. By doing so, educators and publishers can foster a substantial change in children's actions and attitudes.

TEACHING IDEAS AND STRATEGIES

Multicultural children's literature lets children experience the lifestyle of others and thus affect their attitudes and values (Arnez, 1969 and Pate, 1988). Literature acquaints children with people who belong to other groups. However, like any social contact, familiarity with other groups through literature may reinforce stereotypes and misconceptions. If inappropriate teaching strategies are used, literature will reinforce rather than mitigate the development of racial bias. Through proper use of instructional strategies, this sensitization can increase racial openness and interest in social justice (Banks, 1970). Teachers, of course, must first explore and define their own attitudes about various ethnic groups if they hope to present a non-judgmental atmosphere for their students (Rudman, 1984).

In her book, *Print and Prejudice* (1976), Zimet concludes that "while it would appear that much of the long term influence of reading depends upon its reinforcement in the home and community, the potential for changing a point of view has been demonstrated by the immediate effects books do have on children's beliefs."

Response to literature research indicates that the use of literature does affect children's attitudes and concepts. Reading or listening to literature is important in children's value development. Research not only suggests that reading or listening to literature affects attitudes, but also that the active discussion of these values is just as important (Berg-Cross, 1978 and Monson and Shurtleff, 1979).

Literature contributes to a child's development of values. It is important that adults lead them in active discussion of these values in order for students to empathize and identify with certain individuals (Gimmestad and De Chiara, 1982). To encourage positive attitudes toward racial groups, both quality discussions and quality literary selections are necessary. Teachers need to help students focus on the understandings of others, to clarify misconceptions, and to share relevant experiences and feelings.

Moreland has stressed that "we need to realize that, although sound knowledge is necessary to combat false information, it is not sufficient to change attitude. Facts do not speak for themselves; rather they are interpreted through the experience and biases of those hearing them" (1963, p. 125).

Multicultural literature presents opportunities for minority children to see themselves in authentic situations and helps them foster pride in their culture (Nieto, 1986).

Multicultural literature helps the reluctant reader. Reading is easier for a child when 75% of the book is recognizable both in language and situation than when only 10-15% of the book is familiar (Myers, 1989, p. 6). To some extent, the reluctant reader becomes uncomfortable and anxious in situations in which he or she has the additional burden of interpreting different lifestyles and cultures and rejects the material. (Walter Dean Myers, 1989; and Hansen, 1984).

To best use books on Asian Pacific Americans, educators need to be open to teach multi-points of view. It is important not to overgeneralize the differences between cultural groups because many times the differences within groups may be larger than the differences between groups. In our need to utilize Asian Pacific American literature, we must strive to expose our students to :

1. the multiple points of view of different Asian Pacific American authors/illustrators on a variety of topics and themes.
2. the multi-points of view on the same topic and theme (e.g., historical fiction novel on the Japanese American concentration camp by Uchida in comparison to novel by Sone)
3. allow all students to compare reader responses with one another.

Folktales

Folktales provide an excellent evolutionary bridge from ancestral cultures to Asian Pacific American perspectives. Folktales set the scene for discussion and discovery of universal themes and plots. Reading comprehension, science, and social studies concepts can easily be integrated into folktale units.

Teachers can develop a bulletin board of a world of folktales for their students. A map of the world helps students identify various folktales and their country of origin. Yarn and pin markers from the country of origin can be used to label folktale variants. e.g., Red colored yarn to label the Cinderella tales, blue colored yarn to label Hare and Tortoise tales.

A start might be for students to read the many variations of Cinderella:

- The Girl Who was Saved by a Talking Bird-Filipino tale
- The Jewel Slipper or Tam and Cam-Vietnamese tale
- Yeh Shen-Chinese tale
- Little Burnt Face-Native American tale
- Tattercoat-English tale
- Moss Green Princess-African Swazi tale
- Ash Pet-Virginia and North Carolina Grandfather tale
- Cinderella-French tale (Perrault) and German tale (Grimm)
- Vassilissa the Fair-Russian tale

Students can compare and contrast plot and theme similarities. They can focus on how characters and/or setting changes the tale according to the country of origin. Students should also explore possible reasons for the contrasts: Are they different because of geographical areas and climate, cultural and social patterns, religious beliefs, and/or educational influences? Given the common essential elements of a selected folktale, such as Cinderella, let students create a modern version. This concretely reinforces the timelessness of universal folktale themes as well as their differences due to place, culture, and so forth

Other variations might be based upon the following:

Little Shell (Filipino/Visayan) with Issunboshi-Little One Inch (Japanese)

Issunboshi (Japanese) with Tom Thumb

Crocodile's Tale (Filipino) with Gingerbread Boy

Urashima Taro (Japanese) with Rip Van Winkle and/or Pandora's Box

Momotaro (Japanese) with Superman (thanks to second grader, Maggie Brown)

Two of Everything (Chinese) with Magic Pot and/or Magic Porridge Pot

Older students can investigate how folktales were used in the writings of Filipino authors as well as with Yep's folk tales (1989). For example they might read an original retelling of a Chinese folktale and compare it with Yep's Chinese-American retelling.

Playing with Language

Momo's Kitten (1977) and *Umbrella* (1958) by Taro Yashima are two simple tales of an Asian American girl growing and learning to be responsible and independent. The two stories also contain different onomatopoeiac words — the sound of rain falling on an umbrella/bon polo bon polo/*v* splish splash and a cat saying neow, neow instead of meow, meow. For kindergartners, this is a great opportunity to make comparisons of different sound words from various cultures.

Point of View

Rather than teaching didactic lessons from literature, teachers can help their students jump into the story and take the point of view of a character (Sebesta, 1963). In becoming the character, students can better understand motives and actions. Further, by utilizing the literature we allow children to safely discuss their own prejudices and experiences as they discover the uniqueness of story characters (Roney, 1986).

According to Piaget's developmental stages, children are egocentric understanding concepts only in relationship to themselves and find another's point of view difficult to understand. At the same time Maslow's hierarchy of needs indicate people strive for a sense of belonging and safety. Therefore, the "you are" type questions help students to further their understandings of similarities, explore differences, and establish the comfort zone of knowing "you belong."

An example of a point of view question based on this discussion might be: "You are the teacher. What would you have said to Bruce when he asked 'Aren't your eyes supposed to slant up or down? Or a question based on a Japanese folktale, Urashima Taro, "You are Taro. Why did you disobey the warning of the Sea Princess?" Pursue with your students how things, feelings, and/or actions are similar even though names, appearances, or cultures might be different. Then further the discussion with acknowledging and accepting the differences.

In addition to taking the identity of various characters, students can learn to do the reverse. They can find elements within the story that are related to their own life experiences in order to make book reading/listening identifiable and applicable with its universal themes. An example of a "relating self" type question might be: "Tell about the time someone laughed at you for doing something different. What did you do or say in response? Tell how your reactions might have been like the character in the book." Or, based on the tale of Urashima Taro, "Tell about the time you were so curious you opened a box even though you were warned not to. How might Taro's feelings be similar to yours?"

Cross Cultural Experiences
Comparisons

Children's books that focus upon the relationship between the young and elderly and about life and death are scarce. *First Snow* (1974), by Coutant and Vo-Dinh, is a beautiful story of a young Vietnamese American girl who learns from her grandmother the meaning of death. This simple story provides the basis for excellent discussions on how different cultures view life and death, about the Buddhist religion, and about extended family functions and responsibilities. Students can compare this story to other stories based on the theme of the elderly and death, such as Miska, Miles. *Annie and the Old One,* (1971) NY: Little, Brown.

Another Look At History

Given the factual historical accounts of the World War II internment of persons of Japanese ancestry, students can read Uchida's *Journey to Topaz* (1971) and *Journey Home* (1978), and make comparisons. Strategies using the "point of view" an/or "relating self" type questions can be used to vicariously experience the life of the young at camp. A comparative biography might be Monica Sone's *Nisei Daughter* (1979) or Japanese-Canadian Joy Kogawa's *Naomi's Road* (1986).

Laurence Yep's novel *Dragonwings* (1975), can also be used as the basis for historical comparisons to Chinese American History. An interesting side investigation might be to find out about the true accounts of the Chinese American aviator, Fong Joe Guey and his airplane, and to uncover how this real life situation became the basis for Yep's novel.

Role Playing

Role playing as outlined by Shaftel and Shaftel (1967) can be used with various chapters from Yep's books. According to Pate (1988), studies at the fifth grade level and the high school level have demonstrated that the level of prejudice is reduced considerably by empathic role-playing or other vicarious experiences in teaching activities. The students should read only part of the chapter, from the beginning to where the problematic situation is introduced. Then the students should be guided in the role-playing activity by first defining the problem, delineating alternatives, exploring the alternatives through dramatization, and finally making a decision as to what was the best alternative.

Through the use of "point of view" and "relating self" questions and role playing strategies, teachers can use Yep's *Child of the Owl* (1977) and *Sea Glass* (1979) to help build the self awareness and concept of Asian Pacific American students. Through these books students will be able to see how folk tales are a viable part of the Casey's Asian American culture as well as struggle with Casey's and Craig's need to find their identities as a street-wise kid as well as a Chinese American.

RECOMMENDED LIST OF ASIAN PACIFIC AMERICAN CHILDREN'S LITERATURE

Below is a selected annotated list of suggested Asian Pacific American children's literature. It is a very narrow representation of what ought to be.

Missing from this compendium, for the reasons presented in this chapter, are quality works representing other Asian Pacific Americans. It would be great if we could have more represented works to compare and contrast. It would be my hope that another decade will not pass before we can have a wealth of literary works representing the multipoints of views of all Asian Pacific Americans.

Anno, Mitsumasa. (1983). *Anno's USA*. New York: Philomel Books. (primary and intermediate). From an eastern immigrant's point of view, a lone traveler approaches the New World from the West in the present day and journeys the US backwards through time, departing the East Coast as the Santa Maria appears over the horizon.

Bang, Molly. (1985). *The Paper Crane*. New York: Greenwillow. (primary). A stranger enters a restaurant and pays for his meal with a paper crane. The visitor and his paper crane bring prosperity to the restaurant.

Belknap, Jodi Parry. (1973). *Felisa and the Magic Tikling Bird*. Norfolk Island, Australia: Island Heritage. (primary). A narrative set in the Filipino community in Hawaii. Felisa, who is handicapped, learns to dance the Tinikling while gaining insights about herself from her grandmother and a Tikling bird.

Coutant, Helen and Vo-Dinh. (1974). *First Snow*. New York: Knopf. (primary). A sensitive story of a young Vietnamese American girl's first experience with a New England snowfall paralleling the death of her grandmother.

Ignacio, Melissa M. (1977) *The Philippines: Roots of my Heritage*. Filipino Development Associates. (intermediate and up). The tellings of a journey of a Filipino American teenager.

Lord, Bette Bao. (1984). *In the Year of the Boar and Jackie Robinson*. New York: Harper & Row. (intermediate). A story of family relationships and cultural difference, Shirley Temple Wong and her mother leave China in 1947 to begin a new life in Brooklyn.

Say, Allen. (1990). *El Chino*. Boston: Houghton Mifflin. (primary-intermediate). A biography of Bill Wong, the first Chinese bullfighter. Bill, a Chinese American who grew up in the Southwest was often told by his father that "in America, you can be anything you want to be." Hence, Bong Way "Billy" Wong, became "El Chino."

Say, Allen. (in press). *Grandfather's Journey*. Boston: Houghton Mifflin. (primary-intermediate). A poignant telling of Allen Say's grandfather's immigration to the United States and return to Japan.

Say, Allen. (1988). *A River Dream.* Boston: Houghton Mifflin. (primary). A contemporary story of a young boy who lies in bed with a fever and receives a gift from his uncle, his personal fly box. Embarking on a fantasy fishing trip, Mark joins his uncle and learns to make choices in life — keeping his prize fish or setting it free.

Say, Allen. (1989). *The Lost Lake.* Boston: Houghton Mifflin. (primary). A young boy and his father become closer friends during a camping trip in the mountains.

Suzuki, David. (1987). *Looking at the Body.* Toronto, Canada: Stoddart Publishing. (intermediate). A book filled with science facts, projects, and activities written by Japanese Canadian professor and broadcaster-host of The Nature of Things. (Part of a series of science literature for children.)

Takashima, Shizue. (1971). *A Child in Prison Camp.* New York: William Morrow. (intermediate). A first hand narrative of Japanese Canadians who were taken from their homes and relocated in internment camps.

Uchida, Yoshiko. (1983). *The Best Bad Thing.* New York: Atheneum. (intermediate). A sequel to *A Jar of Dreams,* this story filled with family obligations, tells of Rinko's adventures during her summer vacation helping Mrs. Hata, a widow and mother of two young boys. After a series of unfortunate accidents, three good things follow which convince Rinko that spending summer with Mrs. Hata was the "best bad thing" that ever happened to her.

Uchida, Yoshiko. (1985). *The Happiest Ending.* New York: Atheneum. (intermediate). The final to the trilogy, *The Best Bad Thing,* this story tells of Rinko's attempts to prevent the arranged marriage between Mrs. Hata's 19-year-old daughter and an elderly Mr. Kinjo. The story shows the struggles between the values of the old Japanese and Japanese Americans.

Uchida, Yoshiko. (1991). *The Invisible Thread.* Englewood Cliffs, NJ: Julian Messner. (intermediate). An autobiography of Nisei author, Yoshiko Uchida. This children's author relates her experiences growing up in Berkeley, California and in American's concentration camp as a second-generation Japanese American. Through her writings she shares her belief "that it is important for each of us to cherish our own special heritage" and that "we must all celebrate our common humanity."

Uchida, Yoshiko. (1981). *A Jar of Dreams.* New York: Atheneum. (intermediate). The first of the trilogy, introduces 11-year-old Rinko, who like other Japanese Americans living in California, struggles to gain acceptance while maintaining pride in her Japanese heritage.

Uchida, Yoshiko. (1978). *Journey Home.* New York: Atheneum. (intermediate and up). A sequel to *Journey to Topaz,* this is the story of 12-year-old Yuki and her family who return to their home in Berkeley after being imprisoned in one of American's concentration camps during World War II.

Uchida, Yoshiko. (1971). *Journey to Topaz.* New York: Scribner's. (intermediate and up). A portrayal of a young Asian American girl's experience during the evacuation of 120,000 persons of Japanese ancestry from the West Coast during World War II.

Uchida, Yoshiko. (1976). *The Rooster who Understood Japanese.* New York: Scribner's. (primary). Story of a young Asian American girl helping out her next door neighbor.

Uchida, Yoshiko. (1972). *Samurai of Gold Hill.* New York: Scribner's. (intermediate and up). A narrative based upon the historical account of the Wakamatsu Colony, one of the first immigrating parties from Japan, and on the findings of a grave on Gold Hill, north of Sacramento, California, "In Commemoration of Okei Died in 1872 19-years-old, A Japanese girl.

Yashima, Taro and Mitsu. (1961). *Momo's Kitten.* New York: Viking Press. (primary). Momo, a young Asian American child, finds lost kitten and takes responsibility for caring for it.

Yashima, Taro. (1958). *Umbrella.* New York: Viking Press. (primary). Momo receives a new umbrella for her birthday and then waits in vain for a rainy day for a chance to use it.

Yep, Laurence. (1977). *Child of the Owl.* New York: Harper & Row. (intermediate and up). Casey, a Chinese American girl is sent to live with her Paw-Paw, her maternal grandmother, in San Francisco's Chinatown, where she learns about herself as a Chinese American.

Yep, Laurence. (1975). *Dragonwings.* New York: Harper & Row. (intermediate and up). Based upon the factual accounts of a Chinese immigrant who built a flying machine during the Wright Brother's era, this is a novel of Windrider and his son Moonshadow who successfully build a flying machine during the early 1900s. The story also reflects realities encountered by the immigrating Chinese.

Yep, Laurence. (1991). *The Lost Garden.* Englewood Cliffs, N.J.: Julian Messner. Laurence Yep warmly writes his autobiography. Growing up as a Chinese American in San Francisco, Yep relates how he uses his writing "to celebrate his family and ethnic heritage."

Yep, Laurence. (1989). *The Rainbow People.* New York: Harper & Row. (intermediate). A collection of folk tales from Oakland's Chinatown during the 1930s. Yep uniquely presents the oral traditions of Chinese American folk tales by providing cultural and historical theme notes as a preface to each retelling.

Yep, Laurence. (1979). *Sea Glass.* New York: Harper & Row. (intermediate and up). A narrative of a Chinese youth who fails to measure up to his father's ideal of an All American sports player and who is consider a "fat Chinese Buddha Man" by friends yet considered a "white demon" by the old Chinese of the neighborhood. With the sensitivity and insight of "Uncle" Quail, Craig begins to find his own niche and self-esteem. Yep again interweaves the themes of conflict between generations, ethnicity, self-worth and family expectations.

Yep, Laurence. (1991). *The Star Fisher.* New York: Harper & Row. (intermediate). A narrative of Joan Lee (Laurence Yep's mother) and her family growing up Chinese American in West Virginia.

TURNING THE PAGE

As educators we know about the effects of literature on the development of values and self concepts of our children. We know about the strengths of instruction and discussion with quality pieces of literature. As educators and promoters of literature, we have criteria for selecting quality works.

Unfortunately, we may not be so aware of our subconscious efforts at covert censorship. However, we can operate with a more knowledgeable base when incorporating such strategies as teacher read alouds or accepting standard recommended reading lists by including a diversity of books.

From this surface level change perhaps we can continue to heighten the awareness of educators and authors/illustrators, and encourage more writers and publishers as to the needs of quality Asian Pacific American children's literature to affect a deep structure change in children's actions and attitudes. We need to fill the gaps and have a wealth of literary works representing the multipoints of views of all Asian Pacific Americans.

We have a responsibility to present Asian Pacific American experiences from multi-points of views. We need to provide accurate knowledge about Asian Pacific Americans while facilitating pride in one's identity, as well as providing tools to combat the impact of racism and sexism.

How much longer will books cause Asian Pacific American children to sink in their seats and to crawl under their desks? How much longer will non-Asian American children formulate misconceptions? How much longer will Asian Pacific American children as well as non-Asian Pacific American children continue to turn the pages of the *Five Chinese Brothers?* Or can we turn towards a new page in a new book of Asian Pacific American literature?

REFERENCES

Abrahamson, R., and Shannon, P. (1983). A plot structure analysis of favorite picture books. *The Reading Teacher, 37,* 44-48.

Arnez, N.L. (1969). Racial understanding through literature. *English Journal, 58,* 56-61.

Asian Americans in Children's Books. (1976). *Interracial Books for Children Bulletin, 7.*

Austin, M. C. and Jenkins, E. C. (1987). *Literature for children about Asians and Asian Americans.* New York: Greenwood Press.

Banks, J. A. (1970). Developing racial tolerance with literature on the black inner-city. *Social Education, 34,* 549-552.

Banks, J. A. (1991). *Teaching strategies for ethnic studies.* Fourth edition. Needham Heights, MA: Allyn and Bacon.

Berg-Cross, L. and Berg-Cross, G. (1978). Listening to stories may change children's social attitudes. *The Reading Teacher,* (1978), 659-663.

Bishop, C. H. and Wiese, K. (1938) *The five chinese brothers.* N.Y.: Coward, McCann.

Campbell, P. B. and Wirtenberg, J. (1980). How books influence children; What the research shows. *Interracial Books for Children Bulletin, 11,* 3-6.

Chin, F. et al. Editors. (1975) *Aiiieeeee! An Anthology of Asian-American Writers.* N.Y.: Anchor Books

Child, I. L., Potter, E. H., & Levine, E.M. (1946). Children's textbooks and personality development: An exploration in social psychology of education. *Psychological Monographs, 60,* 1-54.

Frymer, M. Mako knows About Casting Problems. *Seattle Times.* May 17, 1991.

Gimmestad, B. J. and DeChiara, E. (1982). Dramatic plays: A vehicle for prejudice reduction in the elementary school. *Journal of Education Research, 76,* 45-49.

Gollick, D. and Chinn, P. (1990). *Multicultural education in a pluralistic society.* Columbus; Charles E. Merrill.

Grant, C. and Sleeter, C. (1986). *After the school bell rings.* Philadelphia: The Falmer Press.

Jay, G. S. (1991). The end of "American" literature: Toward a multicultural practice. *College English, 53,* 264-281.

Kimmel, E. A. (1970). Can children's books change children's values? *Educational Leadership, 28,* 209-214.

Litcher, J. W. and Johnson, D. W. (1969). Changes in attitudes toward negroes of white elementary school students after use of multiethnic readers. *Journal of Educational Psychology, 60,* 148-152.

Matsuyama, U. K. (1983) Can story grammar speak Japanese? *Reading Teacher,*

Meltzer, M. (1989). The social responsibility of the writer. *The New Advocate, 2,* 155-157.

Monson, D. and Shurtleff. C. (1979). Altering attitudes toward the physically handicapped through print and non-print, media. *Language Arts,* 163-170.

Moreland, J. K. (1963). The development of racial bias in young children. *Theory into Practice, 2,* 125.

Myers, W. D. (1989). The reluctant reader. *Interracial Books for Children Bulletin, 19,* 14-15.

Nieto, S. (1986). Past accomplishments, current needs la luncha continua. *Interracial Books for Children Bulletin, 17,* 6-8.

Office of Superintendent of Public Instruction, State of Washington. (1988). *Reading Curriculum Guidelines, k-12.*

Pate, G. (1988). Research on reducing prejudice. *Social Education, 52,* 287-289.

Richie, D. (1983). *Unconsidered assumptions/unexamined premises: Notes for an inquiry into national cinematic style, using the Japanese film as example.* Lecture delivered at University of Washington. April 6, 1983.

Roney, R.C. (1986). Multiethnicity in children's fiction. *Social Education, 50,* 464-466.

Rudman, M. K. (1984). *Children's literature: An issues approach.* White Plains, N.Y.: Longman, Inc.

Sebesta, S. L. (1967). The neglected art: Thought questions. *Elementary English.*

Shaftel, F. and Shaftel, G. (1967). *Role playing for social values, decision making in the social studies.* Englewood Cliffs, N.J.: Prentice Hall.

Shannon, P. (1986). Hidden within the pages: A study of social perspective in young children's favorite books. *The Reading Teacher, 39,* 656-663.

Shannon, P. (1989). Overt and covert censorship of children's books. *The New Advocate, 2,* 97-104.

Smith, N. J., Greenlaw, M.J., & Scott, C.J. (1987). Making the literate environment equitable. *The Reading Teacher, 40,* 400-407.

Takaki, R. (1989). *Strangers from a different shore: A history of Asian Americans.* New York: Penguin.

Tangalin, A. B. (1987). *On being Filipino: Who/what is a Filipino American?* Lecture delivered at Filipino American National Historical Society Conference, November, 1987.

Waples, D. Berelson, B. & Bradshaw, F. (1958). What reading does to people. *Research in the three R's,* ed. by Hunnicutt and Iverson, 10-17. New York: Harper Brothers.

Weitzman, L. J., Eifler, D. Hokada, E. & Ross, C. (1972). Sex-role socialization in picture books for preschool children. *American Journal of Sociology, 77,* 1125-1150.

Yamashita, D. J. (1991). *The essence of being Japanese-American is eroding.* Presentation, Seattle, WA., May, 1991.

Yep, L. (1991). *The lost garden.* Englewood Cliffs, NJ: Julian Messner.

Zimet, S. G. (1976). *Print and Prejudice. London:* Hodder and Stoughton.

5

Native Americans in Books for the Young

Donnarae MacCann

INTRODUCTION

The American character has been defined from the beginning in relation to the indigenous population, the Native Americans. European settlers who later became the mainstream justified their domination of the American land base by crediting themselves with "civilization" and a providential mission to supplant the American Indian. Cultural historian Henry Nash Smith notes that "one of the most persistent generalizations concerning American life and character is the notion that our society has been shaped by the pull of a vacant continent drawing population westward . . ." (p. 7). This myth about a "virgin land," available to any enterprising European, characterized the thinking in both political and literary circles (for example, in writings of Franklin, Lincoln, Emerson, and Whitman). It is not surprising that this fallacy permeates literature for the young, past and present.

To revise the symbolic foundations of a national consciousness is a formidable assignment, yet this is one of the tasks of teachers if they wish to offer their students a credible interpretation of the American past. Those symbolic foundations are laid during childhood, and they continue to include historical assumptions that downgrade Amerind culture and experience. Books for young people present some of the clearest examples of the metaphysics of Indian-hating — those "deadly subtleties of white hostility that reduced native peoples to the level of the rest of the fauna and flora to be 'rooted out'" (Drinnon, *Facing West,* p. xvi).

In this chapter various forms of that subtle white hostility will be examined in specific books within specific genres. Also more authentic works of Native American literature will be discussed. But it is important to realize at the outset that books with a white bias vastly outnumber those expressing a Native American perspective. Narratives that depict traditional Amerind ways as futile and obsolete (if not dangerous) are numerous, especially in fiction. On the other hand, works portraying Native American lifestyles as culturally viable are few. The conflict between Native peoples and non-Native is still an unequal contest, and the consciousness of the child is still central to the battle since today's children represent the future and will shape whatever socio-political relationships are yet to evolve.

Because of this imbalance, teachers may wish to use some negative examples of literature as object lessons. Otherwise they cannot demonstrate how weighted children's literature is, even today, with stereotypic imagery and the virgin land myth. The extent to which negative images should be shared as a means of illustrating mainstream prejudice depends upon the age level of the class. But in any case, teachers need to be aware of ongoing stereotypes. Those who are in charge of the classroom need to analyze continually the hard evidence that underpins the following prediction:

> Americans in some manner will cling to the traditional idea that they suddenly came upon a vacant land on which they created the world's most affluent society. Not only is such an idea false, it is absurd. Yet without it both Western man [sic] and his religion stand naked before the world. (Deloria, p. 127)

If teachers can overcome the traditional idea referred to here, that myth will no longer misguide classroom activities in literature and history.

However, as we examine Native American characters in books for children and young people, we find the myth largely intact — the assumption about land that includes the correlative assumption that Native Americans were non-persons. Novels contain the most insidious fallacies, but similar forms of bias are discernible in picture books and biographies. Folklore collections, poetry anthologies, and books about history provide some counterbalance.

NOVELS ABOUT HISTORY

False assumptions about Amerind culture are presented in the most recent novels, as well as in those from the past. Kristiana Gregory's *The Legend of Jimmy Spoon* (1990) is a case in point, although the author makes explicit statements about her good intentions. On the jacket blurb she says: "Writing for young readers is my way of sharing with them my love of history and my deep appreciation for our first Americans. Most of, . . . *The Legend of Jimmy Spoon* [is] for my Native American friends." She includes in the book a glossary of terms and a bibliography of nonfictional works —signals to the audience that the novel may be considered culturally and historically authentic. But historical distortions soon make their appearance. In a plot centering upon a white child adopted into a Shoshoni family, Gregory seems ambivalent about the encounter between Native Americans and whites. The captive shows real affection for his new home, but the readers are not allowed to share in that sense of empathy because they see too many cruel and cowardly elements in Shoshoni culture.

First Jimmy is lured from his home under the pretext of taking a short journey to a tribal village. He soon discovers that he is being kidnapped, but he goes along with the new thrill and the joy of receiving a pinto pony. The author has Jimmy serve as the eyes of the reader, teaching the contemporary child about the Shoshoni lifestyle and philosophy.

We are told that the adopting family loves Jimmy because an aging Shoshoni woman dreams about a white replacement for her deceased sons. However, others in the village are depicted as so racist that they try to take Jimmy's life because he is white. Even a medicine man has murderous intentions and treats the child's wounds in a way that will induce infection.

We see Jimmy as he observes Shoshoni games, and we discover that children are often killed or wounded while they play. We watch Jimmy as he witnesses intertribal wars and as he lectures the elders about the evil of such conflict. War is not presented as a practice throughout the world, but as part of a fiercely aggressive Amerind temperament. We see a returning scalping party that has murdered white children travelling in a wagon train, but no context is provided for an understanding of this frontier war. Certainly it is never mentioned that whites initiated the war for the West.

Even in the course of daily life Jimmy is portrayed as superior, as when he challenges an attacking bear, a selfless act on behalf of a friend. We are told that Shoshonis consider it proper and preferable to flee rather than help people in trouble.

At the end of the novel the white settlers' misdeeds are briefly described: abuse of Mother Earth, sales of firearms, fraudulent schemes that exacerbate conflict. These evils are listed, but never woven into the emotional texture of the narrative. In Jimmy's adopted family, the correct response to the settler is a policy of withdrawal and passivity. As Chief Washakie puts it: "This is a sad thing, fighting with *tybo* [whites]. Stay away from their road and stay away from them" (p. 134). Although this *was* the position of a real chief, the author is using this character to symbolize the "good Indian," to lend support to white expansionist politics. Other Native American leaders recognized that appropriation of their lands and liquidation of the buffalo would soon make their way of life extinct. Gregory's story avoids this dimension of the conflict and leads the reader to view Shoshonis as self-destructive and violence-prone, although generally respectful toward "Mother Earth."

In a 1991 "Selective Bibliography and Guide," Naomi Caldwell-Wood and Lisa A. Mitten (two Native American librarians) have this to say about _The Legend of Jimmy Spoon:_

> Based on a true incident, this novel . . . is a mixture of historical accuracy and silly stereotype . . . Jimmy is continually harrassed about being white, even after two years of living with the Shoshoni. This flies in the face of accounts of actual treatment of white adoptees. Several incidents of violence towards women and children have no basis in tribal cultures, and ring very false . . . (p. 7)

Given Gregory's negative portrayal of Native Americans in a 1990 publication, it is not surprising that novels by William O. Steele from the 1950s have been reissued — stories that hark back to dime novels and their sensationalized descriptions of howling "savages." The publisher, Harcourt Brace Jovanovich, updates the new editions with stylized art work, removes all original illustrations, and includes introductory essays by Jean Fritz, a prize-winning writer of histories and biographies for children.

Fritz justifies the reprinting of Steele's _The Buffalo Knife_ (1952, 1990) by asserting that Steele finds such terms as "redskins" and "savages" offensive even while he puts these words into the mouths of his characters. She comments: "Mr. Steele not only writes a good story, he writes good history that accurately reflects the feelings, the worries, the dangers of the times" (Steele, p. viii). She insists that the book "is true to **its** times." But in no instance does she substantiate her claim that Steele reflects 19th century racism while opposing it. She offers no examples that suggest a narrational voice in contradiction to the leading fictive voices. In fact, Steele's affinity with his white characters is evident throughout in scenes that treat Amerinds as the sole warring parties.

The novel features Isaac and Andy, two boys symbolizing the contrasting values of town and country. As their families travel by flatboat into so-called new territories, the Chickamaugas lurk on the riverbank or attempt to board the boat and scalp its inhabitants. The white expansionists are characterized as innocents moving to a largely empty space. The point is never made that they are about to dispossess the indigenous population of its land, its livelihood, and even its right to exist. To legitimize the settlers' territorial aims, Steele associates the Amerinds with the British. Andy draws the comparison as he speculates about the Tennessee Valley:

> Some day Americans would live there though. They had already run the British out of this country, just about, and some day the Indians would leave, too. Then men like his Uncle Az, the brave and reckless Long Hunters, would range all through that land and find the best places for people to settle and start new towns. (p. 16)

Given this dream of complete territorial dominance on the part of the whites, it is hard to see how Steele can then portray Native Americans as the attackers. But he reinforces that idea repeatedly. Even a casual remark causes a bitter reply from Andy's father:

> "Yonder's the first star," said Isaac, pointing. "Wonder are there any Indians up there?"
>
> "Wherever there's people there's Indians to fight 'em, I reckon," said Mr. Brown wearily. (p. 102)

Indians, it seems, are *not* people, but nowhere in the novel is an opposing position stated. Steele treats the white settlers as peaceful folk, minding their own business, while the land's original inhabitants (with "cruel unwinking eyes") are presented as an alien menace. In fact, when Andy brags to his uncle that he has shot an Indian, no questions are raised about the circumstances. It is assumed that all Chickamaugas are the enemy, and Uncle Az rumples his nephew's hair affectionately at the news of the shooting (p. 119).

Steele does proclaim that the Cherokee nation is friendly, since the Cherokees "don't hardly ever give any trouble [to the whites]." But because the Chickamaugas have the temerity to defend their homeland, they are grouped with all the alleged undesirables. Uncle Az explains:

> All the Indians that didn't want to be friends with the white men left the Cherokee Nation, and they're the ones we call the Chickamaugas — along with some no-good Indians from other tribes, runaway slaves, and even some white men that are just plain mean and shiftless. (p. 15)

Even runaway slaves are disreputable in Uncle Az' eyes, and Steele never contradicts this viewpoint. Even the prize-winning historian, Jean Fritz, finds nothing here to criticize.

As the climate was ripe in the 1990s for the reintroduction of white supremacist novels from the 50s, so was the literary community in the 1970s receptive to a retold captivity narrative dating from 1857. Evelyn Sibley Lampman's *White Captives* (1975) is based upon the Reverend R. B. Stratton's *Captivity of the Oatman Girls, Being an Interesting Narrative of Life Among the Apache and Mohave Indians.* It is a novelistic retelling and, according to Lampman, an effort to treat the captivity of Olive and Mary Ann Oatman "a little more dispassionately." Lampman does include a few Amerind characters who supply the captives with food, but there is nothing resembling a multicultural perspective in the book as a whole. Lampman's treatment of the Apache and Mohave cultures makes them utterly cruel and fearsome.

Lampman continually refers to the white captives as slaves and depicts the Native American nations as obsessed with trading, working, and humiliating their white and non-white slaves. In one scene the Amerinds crucify on a cross one homesick captive who tries to run away. In Lampman's group portraits, the Apaches and Mohaves have no viable economic systems, no reverent religious practices, and no methods of health care other than a system that expedites Mary Ann's death. Most members of the Oatman family are killed as an eye-for-an-eye gesture, as retaliation for the capture of two Amerind women by white frontiersmen, but the raid on the white caravan is treated on stage. We see nothing of the brutality inflicted by the whites, whereas the Native raiders are portrayed as using special cunning in dispatching the Oatmans. As for the surviving sisters, they are kicked, spit upon, and pelted with dirt.

In appraising this novel, mainstream book critics emphasized what they viewed as Lampman's cultural balance, that is, the presence in the story of good and bad Indians and good and bad whites. This argument is somewhat flimsy since the only good **society** presented to the reader is white and Anglo, and the bad societies are Amerind. The "primitiveness" of the latter is so extreme that the Native nations appear to warrant and induce their own obliteration. The problem with the literary critics is the same as the problem embedded in the novel: they credit the book with a culturally pluralistic position because the plot sets up one Anglo raid in direct relationship with one American Indian raid, but the lifestyles of Amerinds are portrayed in white supremacist terms.

Because cultural portraits of Native peoples are so negative in children's novels, the white settlers seem vindicated in their aggression. In the 1930s this kind of message was treated explicitly, as in Laura Ingalls Wilder's *Little House on the Prairie* (1935) when one white settler states openly: "Treaties or no treaties, the land belongs to folks that'll farm it. That's common sense and justice" (p. 211). To counter this perception of justice, teachers need to become informed about actual land use by Native American groups. The wheat-growing economy of the Laura Ingalls family can be studied in juxtaposition with many kinds of Amerind harvests: corn, squash, Indian potato, wild bean, cranberry, blueberry, lily root, muskrat, to mention just a few.[1] More important, the blatant disregard for international law ("Treaties or no treaties the land belongs to [us]") needs to be soundly condemned. Neither the author nor the protagonists in this novel refute such arrogance, although Wilder does place the speaker among the more openly bigoted members of the community. In general, Indian-hating is a large part of *Little House on the Prairie,* but the book still receives continuous and unqualified mainstream support.

Even in the fantasy genre the displacement of American Indian societies can be an underlying theme, as in Lynne Reid Banks' *The Indian in the Cupboard* (1980) and *The Return of the Indian* (1986). These narratives are set in modern times (an English schoolboy is the leading character), but the cultural content is rooted in the image of the Indian as presented in Hollywood westerns and dime novels. Little Bear is a plastic toy Indian who comes to life in the boy's magical cupboard, but remains just three inches in height. He grunts and snarls his way through the story, attacking the child, Omri, with a hunting knife, and later attacking a traditional enemy, a three-inch cowboy. At every turn of the plot, Little Bear is either violent or childishly petulant until he finally tramples upon his ceremonial headdress as a sign of remorse. The historical culpability of the cowboy and others who invaded Amerind territory is ignored. Native Americans are seen as the primary perpetrators of havoc, even as they defend their own borders.

A similar skewing of history occurs in many children's novels, a number of which are described in Laura Herbst's 1975 article, "'That's One Good Indian': Unacceptable Images in Children's Novels." And while we may not be too surprised by what she reveals about old books and their biases (e.g., *The Matchlock Gun,* the 1941 Newbery prize novel), we should be surprised by the sensationalism and stereotyping that continue into the present. Walter D. Edmonds, in that old Newbery winner, was honored for this kind of description:

> [The Indians] hardly looked like men, the way they moved. They were trotting, stooped over, first one and then another coming up, like dogs sifting up to the scent of food. (p. 39)

In 1986, Lynne Reid Banks is applauded by book critics as she portrays Algonquins in *The Return of the Indian* with faces like "wild, distorted, terrifying masks of hatred and rage" (p. 158). Although Banks is writing fantasy, she is misrepresenting the Algonquin of the past as a means of amusing the white child of today.

NOVELS ABOUT MODERN TIMES

Native Americans in modern settings are typically embroiled in conflicts between old and new societies, or between Anglo and Amerind parents. As in the novels about the frontier, authors frequently includes notes about their research — their visits to reservations, discussions with museum archivists, readings in anthropology, and so on. But this is no guarantee of a multicultural approach. White supremacist elements are discernible in recent works about interracial families and about treks into the wild in search of one's heritage.

In Welwyn Wilton Katz's *False Face* (1988), a distortion of Native American religion is placed at the core of a modern day horror story. Whites who have experienced a bitter divorce come into possession of two ancient Amerind masks, one exerting a magical force that causes murderous impulses and the other supplying protection. The plot spins around who has which mask. Eventually Tom, a boy of interracial parentage, returns the masks to the bog from which they were excavated.

Familiar stereotypes are used in characterizing Tom. His mother informs him that since he is a careful and thoughtful organizer, his white side is asserting itself. The text reads: "She was reminding him he wasn't all Indian. Reminding him that maybe there were things in him that were white" (p. 55). The implication is that Tom's Indianness would not equip him for modern, managerial tasks. Indians, it seems, have not caught up with contemporary life, as a museum curator infers when she says to Tom: "Most of the Indian community is still getting used to the idea of archeology" (p. 57). And when this teenager turns to the Amerind community for advice about the false face masks, a Native elder dismisses him curtly:

> "What have you to do with *faces?* What has any white person to do with them?"
>
> There was a pain in Tom's stomach, sharp and achy as a sickness. White person. Was that what they thought about him? Was that what they had always thought? (129)

Not only is the Amerind tradition presented as a form of destructive magic; the people on the reservation, Tom's former home, are characterized as vindictive and racist.

In describing the problems in this book, Naomi Caldwell-Wood and Lisa A. Mitten write:

> The portrayal of the Iroquois and nonsense presented about the mask are way off base and very insulting . . . Katz conjures up a ridiculously evil power that is supposed to inhabit the false face mask and alter the personalities of characters who attempt to possess the mask. This goes beyond the wild fantasies of a creative author. False face masks are an integral part of traditional Iroquois religions practised today on the very reserve that Katz describes so well. Her description of the mask as an absolute evil amounts to religious intolerance and goes far in fostering the conception of native, non-Christian religions as savage pagan rituals. A very harmful book. (6)

Similarly in Jean Craighead George's *The Talking Earth* (1983), Native American traditions and the keepers of those traditions are depicted as inscrutable and potentially dangerous. A Seminole teenager, Billy Wind, has experienced the world of the reservation and the world of the Kennedy Space Center School. From the latter she has gained sensitivity to the earth and its problem. From the Seminole elders she has access to a more subjective level of understanding and sensitivity, but she rejects their teachings because they are embodied in myth and symbol. Billie is, therefore, sent to the Everglades on a lone quest for the "things that cannot be seen with the eyes." But the whole venture comes across as a hateful trick, a punishment contrived by old men who cannot tolerate discrepancies between Western science and ancient lore. While George probably intends to uphold at least some Amerind values, she undercuts this possibility by her contrived generational conflict and her unfavorable collective portrait of the Seminole people.

George's novel falls within a well-known subgenre in children's literature — the Robinsonnade, a celebration of survival skills reminiscent of Daniel Defoe's 18th century novel, *Robinson Crusoe* (1719). When such a story is set in modern times, the narrative's locale is often the Arctic as in Gary Paulsen's *Dogsong* (1985) and Scott O'Dell's *Black Star, Bright Dawn* (1988).

These authors capitalize upon the hazards of climate and terrain, and add to the Robinsonnade formula a romanticized, mystical relationship between humans and dogs. Paulsen makes the most of such opportunities for empathy and excitement. In the process, however, he misrepresents the Inuits — the group both Paulsen and O'Dell label "Eskimo" (a term unknown in the Inuit language, but meaning "eaters of raw meat" in the tongue of neighboring American Indian groups [Hirschfelder, p. 2]). Paulsen's *Dogsong* encourages the notion that the Inuit nation is a dying civilization, the decline stemming largely from cultural weakness. In the novel, no indigenous tradition can withstand the lure of the invaders' culture. Among the three leading male characters, white society has taken its toll but the blame falls most heavily upon the victims. The 14-year-old hero lives with his father because his mother deserted her family for a white lover. The father's chronic drunkenness is remedied only by means of a fearsome "hellfire and damnation" doctrine preached by missionaries. The village elder, Oogruk, loses a wife who is drawn away by the enticements of a mining town and its parties. And Oogruk's knowledge of a unique ecological system is passed down to just one receptive youngster before he kills himself. With such destructive tendencies, it is a wonder that this people survived for centuries.

Scott O'Dell's *Black Star, Bright Dawn* brings together the dangers of a lethal climate, a cross country sled race, and a volatile lead dog who is part husky but mostly wolf. The plot spins off from an 18-year-old's move to a large Inuit community — a move necessitated by her father's nearly fatal entrapment on the ice and the phobia that follows. Most of the novel is devoted to the sled race in which Bright Dawn stands in for her father and has a similar accident.

Only the presence of Oteg, a father-figure during the course of the sledding competition, enables O'Dell to introduce his views of the indigenous culture. Oteg is respected as a mine of information (he is a veteran of the Iditarod Race), but O'Dell uses him primarily for comic relief. We learn that when Oteg "walked he looked like a bear." When Oteg introduces himself to Bright Dawn he gives his chest a comical thump. In describing the death of a daughter, his tone is flippant: "Panee died one day long ago. Too bad. She was a pretty girl. Now I have only nine [daughters]" (p. 47). As for Oteg's religious practices, they come across as farce:

> Oteg went to his sled and came back with a handful of knives . . . Many people in Ikuma . . . believed that they would change the weather by cutting it into pieces, just as they wished it to be.
>
> Oteg did a dance in the snow. He shook the bundle of knives above his head and muttered, "Wind, who blows cold from the north, we've had

enough of you. We do not want to freeze and soon we must travel fast. Speak to your sister, South Wind. See that she replies." (p. 47)

Given Oteg's highly whimsical conversations with the elements, it is no surprise that Bright Dawn rejects her traditional religion, adding Inuit to Christian concepts only when frightened by the dark.

Perhaps the main difference between such novels about contemporary life and those published earlier is in the treatment of cultural assimilation. In the books already described, authors typically hint at an intellectual struggle between old and new lifestyles and belief systems. In the 1950s questions about Anglo superiority were not usually raised. In Evelyn Sibley Lampman's *Navaho Sister* (1956) the protagonist cannot accomplish white assimilation fast enough. Sad Girl revels in bedroom furniture and indoor plumbing. Going to an Indian Bureau school is the thrill of her life:

> She didn't know that [the brick building] was old and bravely made over. She saw only the bright paint and fresh curtains, and she found it hard to believe she was going to live in all this luxury . . . There was a rug on the floor, so large that she marveled at the size of the loom which must have made it. Instead of stripes and a conventional design, the rug had roses woven into it, a feat for any weaver. (p. 47)

In the book's last illustration, we see utter contentment and joy in the face of Sad Girl. She has shed the "sad" side of life which, as Lampman presents it, is the Navaho side.

For a powerful refutation of this attitude, we have Craig Kee Strete's *When Grandfather Journeys into Winter* (1979), a novella that depicts an Amerind elder's sacrifices for his grandchild, and *The Bleeding Man and Other Science Fiction Stories* (1977), six narratives with either implicit or explicit Native American themes. These short stories are brilliantly metaphoric and mostly suited to a skilled, well-read middle school and high school audience. In the futuristic "White Brothers from the Place Where No Man Walks," a prophet explains the past and future Amerind/white relationships. "When They Find You" is a love story about an interracial marriage on a distant planet. The couple's fate parallels the fate of such couples on earth. "A Sunday Visit with Great-grandfather" is a superbly whimsical ghost story with an indirect critique of Indian Bureau schools, and "The Bleeding Man" exposes the murderous experiments conducted by professionals and tolerated by "scientific" societies. Strete's poetic, philosophic voice, as well as his willingness to handle difficult political themes, make his work for young adults exceptional. He is himself a Native American.

Another book for middle schoolers is A. E. Cannon's *The Shadow Brothers* (1990), a novel praised by Amerind librarians because it deals honestly with a Native American teenager in an otherwise all-white school.[2] The leading character, Henry Yazzie, has been adopted into a non-Native family after the death of his mother. But after unsettling and sometimes racist encounters with schoolmates, Henry recognizes the importance of understanding his father (a reservation police officer), his grandfather, and his Navaho identity.

In Barbara Girion's *Indian Summer* (1990), the culture conflict occurs with younger children. Joni, a white 10-year-old, lives with an Iroquois family when her father takes a summer job as reservation pediatrician. Her five-year-old brother candidly expresses his biases, while Joni reveals what that bias is like when it has become an insidiously veiled hostility. As a novel the book is somewhat repetitive in its plot incidents, but as Amerind critics have emphasized, this is a work of fiction that "manages to touch on a number of issues important to contemporary Iroquois without being preachy" (Caldwell-Wood, p. 3).

The five-year-old in this novel illustrates the way early impressions are formed. Even at his tender age he is a product of the mass media and has learned Indian stereotypes. The picture book is the medium geared specifically for children at this age level — a medium that can circulate valid or invalid imagery.

PICTURE BOOKS

Native peoples are typically amalgamated into one generalized Indian in picture books. As this white-created symbol was utilized in countless Hollywood movies (a character imbued with a few standard motifs), so in the picture book the stereotypes involve a handful of motifs. Robert B. Moore and Arlene B. Hirschfelder studied 75 books that **included** Native Americans but were not specifically **about** them and discovered the following over-generalized features:

> Native people always wear feathers or headdresses; they frequently brandish tomahawks; they live in tipis; the women usually have babies on their backs; the men are fierce and violent; they lurk behind trees; they spend much time dancing on one leg; and their existence is dependent on the proximity of cowboys. (p. 51)

When Moore and Hirschfelder saw that Native people were represented in picture books totally unrelated to Amerind character and experience (as in Maurice Sendak's alphabet book, *Alligators All Around* [1962]) they understood more about the pervasiveness of the mythical Indian. Distorted images were standard fare in picture book sub-genres.

This misuse and over-representation continues in recent picture books. Virginia Grossman's *Ten Little Rabbits* (1991) is a variation on the counting book, showing numerical groupings of rabbits with each animal decked out in Amerind clothing. Specific patterns are explained in relation to specific nations in the afterword, but as critics Caldwell-Wood and Mitten point out, "the impression given is one of generic 'Indianness,' and once again animals 'because' Indians simply by putting on certain articles of clothing, relegating an entire race to the status of a role or profession" (p. 7).[3]

In Patricia Polacco's *Boat Ride with Lillian Two Blossom* (1989), an elderly Amerind woman is a phantom figure who suddenly materializes out of the woods and disappears in the same mysterious manner. The text describes her as "ancient . . . and a little mussed up." She clearly terrifies the small children she encounters. But when she makes a boat fly and magically changes into a young woman, her appearance is supposedly less threatening. In her new form she tells the children fanciful anecdotes about the origin of rain, wind, light and so on. Lillian Two Blossom, as this woman is called, is not only the conventional generic Indian; she is depicted as a homeless, witch-like being — a person whom "folks . . . didn't know where she came from or where she went . . ." She is not an extinct Indian, but she is a highly anomalous one.

In Mercer Mayer's *Liverwurst is Missing* (1981), the stereotypes are the sort that would probably have been avoided if some other minority group had been selected for comic relief. Admittedly the story is a farce and lampoons all kinds of folks, but the Amerinds are anachronistic as well as foolish. In a purely modern setting, Steven Kellogg (the illustrator) makes the Indians unaccountably naked except for headdresses and pants. Mayer calls them "Wackatoo Indians" and names the leader "Chief Sorefoot." They have all escaped from the "Asphalt Flats Reservation" and are said to be on the warpath when spotted by some ex-cavalrymen. This is the level of "fun" that you find in 19th century cartoons about alleged cannibals. The humor is actually ridicule. Only when racial and cultural equality is among the underlying premises from which a story evolves — only then can we speak of humor. Equals can poke fun at one another; unequals are arranged in a social hierarchy and those at the bottom are laughed at — not laughed with.

Picture books that include gratuitous images of Native Americans (as in alphabet books and stories about playing Indian) tend to reinforce misunderstanding, especially when the images suggest violence. For example, a bear in ceremonial headdress is on the warpath with a tomahawk in Marianna Mayer's *The Brambleberrys Animal Book of Big and Small Shapes* (1987, 1991). A child in a nursery school wears a feathered headband and brandishes a tomahawk in Miriam Cohen's *Will I Have a Friend?* (1967). In Maud and Miska Petersham's *The Rooster Crows; A Book of American Rhymes and Jingles* (1945) a child in overalls is pursued by a youngster with headdress and tomahawk. Maurice Sendak's *Alligators All Around* — another example with the tomahawk image — has already been mentioned. One book of this sort would not induce fear in a child, but there are scores of similar images and each one can reinforce the notion that Amerinds are cruel and aggressive.

There is no doubt that many children do view Native Americans in this light. Moore and Hirschfelder report on child attitudes and responses in their study of picture books. Children described Amerinds in their own writings:

> They heurt [sic] lot of people in the world.
> Thousands of people were kild. [sic]
> I think they are killers to americans. [sic] (p. 47)

And in describing one of his drawings a child stated: "He's a bad Indian and an ugly one. And he kills" (p. 47).

Materials that are free from violence or contain it within the authentic trickster tradition have become more numerous in recent years. Jamake Highwater's *Moonsong Lullaby* (1981) is a hymn about the wonders of nature and includes stunning photographs by Marcia Keegan. The book's one flaw is its factual inaccuracy. Doris Seale, a Native American book critic, objects to the scenes in which rabbits and foxes sleep at night while the hawk goes hunting. In fact, hawks hunt by day and rabbits and foxes are abroad after dark (p. 35). Amerind sources have exposed Highwater as a non-Indian, a fact that may explain some of this indifference toward the realities of Mother Earth.[4]

Big Thunder Magic (1990) is by the Amerind, Craig Kee Strete (illustrations by Craig Brown) and is a thoughtful contemporary allegory about a Native American's trip to the city with his favorite sheep. Only the ghost who tags along is able to perform the rescue that saves them. It is a sadder but wiser pair who return to the Pueblo.

Jane Mobley's *The Star Husband* (illustrated by Anna Vojtech, 1979) is a romantic tale about ascending into the heavens to marry a star. In time the young woman longs for her village and returns to earth to become the Wise

One of her tribe. Only after her death does her spirit move back into the heavens; you can see her even now — the star beside the moon (her son), the first star to shine. Mobley has been criticized for failing to identify her sources, but the book's illustrations give it added strength. Vojtech is praised for using Native American rather than European facial features and for the overall beauty of her images.[5]

Another picture book rendition of a folktale is *Iktomi and the Berries* (1989) by Paul Goble. This is the first of a series of "Iktomi" trickster tales, all distinguished by Goble's excellent illustrations and all "capturing flawlessly . . . the flavor of Indian humor and the easy blend of cultures so common in contemporary Indian America" (Caldwell-Wood, p. 3). Goble sets up the narrative in three different typefaces as a way of guiding storytellers in their interpretations and their interactions with listeners. In a prefatory note, he explains Iktomi's cultural history within the Lakota Sioux nation.

These stories are related to the "noodlehead" sub-genre in world folklore, yet sometimes Iktomi's "cleverness" proves beneficial, as when he invents tipis and moccasins. Typically his mischief is highly slapstick — i.e., both rowdy and absurd — as when he sees berries reflected in a stream and nearly drowns himself in trying to grab them.

Goble rightly emphasizes the characterful oral style as well as the humor. He avoids a conventional prose format, a textual layout that tends to obscure the liveliness of Amerind literature, although that straight prose style is generally the way Amerind stories reach the public.

In his serious tales about the history and lore of Amerind nations, Goble returns to a more conventional style as in *Crow Chief* (1992). In this Plains Indian story, crows are white birds that cause much havoc. They continually warn the buffaloes of approaching hunters and the result is near-starvation in the human population. This imbalance in nature is cured by the prayers of the people, the intervention of Falling Star (a character similar to a Christ-figure in Christian tradition), and a stratagem that ultimately turns the crows black. "Falling Star," explains the narrator, "still travels from one place to another to help people. One day, when we need him, he will come again."

FOLKLORE AND POETRY

Native American folktale anthologies have had a long history. Charles A. Eastman (Ohiyesa) was a member of the Sioux nation and author of *Indian Boyhood* (1902), a compilation of Sioux tales with a frame story reminiscent of 19th century children's fiction. The frame story, in particular, reflects the New England influence in Eastman's life. He graduated from an Ivy League college, was converted to Christianity, married a white New Englander, and returned to Wounded Knee to practice medicine. He uses a fictional uncle and nephew in the didactic frame story, but if you screen out that material, you find narratives rich in imaginative power and in reverence for the natural world.

Indian Tales (1953) by Jaime deAngulo are based upon the oral tradition of California Indian nations. DeAngulo was an amateur anthropologist who expressed a certain condescension toward the tribes he visited. He wrote:

> You wonder whether you are dropping back into childhood and the wonder-time of stories, and fairies, and miracles, and marvelous things. (p. 5)

As for the national specificity that today's Amerinds encourage in works for children, deAngulo consciously ignores it:

> I have not paid very much attention to scientific accuracy. I have mixed tribes that don't belong together. I have made some people live in a type of house that belonged to a different section of the country . . . So don't worry about it. If you find yourself getting interested in the subject, go to the literature. (p. 5)

Anthologists today seldom express such a blatant disinterest in the subject of their own books. In his introduction to *Why the Possum's Tail is Bare and Other North American Indian Nature Tales* (1985), James E. Connolly provides information about language groups, forms of subsistence, political organization within tribes, migrations, and much more. And he ends his preface with this stress on specificity:

> With their differences understood [the differences between tribes] we can contemplate what these stories and their storytellers had in common: keen observation of nature, desire to teach virtues, and respect for all living things. (p. 13)

Such careful, empathetic editors produce the best contemporary folk collections. The artist/writer Richard Erdoes edits *The Sound of Flutes and Other Indian Legends* (1976) and names the storytellers (Lame Deer, Jenny Leading Cloud, Henry Crow Dog, and others). In the title story, a young hunter discovers how to make the first flute and uses it in his courting. The beauty of the instrument and the charm and humor of the romance are poetically described by Henry Crow Dog, who concludes his tale in the role of a wise councilor: "And that is how Siyotanka the flute came to be — thanks to the cedar, the woodpecker, the wind, and one young hunter who shot no elk but who knew how to listen" (p. 9).

Paul Goble, the illustrator, captures the legends' beauty and dignity. He is praised by Amerind book critics for his "understanding of Native Americans' feelings and ideas," and for his "fine sense of earth tones and space."[6]

Tonweya and the Eagles and Other Lakota Indian Tales (1979) by Rosebud Yellow Robe contains stories with multiple levels of meaning, as well as introductory material about the author's parents and grandparents. The close association between tale teller and story provides a clue to the vitality in these tales.

Like Rosebud Yellow Robe, Joseph Bruchac is a Native American collector, editor, and storyteller. He retells traditional tales in his book *Iroquois Stories: Heroes and Heroines, Monsters and Magic* (1985) and on the cassette tape "Iroquois Stories" (1988). There is an appealing blend of humor and insight in both versions, but the tape has a special charm and can serve as a guide to the art of Amerind storytelling. As a skillful performing artist, Bruchac does not distract listeners from the substance of the story, but draws them close to its spirit. He mixes a quiet, reverent style, for example, with sudden fierce growls, making the villainy of a character delightfully palpable.

Poetry, as well as storytelling, is a vital part of Amerind life. Arlene Hirschfelder reports that in the Inuit language, the word for poetry is appropriately the same word as the one meaning "to breathe (p. 140)." The two art forms, poetry and folk narrative, are beautifully united in Dennis Tedlock's *Finding the Center: Narrative Poetry of the Zuni Indians* (1972). This work was published as an adult book, but should be used by teachers for its poetic rendering of such an important story as the Zuni version of Cinderella; "The Girl Who Took Care of the Turkeys."[7]

In *Dancing Teepees: Poems of American Indian Youth* (illustrated by Stephen Gammell, 1989), Virginia Driving Hawk Sneve, a member of the Sioux nation, collects traditional Native poems as well as some of her own and other modern poets. She begins with Black Elk's "The Life of a Man is a Circle:"

The life of a man is a circle from childhood to childhood, and so it is in everything where power moves. Our teepees were round like the nests of the birds, and these were always set in a circle, the nation's hoop, a nest of many nests, where the Great Spirit meant for us to hatch our children. (p.8)

A battle song evokes the strong and intimate relationship between a Lakota tribesman and his horse:

My Horse, Fly Like a Bird

My horse, fly like a bird
To carry me far
From the arrows of my enemies,
And I will tie red ribbons
To your streaming hair. (p. 30)
— Virginia Driving Hawk Sneve adapted from a Lakota song

Aline Amon is a gifted graphic artist who collected Native American chants and poems in *The Earth is Sore: Native Americans on Nature* (1981). Her aim, she says, was to make a strong statement about the preservation of the natural environment, and for this purpose she sought out the eloquent poems of Amerinds. The following is a Chippewa children's chant:

To a Firefly

Flitting white-fire insect,
waving white-fire bug,
give me light before I go to sleep!
Come, little dancing white-fire bug,
come, little flitting white-fire beast,
light me with your bright white flame,
your little candle! (p. 25)

Among Amon's selections for older readers is the following Inuit song recorded by a Danish explorer in the 1920s:

One Great Thing

I think over again
my small adventures,
when I drifted out with a shore wind
in my kayak
and thought I was in danger.

My fears,
those small ones,
that I thought so big,
were for all the vital things
I had to get and to reach.

And yet, there is only
one great thing —
to live to see, at home or on journeys,
the great day that dawns,
and the light that fills the world. (p. 13)

— Kitlinguharmiut
Eskimo [i.e., Inuit]

Such a poem brings the reader close to the subjective level of Amerind experience, a level less noticeable in historical and biographical works. Generally speaking, the histories published over the last few decades hold up better than the biographies.

HISTORIES AND BIOGRAPHIES

In the field of history, books are now available that help children unlearn stereotypes. Arlene Hirschfelder's *Happily May I Walk: American Indians and Alaska Natives Today* (1986) was written with this purpose in mind. Hirschfelder is the education consultant to the Association on American Indian Affairs, and presents an overview of contemporary Amerind culture, as well as the historical information that enables readers to understand that culture. She organizes each short chapter so that we learn where the different Native American nations are located, how they are governed, what control is exercised over land and other resources, how arts, sports, and religious practices are part of daily life, how both mind and body are addressed in healing, the manner in which children are educated, and much more. With such information, children can envision a vast continent that was the home of numerous Amerind societies. They can comprehend the rational development of these nations and the cultural values they still embrace.

For the youngest classes, teachers can use *The People Shall Continue* (1977, 1988) by Simon Ortiz, illustrated by Sharol Graves. It reads like an epic poem and includes just a few implicitly presented themes. These include the unity of earth and living things, opposition to invaders, the emergence of new leaders, the tragedy of reservation life, and finally the solidarity that should unite all oppressed peoples. The compression of so much history tends to obscure the gravity of the long 1500-1900 era, but teachers can use this book to prepare the way for more detailed studies.

By the time children are in about the fifth grade, they will be ready to hear a reading of *Night Flying Woman: An Ojibway Narrative* (1983) by Ignatia Broker. Broker centers her story on the life of her great-great-grandmother, but the book is about the compulsory exodus of a whole people and functions more as a history than a biography. The author's family was caught in the uprootings that preceded final resettlement on the White Earth Reservation. Broker reveals the chaotic impact of official U.S. policies on the 19th century Ojibway civilization, and offers her readers a warm, detailed account of family life and the struggle to survive in a time of periodic dislocation.

Richard Erdoes' *Rain Dance People; The Pueblo Indians, Their Past and Present* (1976) is a well-researched but less personal history. Art, religion, communal government, incursions by settlers and missionaries, compulsory boarding schools — these are a few of the subjects Erdoes includes.

As Erdoes does not gloss over the so-called "winning" of the West and its injustices, so *Let Me Be A Free Man: A Documentary of Indian Resistance* (1975) counteracts the Euro-American perspective. This is an incisive collection of quotations by such leaders as Sitting Bull, Geronimo, Vine Deloria, and Dennis Banks. Whether one teaches younger or older students, this anthology edited by Jane B. Katz is important. It enables a listener to hear the language of the Native American struggle in its purest form.

The recent collective biography of Amerind leaders, Russell Freedman's *Indian Chiefs* (1987), is a similarly powerful book to share with the young. Freedman begins with a brief review of the white/Amerind struggle and explains at the outset that the term "chief" is something of a misnomer. The different nations had many degrees of leadership, sometimes a military chief, a civil chief, and a principal chief ranked as first among equals (p. 8). The interplay between leaders at various levels is clearly seen in Freedman's essays covering six nations and six leaders: Red Cloud, Satanta, Quanah Parker, Washakie, Joseph, and Sitting Bull. Although personal facts are not emphasized, the reader does gain a glimpse of the families and upbringing of these individuals, as well as a better understanding of the difficult choices they all confronted as they devised strategies for dealing with whites. Freedman quotes each leader, finding statements that sum up some important chapter in their lives such as the meaning of defeat for Quanah

Parker, seen in his quip, "This was a pretty country you took away from us" (p. 53).

Given such excellence in nonfiction, it is surprising that much biographical writing is of a lower caliber. In part this problem stems from the conventional practice of fictionalizing biographical narratives for children. For example, in works about Sacajawea, Pocahontas, Squanto, and other famous Indians, heavy fictionalizing is the norm. Some forms are more objectionable than others, but Eurocentric biases are usually infused in the storylines. Ann Donegan Johnson's *The Value of Adventure: The Story of Sacagawea* (1980) contains a plotline in which Sacagawea must choose between loyalty to her own Shoshoni people and Lewis and Clark. She chooses the latter exclaiming, "I did only what I had to." When her hot-headed brother, the "chief," says he will never look at her again, she is content with her outcast status because she has helped the "white captains." She sees the march to the Pacific as unexplainably noble.

In Kate Jassem's *Sacajewea, Wilderness Guide* (1979) the brother of Sacajawea does **not** go off in a huff. Instead he embraces her and says that she must help Lewis and Clark and return to tell him "about the great water" (p. 43). Little is known about the actual role of Sacajewea in the expedition, and authors apparently think they are at liberty to concoct any kind of plot. But in both of these books, the land is presumed uninhabited and unexplored, just because it is new to the "white captains." In addition, the Johnson book contains pernicious cartoons and the Jassem book has a variety of other errors (e.g., Jassem calls Sacajewea a princess although her society had no concept of royalty; she also claims that Sacajewea was the first woman to cross the Rockies — an unlikely assumption; and the illustrator gives Sacajewea a necklace that could have been made only by Amerinds in the Southwest).

The Double Life of Pocahontas (1983) by Jean Fritz is a more ambitious biography, but Fritz seems interested in contriving a romance rather than shedding light upon her subject. The author admits that Pocahontas may have saved John Smith on her own initiative, or her father may have arranged the rescue as a means of adopting Smith and gaining gifts in exchange. But she builds a tale in which Pocahontas unaccountably pines for Smith, grieves for Smith, converts to Christianity in order to join Smith in heaven and so on. Both before and after her two marriages, Pocahontas' heart struggles with "storms of feeling" for John Smith and for little else. Fritz does describe in some detail the violence in both English and Algonquin communities, but her epilogue makes the British look like mere bunglers, while the Amerinds are portrayed as invaders and butchers. In the end, her analysis implies that the sin of the English settlers was simply that they were so numerous.

Lisa Eisenberg's *The Story of Sitting Bull, Great Sioux Chief* (1991) includes the proclamation: "No part of this biography has been fictionalized." But the narrative mode is fictional — i.e., the author imagines what is said and thought at specific moments in Sitting Bull's life and reports her imaginings to the reader. She conveys the idea that this Amerind leader generally thought thoughts of pride and bravery; she does not round out the portrait. Yet Eisenberg goes much further than is customary in discussing the politics and manueverings of the Sioux/white conflict. She exposes white culpability and does not hedge on that point.

Eisenberg minimizes fictionalization but does not abandon it. Yet her work represents a better understanding of cultural and political issues than does Kate Jassem's *Squanto, The Pilgrim Adventure* (1979). Jassem brings her short biography to a close by quoting pilgrim leader William Bradford, by emphasizing his belief in a divinely arranged mission: "Squanto was a special instrument sent by God for the Pilgrims' good." To quote that myth without any sort of rebuttal — to make it the climax of the narrative — is to prolong the illusion that "white is right."

The invocation of God on behalf of white expansionism brings us full circle. At the opening of this commentary, the "virgin land" rationale was referred to as "one of the most persistent generalizations concerning American life and character" (Smith, p. 7). That position implied that a great void awaited the white colonizer. In that alleged emptiness, however, new European settlements could be maintained solely by means of military **force.** The paradox here is obvious, but it has been masked by repeated allusions to Providence — a pretext still imposed on the young learner.

CONCLUSION

To move beyond the miseducation of children, different strategies are needed for different literary genres. Book selection practices need to take account of the many subtleties in symbolic forms of literature, especially in novels and picture books. Since stereotyping is not always obvious to people surrounded by mainstream culture, Native American librarians and other have supplied useful guidelines. For example, Caldwell-Wood and Mitten prepared a "What to Look For" list which they adapted from two excellent sources: Raymond William Stedman's *Shadows of the Indian: Stereotypes in American Culture* (1982) and *Through Indian Eyes; The Native Experience in Books For Children* (1992) edited by Beverly Slapin and Doris Seale. Here is a slightly abridged version:

1. Is the vocabulary demeaning? (Are terms such as "squaw," "warrior," "savage" used?)

2. Do the Indians talk like Tonto or in the noble savage tradition?

3. Are the Indians all dressed in the standard buckskin, beads and feathers?

4. Are the Indians portrayed as an extinct species?

5. Is Indian humanness recognized? (Do animals "become" Indians or children "play" Indian?)

6. Do Native Americans appear in alphabet and counting books as **objects** that are counted?

7. Do Native American characters have ridiculous imitation "Indian" names such as "Indian Two Feet" or "Little Chief'?

8. Is the artwork predominated by generic "Indian" designs? Or has the illustrator taken care to reflect the traditions and symbols of the particular people in the book?

9. Is the history distorted, giving the impression that the white settlers brought civilization to Native peoples and improved their way of life? Are terms like "massacre," "civilization," "superstition" used in such a way as to demean Native cultures and indicate the superiority of European ways?

10. Are Indian characters successful only if they realize the futility of traditional ways and decide to "make it" in white society?

11. Are white authority figures (teachers, and so forth) able to solve the problems of Native children that Native authority figures have failed to solve? (**Are** there any Native authority figures?)

12. Are the perceptions of women as subservient drudges present? Or are women shown to be the integral and powerful part of Native societies that they are?

13. Most importantly, is there anything in the book that would make a Native American child feel embarrassed or hurt to be what he or she is? Can the child look at the book and recognize and feel good about what he or she sees?

A critical tool designed for children — the filmstrip "Unlearning Indian Stereotypes" (1978) — enables teachers and young people to watch Amerind youngsters as they critique biased books. This is an ideal point of departure for discussion. The filmstrip's accompanying booklet, "A Teaching Unit for Elementary Teachers and Children's Librarians," provides role-playing and other classroom strategies. But such lessons do not diminish the teacher's need for skills in multicultural book selection. Nor does it obviate the need to recognize specific historical circumstances *vis-á-vis* specific ethnic groups. For Native Americans, the problem is not only stereotyping **per se,** but the large quantity of publications that misrepresent them. In a bibliography published by the Association on American Indian Affairs, Mary Gloyne Byler sums up the difficulty:

> Most minority groups in this country have been, and are still, largely ignored by the nation's major publishing houses ... American Indians, on the other hand contend with a mass of material about themselves. If anything, there are too many children's books about American Indians. (p. 27)

With regard to folktales and poetry, teachers need to make every effort to perfect their oral performance. Stories should be told to live audiences, and if teachers have no opportunity to see Amerind storytellers and study their styles, they can still gain some impressions from Dennis Tedlock's poetic renditions and Paul Goble's comic treatment of trickster tales. Both authors stress performance aspects of tales.

In appraising works of history and biography, perhaps the best strategy is in studying critiques produced by Native American critics. *Interracial Books for Children Bulletin,* a periodical published regularly for more than 20 years, contains numerous reviews written by Amerind scholars and educators. Volumes seven through thirteen were indexed in 1982 (in volume 13, #8) and this makes a great many critiques readily accessible. Although the *Bulletin* is today published infrequently, past issues offer a wealth of models to follow.

Doris Seale, who has already been quoted, wrote the many book reviews contained in *Through Indian Eyes: The Native Experience in Books for Children.* The spirit as well as the insight that is noticeable in her critiques is not available to non-Amerind reviews and makes *Through Indian Eyes* an exceptional resource tool. She covers in detail books that are well-known because widely promoted in the mainstream book Establishment (books by Scott O'Dell, Elizabeth George Speare, Jean Fritz, and many more).[8] In evaluating such works, an authentic Native American viewpoint is indispensable.

In addition to examples of Native American literary criticism, informative adult books will increase our capacity to judge books about Amerinds. Here is a short list: *Chronicles of American Indian Protest* edited by the Council on Interracial Books for Children (1971, 1979); *The Indian in America's Past* edited by Jack D. Forbes (1964); *The Invasion of America: Indians, Colonialism, and the Cant of Conquest* by Francis Jennings (1975); *The Portable North American Indian Reader* (1974, 1977); *The White Man's Indian: Images of the American Indian from Columbus to the Present* by Robert F. Berkhofer, Jr. (1978); *Facing West: The Metaphysics of Indian-hating and Empire Building* by Richard Drinnon (1980).

In his review of Berkhofer's *The White Man's Indian,* Richard Drinnon tells about a status erected at the 1904 Louisiana Purchase Exposition that depicted dancing Indians. The statue's accompanying explanation read: "... the impression made by the group is that of wild frenzy." Drinnon notes the distance between "frenzy (the image in the Euro-American imagination) and the Amerind dancer's reverence as he uses "his body like a prayer" (Drinnon, 'The Red Man's Burden,' 20). This image or perspective gap is one that teachers can do much to overcome. Children's books still contain clichés about American Indian "barbarity," and they can be rejected. The gap can be closed.

DISCUSSION QUESTIONS

1. Native Americans are treated as the primary aggressors in the white/Amerind conflict. Why is such a plotline viewed in the mainstream as appropriate in children's novels? Is it related to national self-definition?

2. Amerinds are frequently portrayed as among the most racist characters in novels. Why is this historical inversion imposed upon child readers?

3. Why have novels changed from an emphasis upon unquestioning assimilation into white culture to an emphasis upon an open discussion of cultural differences? Are outward signs of scholarship (bibliographies, glossaries, consultations) enough to insure that a novel avoids white supremacist attitudes?

4. Why do you think images of Native Americans appear in so many

picture books that have no direct connection with Amerind history or experience?

5. What is the significance of tomahawk-bearing characters in picture books about Indian games or forms of play?

6. Why do you think Native Americans are sensitive to whether or not the specific national origins of folktales are reported to the reader?

7. Why does the use of a fictional narrative mode often open the way for the expression of cultural biases in biographies? How does that mode tend to reduce the possibility of drawing an authentic portrait?

ENDNOTES

1. See the chapter "Livelihood" in *Mountain Wolf Woman, Sister of Crashing Thunder: The Autobiography of a Winnebago Indian* edited by Nancy Oestreich Lurie (University of Michigan Press, 1966) for an account of crop harvesting in the Midwest. See *The Rain Dance People: The Pueblo Indians, Their Past and Present* by Richard Erdoes for similar information about the Southwest.

2. See the annotation in "Selective Bibliography and Guide for "I" is Not for Indian: The Portrayal of Native Americans in Books for Young People" by Naomi Caldwell-Wood and Lisa A. Mitten (American Indian Library Association, 1991).

3. It is conventional for animals to serve as stand-ins for people in children's literature and this convention is not viewed as problematic since mainstream persons have not been consistently dehumanized in children's books. For Amerinds, such dehumanization has been the norm. Animal-Indians tend to reinforce that deprecation unless the narrative is clearly in the folktale mode.

4. See "The Golden Indian" in *Akwesasne Notes* (Late Summer issue, 1984) for an account of the way Gregory J. Markopoulos, a Greek American, has passed himself off as a Native American named Jamake Highwater. According to Hank Adams, the author of this article, "Highwater" was a choreographer and fairly well-known experimental filmmaker prior to 1967. It is his fabricated "Indian" identity that is presented in biographical reference books in the children's literature field.

5. See Donna Lovell's review in *Interracial Books for Children Bulletin* (Vol. 12: 1, 1981).

6. See Daphne Silas' review in *Interracial Books for Children Bulletin* (Vol. 8: 6 & 7, 1977).

7. In commenting upon Tedlock's renditions of folktales, Jerome Rothenberg writes: "We have forgotten . . . that **all** speech is a succession of sounds and silences, and that the narrator's art (like that of any poet) is locked into the ways the sound and silence play against each other. . . . The fundamental language of man [sic] . . . isn't prose at all, but, in the way it turns upon its

silences, is something more like verse." ("Appreciation" in *Finding the Center; Narrative Poetry of the Zuni Indians* translated by Dennis Tedlock, p. xii). In storytelling for children, the oral and poetic qualities are especially important; a dramatic reading is preferable.

8. For additional detailed critiques of novels by such well-known authors as Lynne Reid Banks, Evelyn Sibley Lampman, and Jean Craighead George see "The Ignoble Savage: Amerind Images in the Mainstream Mind," by Opal Moore and Donnarae MacCann. *Children's Literature Association Quarterly* 13.1 (1988): 26-30.

REFERENCES

Amon, A., adapter and illustrator. (1981). *The earth is sore: Native Americans on nature.* New York: Atheneum.

Banks, L. R. (1980). *The indian in the cupboard.* Garden City, NY: Doubleday.

Banks, L. R. (1986). *The return of the indian.* Garden City, NY: Doubleday.

Berkhofer, Jr., R. F. (1978). *The white man's indian: Images of the American Indian from Columbus to the present.* New York: Knopf.

Broker, I. (1983). *Night Flying Woman: An Ojibway narrative.* St. Paul: Minnesota Historical Society Press.

Bruchac, J. (1988). "Iroquois stories." Cassette tape. Greenfield Center, N.Y.: Good Mind Records.

Bruchac, J. (1985). *Iroquois stories: Heroes and heroines, monsters and magic.* Freedom, Calif.: The Crossing Press.

Byler, M. G. (1973). *American Indian authors for young readers: A selected bibliography.* New York: Association of American Indian Affairs, Inc. Introduction reprinted in *Cultural Conformity in Books for Children: Further Readings in Racism.* (1977). Donnarae MacCann and Gloria Woodard, editors. Metuchen, NJ: Scarecrow Press, pp. 27-38.

Caldwell-Wood, N. and Mitten, A. (1991). "Selective bibliography and guide for "I" is *not* for Indian: The portrayal of Native Americans in books for young people. Program of the ALA/OLOS Subcommittee for Library Services to American Indian People. Chicago: American Indian Library Association.

Cannon, A. E. (1990). *The shadow brothers.* New York: Delacorte.

Cohen, M. (1967). *Will I have a friend?* Illustrated by Lillian Hoban. New York: Macmillan.

Connolly, J. E., col. (1985). *Why the possum's tail is bare and other North American Indian nature tales.* Illustrated by Andrea Adams. Owings Mills, MD: Stemmer House.

Council on Interracial Books for Children, ed. (1971, 1979). *Chronicles of American Indian protest.* New York: CIBC.

Council on Interracial Books for Children, ed. (1977). *Unlearning "Indian" stereotypes: A teaching unit for elementary teachers & children's librarians.* New York: The Racism and Sexism Resource Center for Educators (a division of CIBC). Filmstrip, 1978.

DeAngula, J. (1953). *Indian tales.* New York: Hill and Wag.

Deloria, Jr., V. (1973). *God is red.* New York: Grosset and Dunlap.

Drinnon, R. (1980). *Facing West: The metaphysics of Indian-hating and empire building.* Minneapolis: University of Minnesota Press.

Driannon, R. (1978). "The red man's burden." *Inquiry,* 1:16, June 26, 20-22.

Eastman, C. A. (1902, 1933). *Indian boyhood.* Boston: Little Brown.

Edmonds, W. D. (1942). *The matchlock gun.* Illustrated by Paul Lantz. New York: Dodd, Mead.

Eisenberg, L. (1991). *The story of Sitting Bull, great Sioux chief.* New York: Dell Publishing (by arrangement with Parachute Press).

Erdoes, R. (1976). *The rain dance people: The Pueblo Indians, their past and present.* New York: Knopf.

Erdoes, R. (1976). *The sound of flutes and other Indian legends told by Lame Deer, Jenny Leading Cloud, Leonard Crow Dog and others.* Illustrated by Paul Goble. New York: Pantheon.

Forbes, J. D. (Ed.). (1964). *The Indian in America's past.* New York: Prentice-Hall.

Freedman, R. (1987). *Indian chiefs.* New York: Holiday House.

Fritz, J. (1983). *The double life of Pocahontas.* Illustrated by Ed Young. New York: G.P. Putnam's Sons.

George, J. C. (1983). *The talking earth.* New York: Harper & Row.

Girion, B. (1990). *Indian summer.* New York: Scholastic.

Goble, P. (1992). *Crow chief: A Plains Indian story.* New York: Orchard Books.

Goble, P. (1989). *Iktomi and the berries.* New York: Orchard Books.

Gregory, K. (1990). *The legend of Jimmy Spoon.* New York: Gulliver Books.

Grossman, V. (1991). *Ten little rabbits.* Illustrated by Sylvia Long. San Francisco: Chronicle Books.

Herbst, L. (1975). "'That's one good indian': Unacceptable images in children's novels." *Top of the News* (January), 192-198.

Highwater, J. (1981). *Moonsong lullaby.* Photographs by Marcia Keegan. New York: Lothrop, Lee & Shepard.

Hirschfelder, A. B. (1986). *Happily may I walk: American Indians and Alaska natives today.* New York: Scribner's.

Jassem, K. (1979). *Sacajawea: Wilderness guide.* Illustrated by Jan Palmer. Mahwah, N.J.: Troll Associates.

Jassem, K. (1979). *Squanto, the Pilgrim adventure.* Mahwah, N.J. Troll Associates.

Jennings, F. (1975). *The invasion of America: Indians, colonialism, and the cant of conquest.* Chapel Hill: University of North Carolina Press.

Johnson, A. D. (1980). *The value of adventure: The story of Sacagawea.* La Jolla, CA: Value Communications, Inc.

Katz, J. B. (1975). *Let me be a free man: A documentary of Indian resistance.* Minneapolis: Lerner.

Katz, W. W. (1988). *False face.* New York: M.K. McElderry Books.

Lampman, E. S. (1956). *Navaho sister.* Illustrated by Paul Lantz. New York: Doubleday.

Lampman, E. S. (1975). *White captives.* New York: Atheneum.

Mayer, M. (1987, 1991). *The Brambleberrys animal book of big and small shapes.* Illustrated by Gerald McDermott. Honesdale, PA: Riverbank Press; Bell Books (Boyd Mills Press).

Mayer, M. (1981). *Liverwurst is missing.* Illustrated by Steven Kellogg. New York: Four Winds.

Mobley, J. (1979). *The star husband.* Illustrated by Anna Vojtech. Garden City, NY: Doubleday.

Moore, R. B. & Hirschfelder, A. B. (1982). Feathers, tomahawks and tipis: A study of stereotyped "Indian" imagery in children's picture books, in *American Indian stereotypes in the world of children: A reader and bibliography,* ed. by Arlene B. Hirschfelder. Metuchen, N.J.: Scarecrow Press.

O'Dell, S. (1988). *Black Star, Bright Dawn.* Boston: Houghton Mifflin.

Ortiz, S. (1977, 1988). *The people shall continue.* Illustrated by Sharol Graves. San Francisco: Children's Book Press.

Paulsen, G. (1985). *Dogsong.* New York: Bradbury Press.

Petersham, M. & Petersham, M. (1945, 1971). *The rooster crows: A book of American rhymes and jingles.* New York: Macmillan.

Polacco, P. (1989). *Boat ride with Lillian Two Blossom.* New York: Philomel Books.

Seale, D. (1982). Review of *Moonsong lullaby. Interracial Books for Children Bulletin, 13: 2, 3, 35.*

Sendak, M. (1962). *Alligators all around: An alphabet.* New York: Harper & Row.

Slapin, B. & Seale, D. (Eds.). (1992). *Through Indian eyes: The native experience in books for children.* Philadelphia: New Society Publishers.

Smith, H. N. (1950, 1970). *Virgin land: The American west as symbol and myth.* Cambridge, MA: Harvard University Press.

Sneve, V. D. H. (Ed.). (1989). *Dancing teepees: Poems of American Indian youth.* Illustrated by Stephen Gammell. New York: Holiday House.

Stedman, R. W. (1982). *Shadows of the Indian: Stereotypes in American culture.* Norman, OK: University of Oklahoma Press

Steele, W. O. (1952, 1990). *The buffalo knife.* New York: Harcourt Brace Jovanovich.

Strete, C. K. (1990). *Big thunder magic.* Illustrated by Craig Brown. New York: Greenwillow.

Strete, C. K. (1977). *The bleeding man and other science fiction stories.* New York: Greenwillow.

Strete, C. K. (1979). *When grandfather journeys into winter.* Illustrated by Hall French. New York: Greenwillow.

Tedlock, D., trans. (1972). *Finding the center: Narrative poetry of the Zuni Indians.* New York: Dial Press.

Turner, F. W. III. (Ed.) (1977). *The Portable North American Indian reader.* New York: Penguin Books.

Wilder, L. I. (1935, 1953). *Little house on the prairie.* Illustrated by Garth Williams. New York: Harper & Row.

Yellow Robe, R. (1979). *Tonweya and the eagles and other Lakota Indian tales.* Illustrated by Jerry Pinkney. New York: Dial Press.

RECOMMENDED TITLES

Amon, A., adapter and illustrator. (1981). *The earth is sore: Native Americans on nature.* New York: Atheneum. Gr. 5 and up.

Baylor, B. (1976). *Hawk, I'm your brother.* Illustrated by Peter Parnall. New York: Scribner's. Gr. 3-6.

Broker, I. (1983). *Night flying woman: An Ojibway narrative.* St. Paul: Minnesota Historical Society Press. Gr. 5 and up.

Bruchac, J. (1988). "Iroquois Stories." Cassette tape. Greenfield Center, N.Y.: Good Mind Records. All ages.

Bruchac, J. (1985). *Iroquois stories: Heroes and heroines, monsters and magic.* Freedom, Calif: The Crossing Press. Gr. 3 and up.

Cannon, A. E. (1990). *The shadow brothers.* New York: Delacorte. Gr. 7-12.

Clymer, T. (1975). *Four corners of the sky.* Illustrated by Marc Brown. Boston: Little, Brown. Gr. 1-4.

Connolly, J. E., col. (1985). *Why the possum's tail is bare and other North American Indian nature tales.* Illustrated by Andrea Adams. Owings Mills, MD: Stemmer House. All ages.

DePaola, T. (1983). *The legend of the bluebonnet: An old tale of Texas.* New York: Putnam. Gr. preschool-3.

Erdoes, R. (1976). *The rain dance people: The Pueblo Indians, their past and present.* New York: Knopf. Gr. 7-10.

Erdoes, R. (1976). *The sound of flutes and other Indian legends told by Lame Deer, Jenny Leading Cloud, Leonard Crow Dog and others.* Illustrated by Paul Goble. New York: Pantheon. All ages.

Freedman, R. (1987). *Indian chiefs.* New York: Holiday House. Gr. 5 and up.

Goble, P. (1984). *Buffalo woman.* New York: Bradbury. Gr. 3-4.

Goble, P. (1992). *Crow chief.* New York: Orchard Books. Gr. preschool-2.

Goble, P. (1989). *Iktomi and the berries.* New York: Orchard Books. Gr. preschool-3.

Goble, P. (1991). *Iktomi and the buffalo skull.* New York: Orchard Books. Gr. preschool-3.

Goble, P. (1990). *Iktomi and the ducks.* New York: Orchard Books. Gr. preschool-3.

Goble, P. (1983). *Star boy.* New York: Bradbury. Gr. K and up.

Hirschfelder, A. B. (1986). *Happily may I walk: American Indians and Alaska natives today.* New York: Scribner's. Gr. 5 and up.

Katz, J. B. (1975). *Let me be a free man: A documentary of Indian resistance.* Minneapolis: Lerner. Gr. 6 and up.

Mobley, J. (1979). *The star husband.* Illustrated by Anna Vojtech. Garden City, NY: Doubleday. Gr. 1-5.

Ortiz, S. (1977, 1988). *The people shall continue.* Illustrated by Sharol Graves. San Francisco: Children's Book Press. Gr. preschool and up.

Rohmer, H. & Rea, J. G. (1976, 1988). *Atariba & Niguayona.* Illustrated by Consuelo Mendez. Revises Spanish version by Rosalma Zubizarreta. San Francisco: Children's Book Press. Gr. preschool-5.

Rohmer, H. & Anchondo, M. (1976, 1988). *How we came to the fifth world/Como vinimos al quinto mundo.* Illustrated by Graciela Carrillo. San Francisco: Children's Book Press. Gr. 2-5.

Sneve, V. D. H. (Ed.). (1989). *Dancing teepees: Poems of American Indian youth.* Illustrated by Stephen Gammell. New York: Holiday House. All ages.

Steptoe, J. (1984). *The story of Jumping Mouse: A Native American legend.* New York: Lothrop, Lee & Shepard. Gr. preschool-3.

Strete, C. K. (1990). *Big thunder magic.* Illustrated by Craig Brown. New York: Greenwillow. Gr. 1-4.

Strete, C. K. (1977). *The bleeding man and other science fiction stories.* New York: Greenwillow. Gr. 8 and up.

Strete, C. K. (1979). *When grandfather journeys into winter.* Illustrated by Hall Frenck. New York: Greenwillow. Gr. 3-6.

Yellow Robe, R. (1979). *Tonweya and the eagles and Other Lakota Indian tales.* Illustrated by Jerry Pinkney. New York: Dial Press. Gr. 2 and up.

6

We Have Stories to Tell

A Case Study of Puerto Ricans in Children's Books

Sonia Nieto

INTRODUCTION

Approximately 5,000 children's books are published yearly in the United States.[1] Of these, a tiny minority focus on Latino themes or characters, either in the United States or in their native countries, in any substantive way. When such books are published, they frequently do little more than perpetuate romantic images or stereotypes that belie the traditions and day-to-day lives and experiences of Latinos. In stark relief with the neglect and depreciation of the Latino experience in children's books is the reality of the United States as the twentieth century draws to a close: A special 1990 Census report revealed that the Latino population is highly diverse, increasing dramatically, and on the road to becoming the nation's largest minority.[2] According to this report, there are nearly 21,000,000 Latinos living in the United States. They now constitute over 8% of the total US population, a 40% increase since the 1980 census.[3] Of these, about 63% are Mexican American, 11% are Puerto Rican, and 5.5% are Cuban. The remainder are Central Americans, other Latin Americans and Caribbeans. Latinos live in every major metropolitan area in every state and in many rural and suburban areas as well. Although the majority live in three regional areas (the Southwest, the Northeast, and Florida), no area in the United States has remained untouched by the Latino presence.[4]

The apparent contradiction between the dramatically growing numbers of Latinos in the United States and their invisibility in popular children's literature raises a number of issues. One concerns the images that persist in the media. Even when present in children's books, Latinos have often been shown in a number of different, but equally negative, roles: portrayed as either simple, happy-go-lucky characters content to put things off until "mañana," or as hapless victims of "the culture of poverty," Latinos are found swinging sticks at piñatas in fiestas or swinging sticks at one another in gang fights. The result is that neither Latinos nor their non-Latino peers have been well served because the range of images that help define the complexity of their experience within the United States is missing. In addition, many books with Latino characters have been written by non-Latinos who are often woefully unfamiliar with the lived realities of those about whom they are writing. This leads to a related problem of others outside the community making decisions about such issues as what constitutes Latino literature, what genres best represent the cultures involved, and which of the many Latino cultures get visibility. Finally, Latinos are often presented as a monolithic group, as if the vast differences in national origin, geography, native language, race, class, and place of birth, among others, did not exist. The feeling that "if you've seen one Latino, you've seen them all" is perpetuated in children's literature when no provisions are made for such differences.[5]

In this chapter, I will review the recent history of Latino images in children's books written and published in the United States. Using a case study approach, I will explore themes that emerge from the most recent children's books that focus on Puerto Ricans. An attempt is made to include both children's and young adult literature, although the majority of books published focus on the latter, thus limiting the scope of this review. This suggests another issue to be considered, that is, the unavailability of books appropriate for readers of different ages. The use of Latino, and specifically Puerto Rican literature, in the curriculum will also be addressed. The chapter concludes with reflections on the role of publishing companies, educators, and the community in creating and disseminating a Puerto Rican/Latino literature.

A REVIEW OF LATINO CHILDREN'S LITERATURE IN THE UNITED STATES

A paucity of research has been done on Latino children's literature in the United States. The little that has been done has centered on specific groups within the larger Latino category, that is, on Mexican Americans, Puerto Ricans, Central Americans, or others. Given the great differences within Latino groups in, among other things, ethnicity and history in the

United States, this approach is understandable. Isabel Schon, an authority on Latino literature for children and young adults, is among the few who have consistently studied all Latino children's literature: books written in both Spanish and English, published in Latin American countries and in the United States, and reflective of the entire range of Latino groups. Schon has periodically compiled evaluations and annotations of books with Latino themes. Her contribution has been particularly important with regard to books written in Spanish and her books and articles have proven helpful in informing libraries and schools about Latino literature and in providing information to help them update their collections. Since the early 1980s, Schon has reviewed books that range from South American biographies to Caribbean literature to the experience of Latinos in the United States.[6]

Most research, however, has focused on particular groups within the Latino community. One of the first references to Latino children's literature was about Puerto Ricans. As early as 1974, the Council on Interracial Books for Children (CIBC), widely acknowledged to be one of the "best-known purveyors of criteria and guidelines for eliminating stereotyping and bias" in books published a special issue on Puerto Rican themes in children's books.[7] To their surprise, the CIBC discovered that 100 children's books with what could loosely be termed "Puerto Rican themes" had been published since the 1940s. All focused in some way on the Puerto Rican experience, either on the island or in the United States, and had one or more protagonists who were Puerto Rican. The CIBC concluded that the great majority of the 100 books were pervaded by racism, sexism, and an ethnocentric colonialism. Specifically, they said, "Far from finding the books accurate and authentic, the reviewers discovered extraordinary distortions and misconceptions ranging all the way from simple misusages of Spanish to the grossest insensitivities and outright blunders, including editorial errors that in 'non-minority' books would never be tolerated."[8]

The following year, the CIBC followed up with a special issue on Chicano (Mexican American) materials. This time, 200 children's books, including some texts, were reviewed. As with the previous review, the books were characterized by an abundance of stereotypes and "an attitude of benevolent superiority."[9] Some of the images they uncovered defied reality. The best-known stereotypes, that of Mexican men wearing wide-brimmed hats snoozing under a giant cactus, and those of what they called "serapes, piñatas, burros, bare feet, and broken English" were widely accepted and maintained despite the fact that the vast majority of Mexican Americans are urban dwellers and speak English. In textbooks, the situation was just as bad. Most made no acknowledgement of the existence and contributions of Mexicans to what is now the Southwest United States. The same held true for Mexican Americans in the present: "In most instances," the CIBC found, "they are left out entirely. This is so despite the fact that Chicanos constitute the second largest minority group in the U.S."[10]

Ten years after the special issue on Puerto Ricans first appeared, the CIBC asked me to do a follow-up to determine whether newer books were less biased and more accurate than those published prior to 1972. I found 56 titles that had been published in the 10-year period from 1973-1983. A small number of books reflected a more comprehensive understanding of Puerto Rican reality, but the majority were still assimilationist, stereotypical, and pervaded by racist assumptions of inferiority. The fact that more of these books were written and illustrated by Puerto Ricans had a decidedly positive effect on their quality and accuracy. Nevertheless, most continued to be written by non-Puerto Ricans with a limited awareness of and experience with Puerto Rico and Puerto Ricans. My general conclusion was that ". . . there is a need for more books with accurate and positive messages, books sensitive to the true realities of Puerto Ricans in the US and in Puerto Rico."[11]

Until the 1980s, most research had focused on Mexican Americans and Puerto Ricans. Almost no attention had been paid to other Latinos. Even though Central America has been in newspaper headlines and television news for years, its presence in children's books has remained almost inconsequential. Once again, it was the CIBC that undertook the only study of its kind in this area: To analyze some 71 books, including 31 history texts, to determine whether Central America was portrayed accurately in books published for children in the United States. A panel of 15 reviewers knowledgeable about Central America found that it was overlooked in most history books. The fact that Central America is either omitted entirely, given fewer pages, or simply referred to as "a bridge between North and South America" in most books is indicative of the unimportance with which it has been treated. As in previous research, the reviewers found that many of the books were full of racial and ethnic stereotypes as well.[12]

This brief review underscores two realities: A paltry number of children's books focusing on the Latino experience have been published in the United States; and precious little scholarly work has been done in this area. How has the situation changed in the past several years? The following section will focus on a case study of Latino literature to highlight the continuing debate and some specific dilemmas related to using multicultural literature in the classroom.

PUERTO RICAN CHILDREN'S LITERATURE: A CASE STUDY

I made the decision to use a case study approach focusing on only one national origin group precisely because of a major dilemma concerning scholarly work on Latinos, that is, the tendency to lump all Latinos together under one general heading. Although reasons for doing so are certainly legitimate at times, this practice undermines the very way that groups define themselves. One would be hard-pressed, for instance, to find a Latina who would define herself as such; she would be more likely to say that she is a Chicana or a Dominican or a Peruvian. The terms *Latino(a)* or *Hispanic* are useful when we want to express the deep connections among all of us in the Americas who are descendents of native inhabitants, Spanish and other European colonizers, and enslaved Africans, or any combination of these groups. This is a powerful legacy that extends from the southernmost tip of Latin America, to the Spanish-speaking Caribbean, to what is now the Southwest United States. As such, it needs to be recognized and affirmed. Such broad categorizations can nevertheless too easily hide regional or other vital differences that then become invisible. For example, although a Dominican and a Salvadorian may both be Spanish-speaking, Catholic, and middle-class, the largely indigenous heritage of Salvadorians and the African heritage of Dominicans may be hidden if one uses only *Latino* to identify both. The many native languages of the original inhabitants, some of which are still actively used today, may not be apparent if we refer to both Guatemalans and Bolivians as simply *Hispanic.* This general label may hide the fact that for many people in Latin America, Spanish is a second rather than a native language.

The collective legacy of Latinos cannot be denied. Thus, the perspective on Puerto Rican children's literature that I present here will surely sound a responsive chord among other Latinos. A Mexican and a Chilean may both smile at a fondly remembered children's rhyme; a Cuban and a Colombian may share the painful experience of being discriminated against in the United States because of their Spanish accents. But rather than fall into the trap of perpetuating the perceived interchangeability of Latinos, I have chosen to focus on only one group. Because of my own background and experiences, I can speak both more authoritatively and critically about the Puerto Rican experience than about others. Although I do not claim to speak for all Puerto Ricans, I can provide one insider's view and interpretation of children's literature with Puerto Rican themes. In so doing, I hope to open a dialogue and to challenge other Latinos to consider their unique histories and experiences when exploring what it means to develop an authentic literature for children.

PUERTO RICAN CHILDREN'S LITERATURE SINCE 1983

The purpose of using this case study of Puerto Rican children's literature is two-fold. First, it will serve as an example of how Latino children's literature has changed over the past dozen years or so. I was interested not only in the number of books written since 1983, but also in the genres they represent. Also, the conventional wisdom would suggest that the situation has changed, if not dramatically, as least considerably, and that the negative messages about Puerto Ricans found in earlier books would be far less apparent today. The case study will thus also help to document if and how the images of Puerto Ricans in children's books have changed to any appreciable degree. The identity of the authors of the newer books was also investigated. This is a particularly important issue, especially given the fact that the overwhelming majority of books reviewed in 1972 and 1983 were written by non-Puerto Ricans and that many of the stereotypical images in them could be linked directly to this fact.

The second purpose for using this case study is to suggest some directions for the future of Latino children's literature within what is considered mainstream children's literature and curricula. As documented previously, the number of Latinos in the United States has increased dramatically over the past decade and is expected to continue. By the first quarter of the twenty-first century, Latinos will be the largest group of people of color within the nation. The histories, literature, and realities of Latinos within the United States can no longer remain shrouded in mystery or otherwise hidden. This case study may point out some ways in which a more realistic children's literature can be promoted and used in all classrooms.

I began by trying to locate all the children's books published in the United States since 1983 that could be said to deal in any way with Puerto Ricans. To be as inclusive as possible, I considered all genres: fiction, nonfiction, anthologies, book-length stories that included Puerto Rican characters, and revised editions of earlier books. I included Puerto Rican and non-Puerto Rican authors, and considered books for all ages from preschool through young adult. I even included books that *appeared* to be about Puerto Ricans, even if they did not specifically identify the characters as such. As I read these books, three recurring, sometimes contradictory, themes became apparent. These are:

- the continuing invisibility of Puerto Ricans in the field of children's literature
- the absence or neglect of the family and family life in some books, including a reluctance to include anything but the most superficial aspects of culture and a continued stereotyping of Puerto Ricans; and
- the emergence of an incipient children's literature that is beginning to illuminate the Puerto Rican experience.

Each of these three themes will be discussed briefly.

INVISIBILITY

By 1991, the Puerto Rican presence in children's literature in the United States was still almost invisible. Although the number of Puerto Ricans residing in the United States has more than doubled to over two million during the past three decades, one would never know it by their presence in children's books. Only 19 books published or reissued since 1983 were found. (See the complete listing of books at the end of this chapter.) Even this number is misleading because almost a third are books that were published previously and either released in a new edition or reissued by another publisher. If we consider the fact that about 40,000 children's books were published during the same time period, this number is only a tiny fraction of one percent. Compared to 100 books found in 1972 and 56 books published in the period from 1973-1983, 19 books in the years from 1983 to 1991 can hardly be called progress.

What accounts for this apparent backslide in the presence of Puerto Ricans in children's literature? One explanation is the political mood of the country and how it is reflected even in publishing policies and practices. The past dozen years or so have been among the most politically conservative in US history. The fact that many of the gains made during the civil rights movement (including civil rights legislation itself, affirmative action, desegregation, bilingual and multicultural education, programs such as Chapter 1 and Head Start) have been challenged and are indeed under siege, is ample evidence of this conservatism. The recent history of the publishing industry echoes this trend. Whereas Puerto Rican themes might have been more trendy in the early 1970s (20 books were published in 1973, the year when more books about Puerto Ricans were published than ever before or since), the same is not true today. There have been times in the past eight years when *no* books were published (1983 through 1985). The largest number (5, 5, and 4) were published or reissued in 1986, 1988 and 1990, respectively. A progress of sorts, these numbers may represent a renewed and emerging interest on the part of publishers to locate and print a more multicultural literature.

Another explanation for the dearth of Latino, and specifically Puerto Rican, children's literature may have to do with the limited number of published Puerto Rican authors. The percentage of books written and illustrated by Puerto Ricans or other Latinos is now greater than before. Probably not coincidentally, the most blatant of the negative stereotypes found in previously published books has decreased. Nevertheless, a still unacceptably low number of books are written by Latinos and specifically by Puerto Ricans. Of the 19 books reviewed, 11 were written, edited, and/or illustrated by Latinos; of these, however, only seven were written by Puerto Ricans, and four of these were written by one Puerto Rican. In the three anthologies published during those years, 11 Puerto Rican authors were included. Although these numbers are a hopeful sign in that the proportion of books written by Latinos has increased dramatically, the overall number of books is still disappointingly low.

The argument might be made that Puerto Ricans simply do not write as much as others, or that what they do write is not necessarily good literature. The history of Puerto Rican literature, whether in Puerto Rico or in the United States, belies this claim. Numerous anthologies of adult Puerto Rican literature have been published. Some have focused on the Puerto Rican experience in the United States and on literature written in English. These anthologies point to a rich and varied literature that creatively, poignantly, and sometimes tragically describes the many facets of the Puerto Rican reality.[13] The claim that there are no legitimate literary voices within our ranks simply cannot be sustained.

A related argument, that few Puerto Rican authors write for children, has more validity. For example, the majority of books published with Puerto Rican themes has always focused on young adult rather than on younger readers. Even today, only 10 of the 19 books included in this review can be said to be suitable for younger readers. However, the scarcity of Puerto Rican children's literature is probably due to a variety of factors, not simply to the lack of a viable literature. One is the perceived market for such literature. Given the disenfranchisement of Puerto Ricans in general and the subsequent lack of political and commercial clout of the community, it can be safely assumed that the literary needs of the community are not a high priority for most publishers. In addition, most Puerto Rican writers in the United States tend to focus on two of the most representative genres of Puerto Rican literature: short stories and poetry. This is evident in adult anthologies and other resources that have been published.[14] There may be little demand for either short stories or poetry in children's literature in the United States. In fact, very few of the books reviewed in 1972 or 1983 contained either of these genres, although a much larger proportion of the books reviewed in the present case study, particularly those published by small and Latino publishing companies, are short stories. That Puerto Rican writers may perceive an unwelcome market for their work is therefore another possible explanation for their lack of enthusiasm in writing for children.

It is also evident that Latino children's literature has differed from other US children's literature in that it has not been limited to traditional children's themes in mainstream literature. Latino children's literature has revolved around folklore, legends, riddles, games, poetry, and stories in the oral tradition rather than specifically on the childhood or adolescent experience. A good example can be found in the stories, riddles, and poems in *Kikiriki*, one of the few Latino children's anthologies published recently. With selections in English and Spanish (none of which are translated into the other language), this anthology convincingly reflects this tradition. Cirilo Toro Vargas' 15 "adivinanzas" are typical of traditional children's literature from Puerto Rico and his "El gallo que no cantaba" is a funny and charming story about a rooster that could not say "Kikiriki" but could only talk like people. He would instead wake up saying "Amanece!" (dawn is breaking) and only through the intervention of his Fairy Godmother, who explained that his problem was a lack of pure air and pollution, did he overcome this curious malady. Franklyn Varela-Pérez's story of "How the Water of the Bay Turned Silver" is an equally engaging story told in the form of a traditional legend. In the same anthology is Victor Hérnandez Cruz's poem "Taíno," that links the children of Puerto Rico to their ancestors ("your tongue is Taíno/when you eat guava/paste or juice/you can get it at/the store/on the corner"). And Nicholasa Mohr's short story, "A Special Gift," brings readers to the Puerto Rican experience in the urban centers of the United States by telling a story of a child who reluctantly but lovingly releases her apartment-bound bunnies at a sanctuary in New York City. Many of the stories in this anthology, and in the one that preceded it, *Tun-ta-ca-tún,* are typical of the oral tradition of family stories told by Puerto Rico around the kitchen table, whether here or on the island.

Because children's stories have tended to be family or community stories, Puerto Rican children's literature has often been a version of adult literature. The fact that some of this literature is marketed in the young adult category here in the United States, although it may have originally been written and intended for adults is revealing. *Cuentos,* a bilingual collection of Puerto Rican short stories for young adults, is an example of this. An anthology published in the 1970s, *Cuentos* is actually a series of short stories by a superb representation of Puerto Rican authors. Some of the stories happen to be appropriate for young adults because of their style and level rather than because they deal specifically with issues of relevance to young adults. Some of the stories written by Nicholasa Mohr, notably *El Bronx Remembered* and *In Nueva York,* were also originally intended for adults but have consistently been marketed for young adult readers. The same is true of *Silent Dancing,* a beautifully written and evocative collection of autobiographical essays that can be appreciated by only the most sophisticated young adults. The classification of these books in the young adult category is sometimes arbitrary and does not necessarily mean that the themes, language, or content were intended for young adults.

ABSENCE AND DISPARAGEMENT OF THE PUERTO RICAN FAMILY AND A RECURRENT USE OF STEREOTYPES

Although the Puerto Rican family and family traditions are more salient in newer books than ever before, a few books, primarily those written by non-Latinos, continue to demean or exclude the family and to repeat worn stereotypes. The absence of the family as a central concern may be true of children's books in general, but it is a troubling oversight in books that focus on Puerto Ricans. First, the family is crucial to an understanding of the Puerto Rican experience. This focus on family is true of other Latinos as well. Interactions among siblings, relationships between parents and children, and the connections among all family members, including the extended family and those referred to as *como familia* (close friends who for all intents and purposes serve the same role as family) are absolutely indispensable to understand if one is to reflect the Puerto Rican experience with any accuracy.

The characters, story line, and setting of *Secret City, USA* by Felice Holman provide a graphic example of family invisibility. Because this particular book epitomizes family invisibility to an extreme, it will be cited extensively. It should be mentioned at the outset that the author has never claimed that her main characters are Puerto Rican. It is unclear whether they are or not. Their country of origin is never specifically named, Spanish is not used, and most characters have nicknames that even belie a Spanish language heritage. Nevertheless, there are hints of their Latino heritage throughout the book and they live in New York (where over half of the two million Latinos are Puerto Rican). Thus, it is used as a case in point. The very fact that no mention is made of their ethnicity can be taken as a slight; while the protagonists' ethnicity may not be important to the author, it certainly would be to many young Latino readers. No matter what the ethnicity of the characters, however, the same disservice is done to them whether they are Dominican, Cuban, or South American.

What are the hints of Latino ethnicity? The main character, Benno, and his best friend Moon come from what the author calls the "islands" and Jojo, Benno's grandfather, speaks in a "musical language." Benno's cousins who have recently come from "the islands," both have Spanish names (Juan and Paco). And although Jojo's name used to be José, he changed it. There is also a Tío Chico and a number of other references that make it clear that the main characters are indeed Latinos.

Except for Juan and Paco, Tío Chico, and Jojo, the families of the main characters are barely mentioned. After Jojo dies, Benno's family is mentioned only in the most superficial and unflattering ways. The majority of references made to family and community are highly negative. In one scene, the people in the neighborhood are described: "At the sides of the stoops, the men, out of work or on welfare, stand in little groups nodding at each other or punching each other out. . . At the corners, knots of teenage kids or older boys play cards, smoke, deal in drugs or stolen objects. It's the commerce of the slums" (p. 23). Further on, the building is likewise characterized: "Smells that issue from the open doorways are those of too many people closed up together for the winter with bad plumbing and often not much cleaning. All the cooking odors still linger and have turned to garbage stinks" (p. 23). And still later, the neighborhood is described, through Benno's musings, in equally negative terms: "There, the people scream obscenities at each other; do rotten stuff; try to kill each other" (p. 115).

In the midst of these overwhelmingly damaging images of people and community appears the most positive adult character in the book: Marie Lorry, a White woman, a "nice and pretty lady" who is a social worker at a local hospital and the only adult who is supportive of Benno. Her influence on him is more powerful than that of anybody else: "Nobody has been complimenting him since Jojo died. Jojo was the one who used to tell him he was a good person, that he was going to amount to something" (p. 142); and "There has never been another adult in his life with whom he has exchanged so much conversation, except Jojo. There has never been a person who has taken such close notice of what he has done. . ." (p. 163) And, in the final scene, Marie's boyfriend Pete, a reporter for a local newspaper, characterizes Benno and his friends as "otherwise uncared for and sleeping on city streets" (p. 184), this in spite of the fact that both Benno and Moon live with their families. Because of the stories Pete writes about their "Secret City," an abandoned neighborhood that they have begun to refurbish, a private citizen's commission of "outstanding, able, generous people" is formed. No mention is made of their backgrounds, but it is safe to assume that the saviors of these homeless waifs are primarily wealthy and White.

One searches in vain within these pages for strong Latino adults. The curious absence of any reference to family in *Secret City* represents such an extreme example of the denial of the importance of the Puerto Rican family that it is far-fetched and unbelievable. Not only are the families of the children in this story unresponsive, but in fact the only support and love they can find is from communities outside their own. It is true that many Puerto Rican families live in dire poverty and have to contend with unresponsive agencies, crime, drugs, racism, and other negative situations. It is also true that some of these families are dysfunctional, abusive, and neglectful. However, to imply that the majority of Puerto Rican families are so, as this book would suggest, results in a story line that is patronizing and harmful.

Holman's books often portray alienated youth who confront an uncaring world. Furthermore, the theme of homelessness, particularly among children, is an important one that needs to be addressed by all communities. Nevertheless, in misrepresenting Puerto Rican families to such a degree, the author has missed a golden opportunity to present the issue with the validity it deserves. Images such as these are dangerous because they perpetuate the image of Puerto Rican families as monolithic, particularly in their relationships with their children, and characterize them as uncaring and dismissive in the aggregate. They represent a rigidly limited, and therefore incomplete and misleading, perspective of the Puerto Rican community. Blanca Vázquez, wirting about the images of Puerto Ricans in films, could just as easily have been referring to children's books:

> "What was missing from all of those screen images of Puerto Ricans? *Mi abuela,* my sisters, my mother, my father, friends and neighbors. My mother was a sewing machine operator who worked 8 to 5, was never sick or late for work, and came home to raise four girls. My father worked six days a week driving a cab on the night shifts of New York. I'm not seeking to make icons of them (or saying that growing up in a working class Puerto Rican family didn't have its own internal contradictions and history of internalized structures of oppression), but my parents were more typical of Puerto Ricans in the city than the juvenile delinquents and prostitutes on the screen."[15]

Whereas *Secret City* represents an extreme case of the invisibility and inaccurate portrayal of the Puerto Rican family, other books are more subtle in their characterizations. One of the ways in which this is done is through a reluctance to include any but the most superficial aspects of the family culture in the stories. This may be an overreaction on the part of writers to past criticisms about stereotyping and racism, but it also reflects the authors' ignorance of the Puerto Rican experience and uneasiness in dealing with it. The story *Somewhere Green* by Karin Mango includes a Puerto Rican, Angel Rivera, who is the boyfriend of Bryan, the protagonist. Some of the authors' characterizations reveal her lack of in-depth experience with the Puerto Rican community. First, highly unlikely utterances come out of Angel's mouth. When he wants to help her renovate the family townhouse as a surprise for her parents who are away, he says, "Why didn't you tell me, Bryan? It's terriric fun" (p. 64) and he also refers to Bryan and her brother and sister as "lucky devils" (p. 87). Neither of these expressions are believable in the day-to-day language of a New York Puerto Rican. Because Bryan doesn't know the customs of "his Puerto Rican background," she is reluctant to take the initiative in their relationship. "It was pretty sure, though, that girls didn't do the asking in his kind of world" (p. 55). Later, he is portrayed as believing that women simply cannot be architects: "In his experience girls could be teachers or nurses or housewives. If they were less lucky, and lower down the scale, they had to do low-paying menial jobs for survival. The idea of architecture in that context was frivolous as well as freaky" (p. 136-137). Although it is certainly true that there is no great abundance of Puerto Rican female architects, these thoughts are more likely the author's than his.

The depiction of Angel's mother is equally superficial and displays an ignorance of the Puerto Rican community and a demeaning use of the Spanish language. First, Mrs. Rivera is described as screaming his name to call him home: "'An-*hell!*' followed by a lot of shrill, staccato Spanish" (p. 29). Although an English-speaking mother might call her child home in much the same way, it is doubtful she would be so patronizingly characterized. Later, Mrs. Rivera, in describing the protagonist's father, says, "Ah, sí. Tall, blond señor." (p. 93). Using Spanish as a stage prop with which to identify characters' ethnicity has been a common ploy in children's books. Used with much less frequency now than in previous books, it still tends to result in a degrading use of the language. Although code-switching (switching from one language to another) is common in the Puerto Rican community, it is not done in the way that the author has Mrs. Rivera speaking. Very often, authors with little sense of the language will simply insert a word or two that they know in Spanish in an effort to make their stories seem more believable, and will in the process make them less so. It also results in misspellings, misplaced accents, and faulty constructions. ("Erés tan bonita," Angel tells Bryan, misplaced accent and all).

The use of English among Puerto Rican characters is also often stilted and contrived. This is directly related to some authors' ignorance of the way their characters would actually use language. The dialogue in *Secret City* is probably the most annoying in this regard: "Whady'a want? Ya want yer mama and papa don't care whatcha do? (p. 35); "How come is that?" (p. 17) are typical constructions used. This less-than-credible language use is in stark contrast to the dialogue of urban teen-agers used by Walter Dean Myers in *Scorpions*. Set in Harlem, this powerful story is about the friendship between Jamal, an African American boy and Tito, who is Puerto Rican, and the very real dangers young men in urban communities face with gangs, guns, and violence. Myers' use of dialogue is believable and natural. In addition, there is a tacit understanding of the Puerto Rican family. Tito, in explaining to Jamal what grandmothers in the family are like, says, ". . . your grandmother is suppose to take care of you. She said in Puerto Rico everybody treats their grandparents like they were the real mother in the house. She said that your family is more important in Puerto Rico than here" (p.33). *Scorpions* is a good example of children's literature that, while not focusing centrally on the Puerto Rican experience, treats it with respect. There are no cases of misspelled words or trite expressions here.

Illustrations may also help perpetuate incomplete or inaccurate images. Even when the text is good, the illustrations may fall into facile stereotypes. The poetic story *Flamboyan* by Arnold Adoff, with its beautiful descriptions of the girl named for the flame tree and the island of Culebra, is an example. Although the illustrations are dramatic and breathtakingly beautiful, some are also inauthentic. The illustrator, Karen Barbour, who according to the jacket spent time in both Martinique and Hawaii while working on the book, has apparently never been to Puerto Rico. Some of her illustrations are more evocative of Mexican motifs than of the Caribbean; and scenes of women carrying baskets on their heads are more typical of other Caribbean countries than of Puerto Rico.

Stereotypical or incomplete characterizations of Puerto Ricans are not only made by non-Latinos. The anthology *Where Angels Glide at Dawn,* an anthology of stories most of which were originally written in Spanish and translated into English, is a good but uneven attempt to provide a range of Latino voices about the Latino experience. One of the few stories about a Puerto Rican family, "Fairy Tale" by Barbara Mujica, repeats some of the same patterns. The main character is Monica, a 15-year-old Puerto Rican girl living in New York who yearns to go to college. Her mother, Angela, wants her to go to vocational school instead: "Why should the girl be sitting in a classroom when she could be out earning money? It didn't make sense to her" (p. 79). Monica tries to do her studying before her mother gets home because "Angela would make a fuss if she caught Monica studying" (p. 78). A hardly believable characterization, this contradicts the educational aspirations of Puerto Rican parents for their children that are often overly or naively optimistic. Education is generally viewed within the Puerto Rican community, particularly among the poor, as the one sure way out of poverty. Although it is true that some parents might urge their children to go to vocational school because they see it as the only realistic alternative to going to college, one would be hard-pressed to find a Puerto Rican parent who would be upset if she saw her daughter doing homework.

In the same story, Angela, whose "mouth generally worked like a submachine gun" (p. 89), is a bullying, shouting, and name-calling shrew with her husband. Monica's ideas about Puerto Rico are also less than positive: "Monica had never been particularly interested in Puerto Rico. She associated the birthplace of her parents and grandmother with fried onions and black beans, both of which made her feel bloated and gassy" (p. 86). Even putting aside the fact that black beans are more typical of Cuban than of Puerto Rican cuisine, there is an inherent problem with these kinds of images. Certainly all of the characterizations in the story are possible, but because they present primarily negative images, they are also incomplete. What makes this particular story more disturbing is that these issues are simply presented; they are neither broached as dilemmas nor used as a literary strategy for further development within the story.

A more representative Puerto Rican children's literature, however, does just that. The search for an authentic literature is not the search for an upbeat, consistently positive, sentimental, romanticized, or idealized reality. Rather, it is the search for a more balanced, complete, accurate, and realistic literature that asks even young readers to grapple with sometimes wrenching issues. It is literature that is neither sanguinely positive nor destructively negative, but one that attempts to reflect the range of issues and possibilities within the community's experience.

DEFINING A CHILDREN'S LITERATURE: ILLUMINATING THE PUERTO RICAN EXPERIENCE

This brings us to the third, and by far most promising trend: a slowly emerging children's literature that is beginning to reflect the Puerto Rican community in more depth. Before discussing this literature in more detail, let me first define it.

For the purposes of this review, I have chosen to focus on books published in the United States. Most have been written in English, some are bilingual, and a small number are collections that include both Spanish and English. This is not meant to overlook Puerto Rican children's books published in Puerto Rico (the children's books written by the highly acclaimed Puerto Rican writer Rosario Ferré come to mind) or to dismiss Spanish translations of American books or European fairytales (which in any event cannot be classified as Puerto Rican literature). Rather, it is to situate the responsibility for Puerto Rican children's literature on those of us who live in the United States, whether we are Puerto Rican or not. The necessity of opening up the literature to all young people in the United States, regardless of ethnicity or native language, is thus stressed. This multicultural perspective is important for all children because it works against the tendency to ghettoize literature so that only Puerto Rican children read Puerto Rican authors, only African American children read African American authors, and so on.

Puerto Rican children's literature, at least as it stands now, is literature that has been written by Puerto Rican authors. This is not to deny the importance, even the absolute necessity, of non-Puerto Rican authors writing about Puerto Ricans. Walter Dean Myers has done so consistently and convincingly. Milton Meltzer's *Hispanic Americans,* Arnold Adoff's *Flamboyan,* Johanna Hurwitz's *Class President,* among others, are all examples of books that have focused on Puerto Rico or included Puerto Rican characters in a credible way. They are good additions to a field that has far too few such depictions.

It is also conceivable that in the future, authors of non-Puerto Rican backgrounds may be able to write what can be described as Puerto Rican children's literature: stories and other literary genres that capture the mood and texture of the lives of Puerto Ricans in realistic and believable ways. For this to occur, they should probably have had close and enduring relationships with at least part of the Puerto Rican experience. Given the increasing interdependence of communities and the growing awareness of multiculturalism in our society, this may be possible. Myers' work, for example, certainly approaches this situation. Without the willingness on the part of authors to engage in these relationships, however, we are left with only outsiders' interpretations of insiders' lived realities.

Puerto Rican children's literature is founded on the tenets of a *bona fide* Puerto Rican literature and based on the panorama of experiences within the diversity of the community itself. Not afraid to confront sometimes painful realities, it is also not averse to celebrating the small triumphs that individuals and the community can achieve in spite of overwhelming odds. It is quintessentially *good literature.* Alma Flor Ada, acknowledged expert in Latino children's literature, defines literature as good when "it broadens the reader's horizon, validates his or her experiences, invites reflection, and awakens an aesthetic sense."[16] These are precisely the things that good Puerto Rican children's literature can do. Written in English or Spanish or a combination of both, from the island perspective or that of the United States, Puerto Rican children's literature attempts to place before all readers, not only those of Puerto Rican background, an experience that is realistic and free from sentimentality. A synopsis of each of the books that I would include under this category is found at the end of this chapter.

What characterizes this literature and how is it defining the Puerto Rican community? First, excellent Puerto Rican children's literature is excellent literature, period. While based on a particular ethnic experience, its particularity does not necessarily make it provincial; its messages are meaningful for all readers. These messages revolve around themes of growing up, confronting the advantages and disadvantages of difference, learning to accept and respect oneself and others, and developing pride in and a sense of responsibility to one's community.

Second, Puerto Rican children's literature depicts our multiple realities. Whether it is an urban experience, such as that chronicled by Nicholasa Mohr in *El Bronx Remembered,* or set in Puerto Rico, as are Cirilo Toro Vargas' stories, or both as in Judith Ortiz Cofer's *Silent Dancing,* the literature speaks of a variety of experiences, many of which are unknown to some among us. Good literature does not simply replicate our lives, but challenges us to expand our experiences and shed our preconceptions.

Third, this children's literature is based on the tenets of Puerto Rican adult literature. *My Aunt Otilia's Spirits* by Richard García, is a rather harrowing but funny and completely believable ghost story as told within the Puerto Rican experience. *Atariba and Niguayona,* from the same publishing company, is told within the framework of legends and folklore of Puerto Rico. The short stories in the anthologies I've recommended also reflect this history. The books by Lulu Delacre are notable in this regard. Based on songs, rhymes, and games from Latin America, including Puerto Rico, her books will help older readers recall some of the sounds and musical notes of their youth, while teaching others that they are a part of this tradition, whether or not they have experienced it.

Fourth, good Puerto Rican children's literature, although not falling into simple stereotypes, is also not squeamish about posing some difficult and conveniently unspoken dilemmas. In *Going Home,* for example, Nicholasa Mohr confronts the generation gap, the tendency among many Puerto Rican parents to be overprotective, the sometimes unreasonable rules of conduct for females within the family, first love, the difficulty of adjusting to the island with its less-than-sentimental realities, and the pain of being rejected within both the United States and Puerto Rico — and all of this in less than two hundred pages. In the process, both positive and negative portraits of particular characters emerge. The best thing about this book is that it avoids becoming either defensive about being Puerto Rican or idealizing the experience. This, and many of Mohr's other stories, pose difficult issues in frank ways that young readers can understand and empathize with. The stories sometimes broach these issues in hilariously funny ways, as is true of some of the stories of *El Bronx Remembered.*

An incipient literature of this type is not without its problems, however. The books included in the list at the end are not of equal quality. Some are better written and developed than others. Some, such as Lula Delacre's books, have lovely and evocative illustrations; the illustrations in others, such as *Atariba and Niguayona* and *My Aunt Otilia's Spirits,* are bizarre and may reinforce stereotypes of, for example, Taíno Indians as strange and exotic. Some cannot escape the biases and prejudices of their time or of the community which they represent. In *Nilda,* for instance, Puerto Ricans are portrayed primarily as victims. Not surprisingly in a story that takes place during World War II, there are also a number of racist references to "Japs." Others, such as *In Nueva York,* have negative but sometimes depressingly accurate portrayals of women. Nevertheless, books such as these offer young people the chance to be exposed to and discuss issues of oppression and of the community's response and responsibility to confront it.

Although the emergence of a Puerto Rican literature is both exciting and energizing, the news is not all good. The intolerably low number of books with Puerto Rican themes written in the past dozen years is little cause for celebration. A larger percentage of books are being written by Puerto Ricans than ever, but a handful of stories does not constitute a true Puerto Rican children's literature. When we have dozens of books from which to choose, books in English and Spanish and every combination in-between, in every conceivable genre and by a great variety of authors who reflect the many Puerto Rican experiences whether in Puerto Rico, New York, Massachusetts, or even Hawaii, and possibly even books by non-Puerto Ricans written in a sensitive and credible way, only then can we feel that the literature is becoming representative of the many communities that make up the Puerto Rican collectivity. Until then, however, this small number of books is an important beginning because it may point to a future that is more promising than at any time in the past. A number of suggestions for stimulating this literature, and for using it in the classroom, follow.

THE FUTURE OF PUERTO RICAN CHILDREN'S LITERATURE

Whose Responsibility Is It?

At least four different constituencies bear responsibility for stimulating the further development of Puerto Rican literature. These are publishing companies, Puerto Rican writers themselves, the Puerto Rican community, and teachers and schools.

First, publishing companies need to take responsibility because although they might lament the scarcity of Latino authors, most mainstream publishers have done little to discover new talent or to promote those who already have a proven track record. Whether this is because they are reluctant to take a chance on newcomers, because they have not been able to find writers, or simply because they do not perceive a market for this literature is a moot point. The result is that not many more Puerto Rican authors are being published today than 10 or 15 years ago. Those who are writing generally do so for small, alternative, or university presses. It is probably no accident that nine of the nineteen books reviewed here were published by such presses: or that Nicholasa Mohr, one of the most highly respected Puerto Rican writers, has chosen to have some of her previous publications released by Arte Público Press, a company that specializes in Latino literature for all ages, rather than by their original publishers. The Children's Book Press of San Francisco also continues to publish bilingual children's books that are representative of our culturally pluralistic society. Not coincidentally, these two companies have been responsible for publishing more Latino children's authors than all the large commercial companies combined. The sole responsibility, however, cannot rest with them. Large publishing companies with far more resources and more sophisticated distributing networks need to have a major role in finding, developing, and actively promoting Puerto Rican children's literature.

Because there is not an established tradition of writing specifically for children among Puerto Rican writers in the United States, incentives to do so are important. For example, during the mid- to late-1970s, the Council on Interracial Books for Children sponsored an annual contest for African American, Mexican American, Puerto Rican, and American Indian writers. This proved to be a successful way of discovering new talent. A number of the winners went on to successful careers in writing. One of the winners of this contest was *Yagua Days* by Cruz Martel, published in 1976, one of the few books appropriate for younger readers still available. Since the disappearance of this contest, no such incentive has taken its place. If publishing companies believe that the invisibility of the Puerto Rican perspective in children's books is an oversight that needs to be remedied, they need to find ways to do so.

Second, responsibility falls on the Puerto Rican community, particularly on established authors who can act as role models for younger writers. Piri Thomas' *Stories From El Barrio,* first published in 1978 and now out of print, was a wonderful example of this. Known primarily as a writer of adult books, Thomas wrote an engaging, moving, funny, and absolutely truthful collection of short stories about growing up in Spanish Harlem. It is still one of the best books of young adult Puerto Rican literature. The fact that this gem of a book is out of print while damaging and demeaning stories written by non-Puerto Ricans continue to be published is an all too revealing statement about the importance with which such literature is treated. Our own authors need to make sure that their voices are heard by children. Some progress is being made in this area. Pedro Pietri, a leading poet and playwright in the Puerto Rican community in New York, will soon be publishing his first children's book-length poem, *The Little Girl With Make-Believe Hair,* about a young girl whose mother makes her wear a wig to cover her own natural and beautiful curly hair (forthcoming). It is time for more Puerto Rican authors to follow suit.

Third, the Puerto Rican community itself needs to take responsibility for creating a market for Puerto Rican children's literature. Little movement will take place until parents and other community members begin to demand that books representative of the Puerto Rican experience be written, published, and marketed. This also means that reading and the important role of literature need to be nurtured within the family. Although the oral tradition is an important one that should be maintained, the written tradition is equally important in our homes and communities. Until we develop it more self-consciously, we will continue to be at the mercy of unresponsive publishing companies and schools that know little about our literature.

Finally, the role of teachers and schools in learning about Puerto Rican history and culture is crucial. Before teachers can expose their students to the history and experiences of the Puerto Rican people, they first need to educate themselves. This means reading, exploring, talking with people in the community, and in general, being open to learning about the crucial issues that define Puerto Ricans. Resources for beginning to learn about Puerto Rican history and culture are included in the bibliography.[17]

USING PUERTO RICAN CHILDREN'S LITERATURE

Using Puerto Rican children's literature in the classroom should be guided by the same principles as using any good literature. I would suggest three guidelines:

1. Children's literature should permeate the curriculum. No literature should be seen as an appendage to the curriculum. Simply dropping a story or a poem here or there in the curriculum is meaningless unless it is presented within a context of the history and culture. Viewed this way, children's literature can be a key part of the interdisciplinary content to which students are exposed. Although there are few resources for integrating Puerto Rican literature into the curriculum, some are available.[18]

In spite of the scarcity of curriculum resources, teachers can also help make a multicultural children's literature part and parcel of what and how children learn. For instance, *Felita* would be a natural to include in a unit on families in the elementary grades. When studying bodies of water, teachers can read "How the Water of the Bay Turned Silver: A Story About Puerto Rico" by Franklyn Varela-Pérez (in *Kikirikí*). For older students, a unit on identity can include Ortiz Cofer's *Silent Dancing,* which explores the developing identity of a young girl whose family moves back and forth between Puerto Rico and the United States. If children's literature is to be meaningful, it cannot be separated from the rest of the curriculum.

2. Literature can challenge children to become knowledgeable and respectful of others. Using multicultural children's literature will help readers to understand that everyone has a story to tell. Until recently, most stories have reflected a very limited range of realities. Using Puerto Rican children's literature can result in Puerto Rican children developing a healthy respect for their community and in non-Puerto Rican children understanding the importance of different experiences on people's lives. Using a standard of excellence that celebrates only the stories and perspectives of one group is damaging to all children. Rather than viewing experiences different from their own as "weird" or "ethnic," young readers can learn to approach literature with an understanding that we are all ethnic and therefore influenced by our backgrounds and experiences. At the same time, they can learn that ethnicity is only one difference, and that the unique character of every individual needs to be respected and affirmed.

3. Literature should prepare children for a critical love of reading. Exposing children to excellent literature can motivate them to seek all kinds of literature. In addition, it can challenge them to become critical of everything they read. As children learn to interact with and respond to all literature with a more open and flexible outlook, they can learn to be critical and questionning of what they read. The purpose of using Puerto Rican literature is not to romanticize or uncritically accept the experience

it may depict, but to develop the tools to critique both it and the printed word in general.

CONCLUSION

"The teacher read a story about me today!" said an excited second grader to his mother after his teacher had read the class *Yagua Days*. Although this is an everyday experience for children within the majority culture, children from other cultures typically do not have the opportunity to see themselves in books. Not surprisingly, it can be an experience of self-affirmation and pride. But because children's literature in the United States has yet to catch up with the dramatic demographic changes in our society or with growing sensibilities toward diversity, many youngsters develop the impression that books are not about them, their families, or communities, but rather always about "the other." It is the responsibility of teachers and schools to make it possible for all children to see themselves and their experiences reflected in the books that they read. Equally important, they need to make it possible for all children to see the experiences of others different from themselves reflected in the books that they read.

Puerto Rican children's literature is woefully underrepresented in mainstream children's literature. Rather than simply negative images, there are almost *no* images of Puerto Ricans in children's books. Of those few books that are published, some are still full of stereotypical and unconvincing story lines, characters, and situations. Yet in the midst of these negative images, a vibrant, but as yet incipient and tentative, Puerto Rican children's literature is developing. Written by a group of writers who represent a range of experiences, viewpoints, and aesthetics, this literature is demanding a space for the voices of those who have until now remained relatively silent. They are demanding that the mainstream be widened to accommodate us all. They are beginning to let everybody know that we have stories to tell.

ENDNOTES

I would like to thank Roberto Marquez of Mt. Holyoke College for helpful comments on an earlier version of this paper.

1. During 1989, the last year for which complete data is available, 5,413 children's books were published. (*Weekly Record, American Books Publishing Record Data Base,* New York: R.R. Bowker Co., 1989.)
2. U.S. Census Bureau, *March 1990 Survey of 56,4000 Households,* Washington, D.C., 1990.
3. The 1990 Census found over 22,000,000. The discrepancy may be due to the failure of the Bureau to take into account more recent immigration. (See *U.S.A. Today,* April 11, 1991, 1A).
4. Hispanic Community Mobilization for Dropout Prevention, "Facing the Facts: Hispanics in the United States, 1990," Washington, D.C.: Aspira Institute for Policy Research, 1990.
5. Marin, Gerardo and Barbara Vanoss Marin, "Methodological Fallacies When Studying Hispanics," *Applied Social Psychology,* 3(1983), 99-117.
6. See the most recent compilation in Schon, Isabel, *A Hispanic Heritage: A Guide to Juvenile Books About Hispanic People and Cultures,* Series II and III, Metuchen, J.J.: Scarecrow Press, 1988.
7. Bielke, Patricia F. and Frank J. Sciara, *Selecting Materials For and About Hispanic and East Asian Children and Young People,* Hamden, CT.: Library Professional Services, 1986, p. 115.
8. Council on Interracial Books for Children *Bulletin,* "Special Issue on Puerto Rican Materials," v. 4, n. 1&2, 1974, p. 1.
9. Council on Interracial Books for Children *Bulletin,* "Special Issue on Chicano Materials," v. 5, n. 7&8, 1975, p. 7.
10. Council on Interracial Books for Children *Bulletin,* "Special Issue on Chicano Materials," v. 5, n. 7&8, 1975, p. 1.
11. Nieto, Sonia, "Puerto Ricans in Children's Literature and History Texts: A Ten-Year Update," in *Bulletin* of the Council on Interracial Books for Children, v. 14, n. 1&2, 1983.
12. Council on Interracial Books for Children *Bulletin,* "School Books Get Poor Marks: An Analysis of Children's Materials About Central America," v. 13, n. 2&3, 1984.
13. Turner, Faythe, ed., *Puerto Rican Writers at Home in the U.S.A.: An Anthology,* Seattle, WA.: Open Hand Publishing Company, 1991.
14. Examples of these anthologies and references include Algarin, Miguel and Miguel Pinero, *Nuyorican Poetry: An Anthology of Puerto Rican Words and Feelings,* New York: William Morrow & Company, 1975; Meyer, Doris and Margarita Fernandez Olmos, eds., *Contemporary Women Authors of Latin America,* New York: Brooklyn College Press, 1983; Foster, David William, compiler, *Puerto Rican Literature: A Bibliography of Secondary Sources,* Westport, CT.: Greenwood Press, 1982.
15. Blanca Vazquez, "Puerto Ricans and the Media: A Personal Statement," *Centro Bulletin,* v. 3, n. 1 (Winter, 1990-91), p. 7.
16. Ada, Alma Flor, *A Magical Encounter: Spanish Language Children's Literature in the Classroom,* San Francisco: Santillana Publishing Co., 1990, p. 3.
17. Clara Rodriguez's book, *Puerto Ricans: Born in the U.S.A.* (Boulder, CO.: Westview Press, 1991) is a good place to begin because it is an eminently

readable book that includes a short history of the island while focusing on the Puerto Rican experience within the United States.

18. One such curriulum was developed by Roberto Marquez and Sonia Nieto, *Literature and Society of the Puerto Rican People: A Syllabus for Secondary Schools,* Newark, N.J.: Rutgers University, 1985. Other resources include *Caribbean Connections: Classroom Resources for Secondary Schools,* a series of resources including one on Puerto Rico, edited by Deborah Menkart and Catherine A. Sunshine (Washington, D.C.: Ecumenical Program on Central America and the Caribbvean [Epica] and Network of Educators' Committees on Central America [NECCA], 1990 and available from Caribbean Connections, P.O. Box 43509, Washington, D.C. 20010; and *Building Bridges of Lerning and Understanding: A Collection of Classroom Activities on Puerto Rican Culture* developed by Maria E. Perez-Selles and Nancy Carmen Barra-Zuman, Andover, MA.: The Network, 1990. See also the resource list and sample lessons included in Chapt. 11 of Banks, James, A., *Teaching Strategies for Ethnic Studies,* 5th ed., Boston: Allyn & Bacon, 1991.

BOOKS REVIEWED

Adoff, A. (1988). *Flamboyan.* New York: Harcourt Brace Jovanovich.

Carlson, L. & Ventura, C. L. (1990). *Where angels glide at dawn: New stories from Latin America.* New York: J.B. Lippincott.

Delacre, L. (1989). *Arroz con leche: Popular songs and rhymes from Latin America.* New York: Scholastic.

Delacre, L. (1990). *Las Navidades: Popular Christmas songs from Latin America.* New York: Scholastic.

García, R. (1987). *My Aunt Otilia's spirits.* San Francisco, CA.: Children's Book Press, revised edition.

Holman, F. (1990). *Secret City, U.S.A.* New York: Charles Scribner's Sons.

Hurwitz, J. (1990). *Class president.* New York: Morrow.

Mango, K. N. (1987). *Somewhere green.* New York: Four Winds Press.

Mohr, N. (1986). *Going home.* New York: Dial.

Mohr, N. (1988). *In Nueva York.* Houston, TX.: Arte Público Press, revised edition.

Mohr, N. (1986). *Nilda.* Houston, TX.: Arte Público Press, revised edition.

Mohr, N. (1986). *El Bronx remembered.* Houston, TX.: Arte Público Press, revised edition.

Myers, W. D. (1988). *Scorpions.* New York: Harper & Row.

Ortiz Cofer, J. (1990). *Silent dancing: A partial remembrance of a Puerto Rican childhood.* Houston, TX.: Arte Público Press.

Peña, S. C. (1987). *Kikirikí: Stories and poems in English and Spanish for children.* Houston, TX.: Arte Público Press.

Peña, S. C. (1986). *Tun-ta-ca-tún: More stories and poems in English and Spanish for children.* Houston, TX.: Arte Público Press.

Rohmer, H. & Rea, J. G. (1988). *Atariba y Niguayona.* San Francisco: Children's Book Press, revised edition.

Thompson, K. (1986). *Portrait of America: Puerto Rico.* Milwaukee, WI.: Raintree Publishers.

Walker, P. R. (1988). *The price of Puerto Rica.*

ANNOTATIONS OF HIGHLY RECOMMENDED BOOKS IN PUERTO RICAN CHILDREN'S LITERATURE

The following list includes books published since 1983 as well as others still in print that were recommended in the 1983 review (*Bulletin of the Council on Interracial Books for Children,* v. 14, N. 1&2).

Delacre, Lulu, *Arroz con Leche: Popular Songs and Rhymes from Latin America,* New York: Scholastic, 1989.

Twelve of the best-known children's songs and rhymes from the Spanish-speaking world, both in the original Spanish and English translations, are included in this lovely book. The accompanying music is found at the end of the book. The book is beautifully illustrated with scenes which are very evocative of Puerto Rico, Mexico, and Latin America. Particularly recommended for use with young children, it can also be used with older elementary grades to teach some of the actual songs and games played by children in Latin America.

Delacre, Lulu, *Las Navidades: Popular Christmas Songs from Latin America,* New York: Scholastic, 1990.

Another book by the same author, this is a beautiful and authentic book illustrating 12 Christmas songs from Spanish-speaking countries. Descriptions of the traditions associated with each are also included, and the country of origin of each scene is identified. The events are arranged chronologically, starting with Christmas Eve and finishing on the Epiphany (Three Kings' Day). Musical scores are included in back. This wonderful book would be good to use with all elementary grades and can be used to teach music as well as customs in a natural and entertaining way.

García, Richard, *My Aunt Otilia's Spirits,* rev. ed., San Francisco: Children's Book Press, 1987.

> A young boy's recollections of his Aunt Otilia's visits to New York from Puerto Rico and the strange goings-on associated with her spirits.

Martel Cruz, *Yagua Days,* New York: Dial, 1976.

> For younger readers, this delightful story depicts a young boy's first visit to Puerto Rico and his experiences there, including *yagua days,* those days after rainstorms when the children use yagua leaves as sleds to slide down the hills.

Mohr, Nicholasa, *Felita,* New York: Felita, 1979.

> This story about a Puerto Rican family in New York, focuses on Felita, a nine-year-old, and her warm and loving relationship with her family and especially her beloved grandmother, as well as on the struggles the family goes through in moving to a White community. Their decision to return to their own neighborhood and the death of Felita's grandmother are movingly and sensitively told.

Mohr, Nicholasa, *Going Home,* New York: Dial, 1986.

> The sequel to *Felita,* this story focuses on the young girl at eleven, two years after her beloved Abuelita has died. Given the opportunity to go to Puerto Rico for the first time to spend the summer with her uncle, Felita faces discrimination for being a "Niuyorican" in Puerto Rico. This story of the Puerto Rican experience in the United States confronts some difficult issues, including language discrimination in Puerto Rico, in an honest and believable way.

Mohr, Nicholasa, *El Bronx Remembered,* rev. ed., Houston, TX.: Arte Público Press, 1989.

> Mohr's first collection of short stories originally published in 1973, these stories range from comical to tragic experiences of the early Puerto Rican community in the Bronx.

Mohr, Nicholasa, *In Nueva York,* rev. ed., Houston, TX.: Arte Público Press, 1991.

> An interconnected collection set in the Lower East Side of New York City, these stories revolve around the lives of Puerto Ricans trying to survive in New York City.

Mohr, Nicholasa, *Nilda,* rev. ed., Houston, TX.: Arte Público Press, 1991.

> A novel about a young girl's coming of age in New York City during the 1940s. Confronts such issues as the discrimination faced by Nilda and her community, as well as on limited choices offered to women within the community itself.

Ortiz Cofer, Judith, *Silent Dancing: A Partial Remembrance of a Puerto Rican Childhood,* Houston, TX.: Arte Público Press, 1990.

> A beautifully written and evocative autobiographical account of the author's childhood as the daughter of a military father and her family's life shuttling between Puerto Rico and New Jersey, where he was based.

Peña, Sylvia Cavazos, *Kikiriki: Stories and Poems in English and Spanish for Children,* Houston, TX.: Arte Público Press, 1987.

> A series of short stories, poems, and *adivinanzas* (riddles), some of the selections are written in Spanish and others in English. All of the selections were written by Latinos and are presented by grade level from kindergarten through sixth grade. The fact that they are not translated, but rather kept in the language in which they were written, makes this a particularly appropriate volume to use with bilingual programs.

Peña, Sylvia Cavazos, *Tun-ta-ca-tún: More Stories and Poems in English and Spanish for Children,* Houston, TX.: Arte Público Press, 1986.

> This anthology, which predates the one above, also realistically reflects the Latino experience both in the countries of origin of the authors and of the experience as brought to the United States. Selections are in either English or Spanish and include stories by Puerto Ricans Nicholasa Mohr and Franklyn Varela.

Rohmer, Harriet and Jesús Guerrero Rea, *Atariba y Niguayona,* rev. ed., San Francisco: Children's Book Press, 1988.

> Told in the tradition of a Puerto Rican legend, this story focuses on the friendship between two young Taínos, a boy and a girl, and the boy's commitment to help cure her when she gets sick.

Wagenheim, Kal, *Cuentos: An Anthology of Short Stories from Puerto Rico,* Schocken, 1978.

> With English and Spanish on facing pages, this is an excellent collection of short stories, although not always appropriate for high school students. It includes some of the most notable Puerto Rican authors of short stories, some of which are set in New York, and most of which focus on the political and cultural tensions of the Puerto Rican experience.

REFERENCES

Ada, A. F. (1990). *A magical encounter: Spanish language children's literature in the classroom.* San Francisco, Santillana Publishing Company.

Algarin, M. & Piñero, M. (1975). *Nuyorican poetry: An anthology of Puerto Rican words and feelings.* New York: William Morrow & Company.

Banks, J. A. (1991). *Teaching strategies for ethnic studies,* 5th ed. Boston: Allyn & Bacon.

Bielke, P. F. & Sciara, Frank J. (1986). *Selecting materials for and about Hispanic and East Asian children and young people.* Hamden, CT.: Library Professional Services.

Bulletin of the Council on Interracial Books for Children. (1984). School books get poor marks: An analysis of children's materials about Central America, 13, 2&3.

Bulletin of the Council on Interracial Books for Children. (1975). Special issue on Chicano materials, 5, 7&8.

Bulletin of the Council on Interracial Books for Children. (1974). Special issue on Puerto Rican materials, 4, 1&2,

Cooperative Children's Book Center. (1991). *Multicultural literature for children and young adults,* 3rd ed. Madison: University of Wisconsin-Madison.

Foster, D. W., compiler (1982). *Puerto Rican literature: A bibliography of secondary sources,* Westport, CT.: Greenwood Press.

Kanellos, N., ed. (1989). *Biographical dictionary of Hispanic literature in the United States.* New York: Greenwood Press.

Marquez, R. & Nieto, S. (1985). *Literature and society of the Puerto Rican people: A syllabus for secondary schools.* New Jersey: Rutgers University.

Meyer, D. & Olmos, M. F. eds. (1983). *Contemporary women authors of Latin America.* New York: Brooklyn College Press.

Nieto, S. (1985). Children's literature on Puerto Rican themes. *Bulletin of the Council on Interracial Books for Children,* 14, 1&2, 10-16.

Nieto, S. (1987). Self-affirmation or self-destruction? The image of Puerto Ricans in children's literature written in English in *Images and identities: The Puerto Rican in two world contexts,* Asela Rodriguez de Laguna, ed. New Jersey: Transaction Books.

Rodriguez, C. E. (1991). *Puerto Ricans: Born in the U.S.A.* Boulder, CO.: Westview Press.

Pytowska, E. & Willett, G. P. (1989). *A quest for belonging: Empowering adolescents through multicultural literature.* Cambridge, MA.: Savannah Books.

Schon, I. (1988). *A Hispanic heritage, series II and III.* New Jersey: The Scarecrow Press.

Vázquez, B. Puerto Ricans and the media: A personal statement. *Centro Bulletin,* 3, 1 (Winter, 1990-91), 5-15.

7

Ideas a Literature Can Grow On

Key Insights for Enriching and Expanding Children's Literature About the Mexican American Experience

Rosalinda B. Barrera, Olga Liguori,
and Loretta Salas

INTRODUCTION

In much of the current professional talk concerning multicultural literature for children, one of the major premises emphasized is that multicultural literature leads to cultural awareness and understanding, qualities essential to living and learning in a multicultural world. In this chapter, however, we will stress the other side of that coin, namely, the less-discussed premise that cultural awareness and understanding are prerequisites for the development and use of multicultural literature. In a society of plural cultures such as ours, in which relations of power predominate, multicultural literature cannot be created with authenticity nor utilized effectively in the classroom without an adequate degree of cultural sensitivity and insight on the part of the people performing those functions. Simply stated, the cultural sensibilities of the makers and teachers of the literature are crucial to the quality and success of multicultural literature. This is not a radical or new thought, but it is one whose far-reaching implications are just now beginning to be grasped.

As makers of the literature, we have in mind the different people who shape the literature before it reaches its audience — in particular, the writers who create it, the publishers who choose to disseminate it, the illustrators who depict it, and the editors who refine it. As teachers of the literature, we include those individuals who help to mediate literature as a medium for instruction — in the main, teachers, librarians, and teacher educators. The second group has much potential for also "shaping" literature by acting as critics and advocates. The cultural sensibility of all these literature-related professionals is crucial to the development and growth of multicultural literature in the 1990s.

The present multicultural movement in children's literature is the second one to occur during this second half of the twentieth century; the prior one took place during the 1960s and 1970s. Yet between these two periods, the need for cultural awareness and understanding, or just as appropriately, multicultural awareness and understanding, has not diminished but increased in the U.S. The modest gains that were realized in terms of cultural diversification in children's literature during the former era were obviously not maintained during the conservative decade of the 1980s. In fact, during recent literature-focused interactions with various audiences, among them, practicing and prospective teachers, school administrators, publishing personnel, librarians, and fellow teacher educators, we have encountered a palpable lack of knowledge and understanding about cultural and ethnic diversity in general, and lack of insight into specific cultural groups and their collective experiences. In our estimation, there is a "new" generation of literature-related professionals today (post 1960s and 1970s), as well as an "older" generation, that both need to learn more about these topics *vis-a-vis* multicultural literature.

A historical look at U.S. children's literature from the point of view of diversity indicates that cultural homogeneity and insularity have been the norm traditionally, with the range of experience portrayed in children's books mostly confined to that of the dominant society and culture. Such a pattern, of course, does not promote multicultural thinking and development. The number of children's books dealing with the life and culture of diverse ethnic groups in the U.S. has always been relatively small, and the content of such books has left much to be desired. So not only have diverse cultural groups been excluded or omitted from the literature, but when they have been included, their range of experiences or intra-group differences have not been depicted. Even today, as the country's make-up reflects increasing linguistic and cultural diversity, children's literature has a long way to go toward adequatley representing that diversity.

One cultural group long slighted by the world of children's books is the Mexican-American community. In fact, the underrepresentation and misrepresentation of the Mexican American in children's literature is a well-documented professional fact. For almost 20 years now, a number of writings and reports have decried this skewed situation, and have identified specific shortcomings in children's books dealing with Mexican-American life and culture, beginning with the landmark critical report published by the Council on Interracial Books for Children (1975) based on a survey of 200 Chicano-themed books, to succeeding works by various professionals, among them Duran (1979), Schon (1978, 1980, 1989), Reséndez (1985), and Cortes (1992). Additionally, there have been assorted articles in professional journals throughout this time that have called attention to the limited quantity and quality of Mexican-American content and images in children's literature.

In general, however, larger concern for the relative invisibility of Mexican-American content in children's literature has waxed and waned depending on the sociopolitical mood of the country, just as it has for the shortage of literature about other ethnic and cultural groups. Today, Mexican Americans are the largest and fastest growing ethnolinguistic group in the United States, totalling almost 14 million persons who compose more than five per cent (5%) of the country's entire population and more than sixty per cent (60%) of the Hispanic-origin peoples in the U.S. (U.S. Bureau of the Census, 1991). Yet, contemporary children's literature does not provide a realistic sense of this community, neither in terms of quantity nor quality of representation. Although some degree of improvement has been noted in recent years in Mexican-American content, a justifiable conclusion is that serious misperceptions, misconceptions, and overall misinformation on the Mexican American in children's literature persist to the present day.

At this point in time, decisions, plans, and projects for increasing the number of children's books on Mexican-American themes and topics are becoming more frequent again; increased classroom use of these materials promises to follow. For us, these developments are a cause for optimism, but a watchful optimism. Knowing what we know about the past and the present of the Mexican-American experience in children's literature, we are wary of what might unfold in the future (Barrera, in press). All of which brings us back to our opening premise, which we will now articulate in more specific terms. For there to be substantive improvement in how the Mexican-American experience is portrayed in children's literature in the future, there has to be a base of cultural awareness and understanding of that experience undergirding its literary development and intepretation. Without this, the literature will not evolve qualitatively, although there may be more books produced in this area. The same is true with respect to the portrayal of the experience of other cultural groups.

We see several basic understandings or insights into the Mexican American experience as essential to informing the future development and classroom use of Mexican-American children's literature. Metaphorically, these ideas are seeds for growing a "new literature" about the Mexican-American experience, one that will authentically portray the breadth and depth of our history, life, and culture. In this chapter, we pursue five of these foundational understandings, using children's literature mostly from the past decade (specifically from 1980 to 1991) to make and support our case. The specific insights into Mexican-American children's literature that we seek to impart are the following:

- The Mexican-American experience is a diverse, complex, and dynamic phenomenon.
- Authentic portrayal of the Mexican-American experience derives from a particular perspective.
- Mexican-American writers have a vital role to play in interpreting the Mexican-American experience for children.
- The literary potential of the Mexican-American experience has barely been tapped by contemporary children's books.
- Literature about the Mexican-American experience is a source of knowledge and learning for all children.

It should be noted that we do not mean to imply that this particular set of five insights addresses all that may need to be said/explained/clarified about the Mexican-American experience with regard to children's literature. Therefore, in the final part of the chapter, we suggest how such understandings might be refined and supplemented by related insights into the Mexican-American experience, so that ultimately this knowledge as a whole can lead to enhanced understanding about our ethnic community and more informed development and teaching of Mexican-American children's literature.

DEFINING THE MEXICAN-AMERICAN EXPERIENCE

Within the pages of children's literature, the Mexican-American experience tends to be portrayed as a monolithic, unchanging experience. Actually, there has been some differentiation of portrayal across the years, but the composite portrait has not changed dramatically. In the past, the Mexican-American experience was sometimes equated with the Mexican experience (i.e., the experience of the people of Mexico in Mexico); today, there is a tendency to equate it with the Hispanic-American experience (i.e., the experience of different Latino groups in the U.S.), in particular, the immigrant experience of such groups. Although the Mexican-American experience shares a degree of overlap with the Mexican experience (Mexico is the historical homeland of Mexican Americans and the Mexican culture is our root culture) and with the experience of other Latinos (we share a cultural heritage that goes back to the colonization of the Americas), there are significant differences that must not be overlooked. To gloss over these differences means that the uniqueness and range of Mexican-American life and culture is reduced to nothing or los completely; in essence, we become invisible as a people. Consequently, we would like to point out the origins and development of this experience — to provide sociohistorical bearings so to speak — so that it can begin to be better understood.

Generally speaking, the Mexican-American experience is human experience, with all the depth and complexity that accrues to all human experience. But it is also distinctive in nature because it flows from a particular group of people affected by a unique array of forces and circumstances, all of which has led to the formation of a particular frame of reference or perspective on the world. Technically speaking, the historical beginning of this experience was 1848, the year when Mexico ceded almost one-third of its land, its northwestern sector, to the United States after a two-year war preceded by several years of hostilities between the two countries. That land now forms the states of California, Nevada, Utah, Arizona, New Mexico, Texas, and part of Colorado. The political act that formalized those proceedings was the Treaty of Guadalupe Hidalgo, which transformed *Mexicanos* who chose to continue to live in the conquered territories into "Mexican Americans" (Acuña, 1988; Barrera, 1979; McWilliams, 1990).

A noteworthy point about this historical beginning is that the *Mexicano* population was socially and economically diverse, as well as geographically dispersed, at the time. It was a diverse population then as it is now. There were distinct settlements in New Mexico, Texas, California, and Arizona with regional identities such as *Tejanos, Californios,* and *Nuevomexicanos.* Needless to say, the response of the different *Mexicano* groups to political conquest by the U.S. was also diverse (Alvarez, 1985; Gonzales, 1989). However, a big part of the collective experience and memories that bind Mexican Americans as a communal group was shaped by the overall pattern of relations between the dominant Anglo group and the different groups of Mexican-origin people, a pattern of domination and subordination that had been reached in Texas prior to the war with Mexico and "was substantially complete throughout the American Southwest by the end of the nineteenth century" (McLemore & Romo, 1985).

Clearly, a closer look at the history of the Mexican-American people is beyond the scope of this chapter, but in our estimation, that history can inform how one portrays and interprets the Mexican-American experience in children's literature. We can only highlight some of the key points in this discussion. It is important to know, for example, that the Mexican-American community has undergone many changes across generations since 1848; scholars such as Acuña (1988), McWilliams (1990), Barrera (1979), and Alvarez (1985) have chronicled this evolution in detail. Some of those changes include the shift from being a rural to a highly urban population, residential movement from the Southwest to the Midwest and the Northeast parts of the country, the impact of successive waves of immigration from Mexico, and linguistic and cultural change due to the acculturating forces of the larger society and its various institutions, especially the schools. Always in place has been a long-standing backdrop of economic subjugation, social discrimination, political inequality, and educational segregation, to which the Mexican-American community has responded actively, not passively, as the historical record shows.

Today, the Mexican-American population is no less diverse then when it began (Gómez-Quiñones, 1990). It is a heterogeneous population with "distant subgroups . . . manifesting different experiences and different adaptations and strategies to life in the United States" (Matute Bianchi, 1990, p. 210). Some Mexican American are more integrated into U.S. society than others. "As a result, there are class differences, differences in cultural orientation, and differences in ethnic identification and consciousness, as well as differences between immigrant and nonimmigrants" (Matute Bianchi, 1990, p. 210). An even more appropriate summary statement would be that "different experiences have been evident for different individuals during different periods in U.S. history" (Matute Bianchi, 1990, p. 210).

Our purpose in providing this thumbnail sketch of Mexican-American diversity is to contrast it with the traditional view of a homogeneous and immutable experience that exists in children's literature. According to contemporary reviewers of Mexican-American content in children's literature, the overall view of Mericans Americans has been highly limited and distorted. It has been one of *huaraches* and *zarapes* (Cortes, 1992), "tortillas and beans" (Schon, 1978, p. 11), "migrants and farmworkers" (Garcia, Hadaway & Beal, p. 253,), poverty, sacrifice, and ensuing social and psychological problems. Several themes have dominated this literature, chief among them, the "white savior" theme, in which Chicano individuals are saved from assorted problems, including themselves, by benevolent members of the dominant white community, and the "no English, no hope" theme, in which Chicanos cannot succeed in life and in solving their problems until they manage to speak English (Council on Interracial Books for Children, 1975; Duran, 1979).

This tedious array of stereotypical content and images appears to have started in the 1940s (Council, 1975) and has been called for lack of a more specific designation "the traditionally available literature on the Chicano child" (Reséndez, 1985, p. 107-108). According to Cortes (1992), books in this vein "offered a pastoral view of how a 'Mexican' (and, by implication, other 'Spanish') was supposed to look and act" (p. 121). Often the content and images were evocative of the Mexican experience, **not** the Mexican American experience, and even then, one can question the type of Mexican experience portrayed. Often this meant old-time Mexican villages, rural Mexican dress, and outdated vocations for the people depicted, features which did not adequately portray Mexican nor Mexican-American life. Sadly enough, 50 years later, variations of this type of view of Chicanos are still contained in children's literature.

For example, the book *My Best Friend Martha Rodriguez: Meeting a Mexican-American Family* (1986) seemingly targets contemporary Mexican-American life for its focus but is heavily about the Mexican heritage, which is an important part, but not the entirety, of Mexican-American culture. *Martha* is so loaded down with traditional cultural content that the story line is secondary; the "story" is there only to move along the parade of cultural information, a series of holidays, foods, games, songs, and family events that is continuous and seemingly endless. We question the overall intent, if not the literary quality, of such a book. Told through the eyes of a Euro-American friend of Martha's, the intended audience apparently is Euro-American children. But one wonders how much cultural appreciation and understanding can grow when a people's culture is presented in this superficial and contrived manner of what we call a "heritage parade."

Martha has been previously criticized for providing nothing more than "a romantic look at Mexican-American family life," one in which Martha's family "is constantly celebrating 'special and not so special events' in a manner that can be labeled traditional or folk" (Garcia, Hadaway, & Beal, 1988, p. 254). To add to this discouraging note, Garcia, Hadaway & Beal (1988) note that *Martha* "is almost a carbon copy of another tradebook assigned [by them] to the white ethnics category, *My Best Friend, Eleni Pappas*" (p. 254). Evidently, these two books reveal a formulaic approach that reduces different ethnic experiences (in this case, the Mexican-

American experience and the Greek-American experience) to a string of cultural holidays, customs, and related aspects.

In a different genre from *Martha,* but still emphasizing a folk or pastoral view of Latinos, if not Mexican Americans, in a highly visible way is the book-collection of nursery rhymes, *Tortillitas Para Mamá and Other Nursery Rhymes* (1981). Although the book claims to be about rhymes and lullabies from the overall Spanish-language community in the Americas, and does not make specific reference to Mexico or the Mexican-American culture, one can find in it much that is common to the Mexican and the Mexican-American traditions. The featured material consists mostly of works from the oral tradition that are still recited, chanted, played, and sung today. However, the authors chose to accompany this enduring material with illustrations that evoke a largely rural, largely indigenous look of the past that probably never realistically characterized all the peoples of the Americas. Thus, the images are not representative of the Latin American community that the authors seek to represent; they tend more toward the stereotypical images that have traditionally represented Mexican Americans and Mexicans in U.S. children's literature.

In summary, the field of children's literature needs to recognize that the Mexican-American experience is a diverse, complex, and dynamic phenomenon. Children's literature appears to have frozen that experience in its pages, but the Mexican-American community has continued to evolve and grow. Granted, overall, we are still a community characterized by high levels of poverty and scholastic underachievement, but contemporary Mexican Americans cut across all social classes, educational levels, and other categorical groupings. That reality is not reflected in children's literature. Instead, the enduring tendency, in individual books and across the literature as a whole, has been to present the Mexican-American experience as a homogeneous, static phenomenon, even to confound it with other ethnic experiences. There has been no balance struck such that the breadth and depth of Mexican-American life and culture can be appreciated.

THE NECESSITY AND CHALLENGES OF AUTHENTIC PORTRAYAL

From the standpoint of multicultural education, authenticity of content and images in children's literature is essential because inauthentic representation subverts the very cultural awareness and understanding that such literature can build. Literary license cannot be invoked as justification for the misrepresentation of other cultures, not even in works of fiction. Makers of the literature have a social responsibility to portray cultural groups authentically; anything less is ignorance at best, or racism, at worst. The unreal pictures of Mexican Americans put forth traditionally in both fiction and nonfiction books are unacceptable in the 1990s. Mexican Americans are no longer just objects to be written about; they are also subjects who read and write and who are going to criticize inauthentic and invalid portrayals of their ethnic community.

One of the salient characteristics of the traditional literature on the Mexican American is that it has been written and illustrated largely by non-Chicanos. On the one hand, this is a reflection of the traditional lack of support for writers of color by mainstream publishing; on the other hand, this also reflects the relative scarcity of Chicano individuals writing for children, who because of a complex of reasons have not entered that field. Given the fact that all writers write from a particular perspective that is partly personal and partly cultural (Anaya, 1985; Sims, 1982; Tapahonso, 1990), it is not surprising that many nonnative writers have been unable to portray with authenticity Mexican-American life and culture. The Council on Interracial Books for Children (1975) found in its investigation of Chicano content in children's literature that "even those authors whose efforts were marked by good intentions could not, in the final analysis, seem to transcend the boundaries of perspectives defined by their white American cultural biases" (p. 7). For the most part, many nonnative writers have been able to provide only outsider perspectives, or tourist-like perceptions (Cortes, 1992), not wholly different from the distant and uninformed views of the larger society. What is sorely missing from the corpus of literature on the Mexican-American experience are insider perspectives that can only be provided by someone from within the culture or by someone outside the culture who has gotten to know the culture well.

We are not creating cultural pigeonholes here by saying that only Chicanos can write about Chicano life and culture, and non-Chicanos cannot. Nor are we saying that Chicanos should write only about Chicano life and culture. We are saying, however, that to write with authenticity about the Mexican-American experience requires a particular perspective on the world (i.e., a world view) that only comes from having lived that experience or having learned about it in depth. Although outsiders may succeed to varying degrees at writing nonfiction about the Chicano, it is extremely challenging to carry off authentic writing in the fiction area. Cortes (1992) notes that "authors from outside the culture have generally been more successful in writing nonfiction, which relies upon factual research and the quality of its presentation, than in depicting the subtle aspects of language, experience, and emotion necessary for a compelling work of fiction" (p. 123). In the rest of this section, we provide a look at the inauthentic and authentic ways in which the Mexican-American experience has been portrayed in recent works by nonnative writers.

Several disappointing effects can result when the writer of fiction does not have native-like understanding of the other culture. In the first place, there can be outright errors in the information provided verbally or visually, that immediately trigger for the Chicano reader lack of insight — and lack of authenticity — into his/her culture. We provide here just two examples of cultural blunders in recent children's fiction about the Mexican American, both of which are highly conspicuous due to their appearance in the opening paragraph of a work. Our first example is from the story "The Cricket," one in a collection of tales for elementary school-age children titled *The Day It Snowed Tortillas,* by Joe Hayes (1982); the second example is from the book *You Can Hear A Magpie Smile* by Paula G. Paul (1980). Incidentally, both writers were apparently living in the Southwest, home to a large portion of the U.S. Chicano community, at the time these works were written.

Hayes begins "The Cricket" with the rather simple, but culturally inaccurate, statement: "This is a story about two men who were *compadres,* which means they were godfathers to each other's children" (p. 24). Unfortunately, the writer's definition of *compadres,* an integral social relationship within Chicano and Mexican culture, is seriously flawed. To be *compadres,* the two men do not need to be godfathers (or *padrinos*) to each other's children, in fact, it would be pretty unusual to find such a highly reciprocal situation involving the children in two families! **One** man would be godfather to **one** of the other man's children — not all of them — and the two would still be *compadres.* They could also call themselves compadres if the child of one married a child of the other. Moreover, the term *compadre* can also be used to refer to a friend or acquaintance. In Hayes' story, the problem is compounded further because not a single godchild figures into the story, so one really wonders what type of *compadres* the two characters are, or why this type of relationship were even mentioned in the first place. To native readers, reference to the characters as *compadres* comes across as a contrived feature of the tale, something used merely to mark it as Hispanic.

Magpie is about the relationship between an eight-year-old Chicana girl, Lupe Montano, and an elderly woman, Manuelita, who live in a small northern New Mexico community. In the second line of the opening paragraph, Paul notes that Manuelita "was a *curandera*. That is a Spanish word for healer, but to some it also means witch" (p. 9). The purported association between *curanderas* and witches becomes a major thread in the story, and is embodied as a source of distrust and dislike for Manuelita by one of the story's characters, Pedro, Lupe's uncle. Lupe's response, on the other hand, is different: she has grown up around Manuelita, has learned her healing ways, and has come to feel only love for her. The reader find it hard to believe that Manuelita could live in this community for a long time and have people looking to her for help if she were believed to be a witch. But the more important point to be made about the story is that in the Mexican and Mexican-American cultures, *curanderas* are treated with respect and admiration, not in the ways described by Paul. Folk medicine, of which faith healing is a part, is an enduring element in both cultures, involving different reasons, some of them economic and religious. The *curandera*-witch association that Paul sets up is more a telling sign of her cultural misunderstanding than a view of the reality of *curanderismo* in the Mexican-American community.

Magpie also reveals a number of other cultural biases, limitations that only exacerbate an implausible story line. One of these is a xenophobic reference to the U.S.-Mexican border and its people. In one scene, Lupe and a friend, Maria, are at a stream of water filling up a water jar, and contemplating whether or not to follow the stream. Maria asks: "What if it leads us to El Paso before it gets to the river? That's a big city. We'll be kidnapped and taken across the border into Mexico and sold as slaves!" (p. 44). In just a few lines, with a few broad strokes, the writer paints a border city, its people, and its neighbors as harmful and sordid elements. But given the rest of the book, and its lack of insight into Mexican-American people, such a statement is not totally unexpected.

Apart from cultural errors such as we have just described, another result when a writer attempts to write fiction about an unfamiliar culture might be a culturally sterile, or acultural, rendering. A good example of this is provided by the story *A Gift for Tía Rosa* by Karen T. Taha (1986). We need to mention at the outset that there is nothing stated in the book that identifies the story as being about Mexican Americans. In fact, the characters could just as well represent other Latino groups; likewise, any one particular group could be inferred. Apart from the characters' names, however, there are only about three other markers to indicate that this story is about Latinos: (a) the word "Hola" is used on page 10 in the address "Hola, Carmelita," and (b) Tía Rosa is described on page 11 as being "like a soft pillow that smelled of soap and bath powder and sometimes of sweet tamales," and (c) Tía Rosa is described on page 19 as having "brown fingers." One could remove the Latino names and these three markers (i.e., Hola, tamales, and brown) and have a non-Latino story line.

In essence, this particular story does two questionable things: First, it does not provide specific or substantive cultural information about Latinos, and two, in so doing, it creates the illusion of a generic Hispanic experience. Its culturally deprived context creates ambiguity and implausibility. For example, if Tío Juan and Tía Rosa are only next-door neighbors to Carmela and her family (evidence to this effect is provided on p. 10), it might be culturally informative for nonnative readers to know why the young girl refers to them as Tío (uncle) and Tía (aunt), cultural information that is not provided. Second, we cannot imagine how as Latino parents to six sons, Tío Juan and Tía Rosa never get visited by one of them; only at the end of the story is there indirect reference to the presence of the eldest son and his family. It is unbelievable that a seriously ill and dying Tía Rosa would not be visited by her immediate or extended family, an integral facet of Latino life. But this is only one of many flaws in this story; overall, the setting is minimal, the characters are vague, and the cultural content is superficial.

In recent years, there has been some improvement in the way nonnative writers have depicted the Mexican-American experience. Much more sensitive, insightful, and authentic portrayals have been produced. Many of these books, however, have focused on a narrow band of the Mexican-American experience, usually the immigrant or schooling experience. At least three books produced recently have treated these two aspects of the Mexican-American life in a much more informed and balanced way: *Hello, Amigos!* by Tricia Brown (1986), *I Speak English for My Mom* by Muriel Stanek (1989), and *Hector Lives in the United States Now: The Story of A Mexican-American Child* by Joan Hewett (1990). All three books focus on family support and Mexican-American socioeconomic and educational progress, albeit with a realistic sense of the difficulties involved. Both *Amigos* and *Hector* are black-and-white photographic essays, in the nonfiction category. The photographer for the former is Fran Ortiz, a Pulitzer Prize-nominated photojournalist, whose face shots in *Amigos* are superb; for the latter it is Richard Hewett, who has done award-winning photographic work for other children's books.

Frankie Valdez, a young boy who lives in the San Francisco's Mission District with his father, mother, four sisters, and three brothers, is the focus of *Amigos*. The book follows Frankie all day long the day of his seventh birthday, from the time he gets ready for school, through classes, to after-school activities, and finally, to a family birthday party. The simple text contains key words in Spanish that can be figured out through the pictures or the context, although a glossary is included at the end of the book. The overall effect is an informative and pleasing treatment of a slice of this young child's life, although we find out little about his parents' background or what they do for a living. Ten-year-old Hector Almaraz, a native of Mexico living in Los Angeles and the eldest of four boys, is the focus of the book by the Hewetts. Apart from his schooling, the book highlights Hector's preparation and celebration of his First Holy Communion and his parents' bid for U.S. citizenship as part of the amnesty process terminating in 1986. In addition to these two events, *Hector* tackles many aspects of the life of its focal subject and his family — social, religious, economic, and educational aspects — and handles them well.

In *I Speak English for My Mom*, a work of fiction, Stanek portrays in an insightful and balanced manner a common reality in the life of many immigrant or first-generation students in this country: having to serve as the English voice for their parents and family in many social situations within the dominant society. This is an aspect of life also mentioned in *Hector*. Lupe is an elementary-school-age child whose father died before she and her mother emigrated to the U.S. from Mexico; now her mother's factory job is in a precarious state due to personnel cutbacks. After apprehension and doubt, her mother enrolls in English classes to be better prepared for future job pursuits. The relationship between Lupe and her mother is tenderly depicted, and the pencil-and-line drawings by Judith Friedman, edged in an Aztec-motif border, complement the story well. Like *Amigos,* this book uses limited Spanish phrases throughout the text, which are immediately defined in the text. Even the environmental print in two of the book's pictures is in Spanish.

Another book by someone outside the culture that conveys with authenticity some of the harsh realities of the Mexican-American experience (or the experience of Mexicans seeking to enter the U.S.) is *The Maldonado Miracle* by Theodore Taylor. Originally published in 1962, this novel for older elementary readers has been reprinted at least two times that we know of, in 1973 and 1986, which speaks to its enduring popularity. Duran (1979) called it "one of the few books by an Anglo author that appears to have captured some of the realities of conditions in migrant labor camps . . . the story is believable enough to give the reader a sense of the farmworker's life" (p. 122). The protagonist is 12-year-old Jose, a boy living in a Mexican coastal community, whose mother has died of cancer and whose father has left for the U.S. in an effort to improve their lives. Jose must be smuggled across the border in California in order to join his father upstate. Jose's precarious adventures in his new environment, some of them dangerous, others humorous, form the balance of the book. Despite the robust way in which all of the book's characters were developed, we found distracting the almost stereotypical depiction of one of Jose's attributes, his artistic talent, that is part of the story line at several points.

In concluding this section, we want to stress that authenticity will continue to be an important criterion for evaluating multicultural literature in the 1990s. Within the context of Chicano children's literature, it has been easier for nonnative writers to portray the Mexican-American experience more authentically in nonfiction rather than fictional works. In either category of writing, however, all writers must be able to recognize their own cultural selves as well as those of the people they wish to portray. Nonnative writers must come to understand that the "cultural capital" they have gained from the dominant society, in particular, the value system and literary tradition of the mainstream culture (Romero & Zancanella, 1990), may be the very things that stand in the way of their producing more authentic works about diverse groups. Some Chicano writers came to this conclusion some time ago; they came to discover that they could not tell the stories of their communal group through the underlying world view of the dominant culture (Anaya, 1985). Nonnative writers cnnot do this either. They can neither understand nor tell authentically the stories of other cultures without confronting their own cultural frameworks and transcending them.

In our opinion, the critical question for multicultural literature at this particular time is not in the area of authenticity, or "Who can write about a culture?" (which by the way, is usually a way of asking: Can mainstream writers write authentically about non-mainstream cultures?). The more critical area is authorship, and the key question is "Who is getting to write the literature?" Multicultural literature implies multiple perspectives on the world and multiple voices. Cultural authenticity will follow and flow naturally when the doors to children's literature are opened to writers from non-mainstream cultures, when different perspectives and different voices are encouraged and supported. We elaborate and prove that viewpoint in the next section.

THE VITAL ROLE OF MEXICAN-AMERICAN VOICES AND PERSPECTIVES

We have already noted that during the 1980s, children's literature about multicultural themes and topics, including the Mexican-American experience, became less visible than in previous years (Reimer, 1992). A significant development in the evolution of Mexican-American children's literature, however, began to take place during the second half ot eh 1980s, largely unknown to the world of mainstream literature. A small number of Chicano professional writers started to write for children. Most of these individuals were respected writers within the growing ethnic field of Chicano literature and had written previously of childhood themes and experiences, but had not produced literary works specifically for young audiences. Interestingly enough, as we will show in this section, their works for young readers clearly break away from the traditional one-dimensional mold to provide glimpses of a multifaceted Mexican-American experience. This important tendency supports our third understanding in this chapter, that Mexican-American writers have a vital role to play in interpreting the Mexican-American experience for children.

We need to point out that this recent development does not represent the first effort by Chicanos to write literature for children. During the 1970s, within the larger context of the civil rights movement and its accompanying mandate for the improvement of educational opportunities for linguistic and cultural minorities, Mexican-American education professionals had as part of the nationwide bilingual education movement involved themselves in producing more culturally-relevant reading and literature materials for bilingual Mexican-American children (Reséndez, 1985; Barrera, in press). Written mostly in Spanish, many of these materials were produced as part of federally-funded school projects and were viewed as instructional in nature. Many of them were written by non-professional writers, often education specialists and scholars, who wrote to funding deadlines and constraints. Needless to say, these materials are of mixed literary quality, but they include some outstanding texts. One scholar-writer who produced exemplary Spanish-language literature for children during this era was Ernesto Galarza, whose "Colección Mini-Libros" was the first significant collection of books for young readers by a Chicano. Overall, much of this body of materials was folkloristic in content and did not reach audiences outside the bilingual education arena, nor were they developed by mainstream publishers.

There is little in the historical record and professional literature about the participation of Mexican Americans in the writing of children's literature earlier than the 1970s. We do not know if Mexican Americans produced any literary works for children between 1848, when the Mexican-American experience began historically, to the 1940s, when the first content and images of the Mexican American began to appear in children's books under the authorship of non-Chicano writers. Even the years from the 1940s to the 1970s have not been studied from the point of view of Mexican-American authorship. We do know, however, that the oral tradition has been an integral part of the Mexican-American community throughout its existence (Anaya, 1985), and that it has touched the lives of children growing up Chicano. This is in contrast to the school context where, until recently, nothing about the literary heritage or history of the Chicano was part of the curriculum. This latter circumstance partly explains the lack of professional concern or knowledge about the involvement of Mexican Americans in the writing of children's literature.

It is much to the credit of the Chicano writers we will discuss here that their respective works for children were developed and published, given the historical patterns we have just described and the overall unsupportive climate of the 1980s. In 1987, four works for elementary school children were published by four different Mexican-American writers: Gary Soto Rudolfo Anaya, Sabine Ulibarrí, and Carmen Tafolla. Soto, a former Pulitzer Prize and National Book Award nominee, wrote *The Cat's Meow*. Anaya, a recipient of the Premio Quinto Sol (national literary award for best written work by a Mexican American) for his novel for older readers, *Bless Me, Ultima,* published *The Farolitos of Christmas: A New Mexico Christmas Story.* Ulibarrí, respected Chicano poet, essayist, and short story writer, wrote *Pupurupú: Cuentos de Niños/Children's Stories.* Tafolla, a Chicana poet and bilingual children's television writer, published *Patchwork Colcha: A Children's Collection.* The first two works are in English; the third is a bilingual parallel (Spanish-English) edition published in Mexico City, and the fourth is a combination of Spanish-language and English-language works. It is very telling that these works for children by Chicanos were published mostly by small and alternative presses, not mainstream publishing, a pattern slow to change in the unfolding story of Chicanos in children's literature.

In *The Cat's Meow,* a story for mid-elementary readers, Soto shows a different side of the Mexican-American experience, one that breaks many of the stereotypes of its traditional literary counterparts. Although the story is a modern fantasy, it authentically reflects aspects of contemporary Chicano life, not unlike those to be found in California, Soto's home state. First of all, the main character, eight-year-old Nicole, is not a Mexican immigrant or a socioeconomically poor Mexican-American child; she is a child who is "part Mexican" (p. 5). Intermarriage and mixed parentage have always been sociocultural realities within the Mexican-American community. Nicole is fluent in English, but also understands some Spanish, a familiar language situation in growing up Chicano. She lives in an ethnically mixed neighborhood, and has friends and acquaintances of different cultural backgrounds, another sociocultural reality for some Mexican Americans. The family can best be described as middle class, and her parents are pretty typical as far as parents go, "so strange" at times, and "like other parents" at other times (p. 16).

The story is light and funny at times, and also has its touching and sad moments. Nicole's cat, Pip, can speak Spanish, which Soto uses deftly throughout the book. Pip's Spanish mentor has been Mr. Langer, a neighborhood resident who speaks seven languages, "one for each day of the week" (p. 20), and who wants to keep Pip's talent a secret. When the secret is leaked, and a media spectacle follows, the reclusive Mr. Langer has no recourse but to leave and to take Pip with him. In all of this, Nicole learns the responsibilities and joys of friendship.

Anaya, in *Farolitos,* blends the traditional and the contemporary to provide an account of how a modern Christmas ritual — the lighting of farolitos, or small lanterns on Christmas Eve — might have begun as an alternative to the older practice of lighting *luminarias,* or small bonfires, to light the way for *los pastores,* the shepherds in processional to view the Christ Child. Anaya's story focuses on Mexican-American life and culture in northern New Mexico, revealing some of the language and customs of that region; however, it also emphasizes many of the values of the larger Mexican-American community, such as family support and togetherness, respect for one's elders, and continuity of tradition.

Three generations of a Mexican-American family figure into Anaya's story: Luz, a fourth grader; her parents; and her grandfather, who lives with them. The central problem is that Luz's grandfather is ill and will not be able to light the traditional *luminarias* on Christmas Eve; thus, the *pastores* will not stop to sing in front of Luz's house. Luz's father who could help works away from home and might not even be home for Christmas. Her concern is both for her Grandfather and the tradition that will be broken. Out of this concern, Luz concocts the idea of replacing the *luminarias* with paper bags filled with sand and lighted votive candles inside, a light source with a bright glow. The resulting paper-bag farolitos are a successful substitute. It should be noted that in the story, Luz's best friend is Reina, a young girl of Pueblo Indian background, a cross-cultural friendship not unlikely in this part of the country. The Christmas traditions of Reina and her family are contrasted to those of the Mexican-American community which Luz represents.

Pupurupú, by Ulibarrí, another New Mexican writer, is a collection of eleven short stories, out of which six are animal tales, some of them variants of well-known animal stories such as "The Three Little Pigs." Four stand out above the others in terms of story line and character development; these are "El Patito Tito" ("Little Duck Ling"), "Caballito del Cielo" ("Space Pony"), "Pupurupú," and "Pulín y Miga" ("Pulín and Miga"). Prominent themes running through these stories include friendship (the latter three stories), growing up (the first two stories), and family love and support (the first two stories). Altogether, the collection shows a wide range of characters and story lines, with the overall result being a synergistic, playful blending of story elements from several cultures — Mexican, American, and Mexican American.

We would like to note that we found the Spanish versions of the stories in *Pupurupú* richer linguistically than the English versions because some of the subtlety and humor of the texts comes from the rhythmical and funny animal names which translated only moderately well into English. Also because the book was published in Mexico, there are some typographical errors in the English versions which were not caught during the proofreading process, although these are not overly distracting.

Patchwork Colcha is a collection of poems, stories, and songs in Spanish and English. All total, there are 15 poems, three short stories, and seven "crazy songs for crazy moments" (p. 43). Like the other three writers just discussed, Tafolla, a native Texan, uses English and Spanish in strategic, skillful ways. In the first of three short stories, "Tacho, el Baby Tacuache," the tale of a tiny possum who lives in the Southwest, Tafolla writes in English, but weaves in Spanish phrases throughout the text. In the next story, "The Day the Armadillo Saw His Shadow," Tafolla writes solely in English with the exception of the main character's name, Arnulfo, an armadillo who wanted to be taller. Her third story, "El Dulcero" (The Vendor), about a street vendor in a San Antonio of former times, is written entirely in Spanish.

Tafolla's songs for children in *Colcha* playfully blend incongruous cultural elements from her multicultural background. The song "Los Tennies" (The Tennis Shoes), written in Spanish, is to be sung to the tune of "Malaguena," a popular Spanish-language song. Another song, "The Foot Monster," written in English, is to be sung to the tune of "La Cucaracha," a traditional Mexican song. Her poetry reflects many different moods, from the gentle opening lines of "Mari and the Moon" to the assertive beginning of "The Discovery" to the scary beginning of "La Llorona".

The preceding four works as a group offer a refreshing contrast to the traditional literature on the Mexican-American experience produced in the past by nonnative writers. These pieces contrast with the latter simply because of their genre — three are fiction, one is fiction and rhyme. They are not nonfiction, which is the genre that has been most culturally informed *vis-a-vis* Mexican-American life and culture when written by non-Chicanos. Fiction and rhyme, however, are not culturally demanding for this quartet of native writers; they have no difficulty calling their intuitive cultural knowledge into play in their writing. (We should not expect differently for any writer writing about familiar cultural experiences.) Secondly, there are bilingual and bicultural elements woven with ease and authenticity throughout these writings that set them apart from the traditional literature on the Mexican-American experience written by nonnatives. Finally, the varied content also distinguishes these native literary contributions from the fairly predictable and stereotypical content that has dominated traditional children's literature on the Mexican American. They truly offer perspectives from inside the culture that reflect the subtle and not-so-subtle intra-group differences that are a natural part the Mexican-American community, while at the same time illuminating the common threads that bind us together as an ethnic group.

Several other works by Chicanos were also published during this second half of the 1980s, adding to the sound of native professional voices beginning to write for children. *Tun-ta-ca-tun,* a Latino anthology of stories and poems for children edited by Sylvia Peña was published in 1986. Peña also edited a forerunner, *Kikirikí,* originally published in 1981 and reprinted in 1987. *Tun-ta-ca-tun* contains two works by Pat Mora, whose two books of poetry, *Chants* (1985) and *Borders* (1986) had begun to establish her as an outstanding Chicana poet. Those pieces are "Tarahumara Indians," a poem ideal for chanting by young children and "The Legend of the Poinsettia," a short story written with Charles Ramirez Berg, that is a modern retelling of the magical origin of this Christmas flower in Mexico.

Children's Book Press, a California non-profit publisher that has steadfastly produced multicultural children's literature since the 1970s, especially about indigenous and Hispanic cultures from the Americas, also published two books with Mexican-American content by Mexican-American authors during this time. One of these, *The Adventures of Connie and Diego/Las Aventuras de Connie Y Diego,* by Maria Garcia, had originally been published in 1978, and was republished in 1987. *Mr. Sugar Came To Town/La Visita del Sr. Azúcar,* adapted by Harriet Rohmer, Children's Book Press editor, and Cruz Gomez, was published in 1989.

The first book treats the topic of differences in skin color through a fantasy tale about a set of twins Connie and Diego, whose skin is multicolored. Laughed at because of this difference, the two run away to find a place where no one will make fun of them. They return wiser and untroubled by their many colors. Chicano artist Malaquias Montoya depicts the twins' adventures in bold colors that appeal to children. *Mr. Sugar* is based on a puppet show by Cruz Gomez performed to teach food and nutrition information to migrant farmworkers and their families in California. This has been called an "allegorical story of the evil that Mr. Sugar represents" (Cortes, 1992, p. 129). The pencil and paper illustrations in *Mr. Sugar* are by an artist of Mexican heritage, Enrique Chagoya.

As the 1990s began, two landmark books in the evolution of Mexican-American children's literature were published, offering further proof that Mexican-American writers (and illustrators) have a significant role to play toward expanding and enriching the multicultural horizons of children's literature. These books were *Family Pictures/Cuadros de Familia* (1990) by Carmen Lomas Garza, a major Chicana artist, published by Children's Book Press, and *Baseball in April* (1990) by Gary Soto, the first children's book of stories by a Chicano to be published by a major publisher.

Garza's book for young readers is a set of 14 pictorial vignettes about her Mexican-American childhood in South Texas. The pictures and stories reveal rich views of the everyday and special-day experiences of rural Mexican Americans in this heavily Mexican-American region, for example, a foods and crafts fair "across the border in Reynosa, Mexico" (p. 4), picking *nopal* cactus for cooking and eating "with chili powder and eggs for breakfast" (p. 14), the healing ritual of a *curandera,* individuals who in the Mexican-American community "are very highly respected" (p. 28). The illustrations and text work beautifully together to provide many more cultural details and insights that have seldom been a part of children's literature on the Mexican-American experience. The importance of family and community permeate the book, and the close-knit but extended social relationships of Mexican Americans are vividly portrayed, both visually and verbally. The pictures follow Carmen's childhood from the time she is five to age 13, when she already knows that she wants to be an artist.

As culturally rich and penetrating as Garza's *Family Pictures* is Soto's *Baseball in April,* a collection of eleven short stories for the middle-school reader. Each story focuses on a different Mexican-American child character, but together the stories offer a panoramic view of growing up Chicano in central California. The book has potentially broad appeal, however, because "while the culture is specific, the conflicts and concerns are universal" (Cortes, p. 148). The memorable characters in Soto's book include seventh grader Alfonso in "Broken Chain," who desperately needs to borrow his older brother's bicycle in order to impress a girl; nine-year-old Jesse and his older brother, Michael, in "Baseball in April," who want to make Little League but do not have the required athletic power; Veronica, the elementary school student in "Barbie," who would like nothing better than to have a slim, blonde Barbie and finally gets her wish; eighth-grader Yollie in "Mother and Daughter," who goes to the fall dance in an almost-new dress that her mother has just dyed, albeit not colorfast; and fifth-grader Manuel in "La Bamba," whose talent show performance at lip synching a popular song goes from embarrassing calamity to unexpected success.

The other characters in this multifaceted work are just as engaging as the ones mentioned above. So, too, are the family members and acquaintances who surround these focal children — people who include their parents, siblings, grandparents, other relatives, friends, classroom teachers, coaches, and neighbors. The overall effect is a rich, interesting literary fabric that provides multiple views of the Mexican-American experience. Soto again skillfully uses Spanish words, phrases, and expressions throughout the stories that provide important cultural grounding, not just superficial marks reaching for cultural semblance; these terms are defined at the end of the book.

In retrospect, on a hypothetical time line or chronology of Mexican-American children's literature, the five years from 1986 to 1990 were significant ones in the development of Mexican-American children's literature. A small number of professional Chicano writers turned their attention to young audiences, and produced works that offered far different views of Mexican-American life and culture than previously afforded in the world of children's books. They wrote with bilingual and bicultural ease, naturally displaying cultural vitality and authenticity in their works. At the same time, they aimed for wider audiences by writing in English or by having their works produced in bilingual (Spanish-English) editions. This did not prevent some of them from also writing solely in Spanish. Overall, the result was not the creation of culturally-insular subtexts, but of texts that have far-ranging appeal, without sacrificing the uniqueness and diversity of the Mexican-American experience. In the next section, we look at the vast potential for Mexican-American children's literature that awaits exploration or has begun to be explored in the 1990s.

LITERARY POTENTIAL AND DIRECTIONS FOR THE FUTURE

The next few years will be critical ones for Mexican-American children's literature. The vital role of native writers needs to be recognized and supported by the makers and teachers of the literature. More Chicano writers need to turn their attention to writing for young children. Already, there are encouraging signs that these two needed developments may be occurring. At the same time, there are a number of not-so-encouraging matters *vis-a-vis* the future of Mexican-American children's literature that must be examined and monitored if the cultural integrity of this body of literature is to be maintained. In all of this, one thing is certain: There is much about the Mexican-American experience yet to been explored in children's literature.

Importantly enough, some of the untapped potential that Mexican-American life and culture hold for children is continuing to be explored at the present time by Chicano writers, who although they continue to write for adult audiences as they have in the past, are now intent on developing works for children and youth. The growing importance of this field to the Chicano writing community is vividly exemplified by the current activities emanating from the Guadalupe Cultural Arts Center in San Antonio, Texas. For two years now, this community center whose main focus is Mexican-American culture has sponsored a Children's Program as part of its annual Inter-American Bookfair and Literary Festival. Two children's authors participating in the two-day children's program in 1991 were Gary Soto and Margarita Robleda Moguel, a prize-winning children's writer from Mexico City and a former resident of San Antonio. The five cultural strands promoted by the center are theater, literature, Xicano music, visual arts, and dance. Ray Gonzalez, Chicano poet and poetry editor of *The Bloomsbury Review* in Denver, is the Literature Director of this thriving center.

One Chicana writer who recently added a new dimension to Mexican-American children's literature is novelist Denise Chávez, author of *The Last of The Menu Girls* (1986). In 1991, Chávez wrote and produced a three-act children's play titled "The Woman Who Knew the Language of the Animals," that had its debut at the Children's Theater Festival at the University of Houston. Chávez has described the play, which is based on a New Mexican folktale, as "a modern melodrama about the *pichilinguis*" (D. Chavéz, personal communication with the first author, March 12, 1991).

Pichilinguis are leprechaun-like figures in Mexican and Mexican-American folklore that are known for their mischievous doings and pranks on human beings (Campos, 1977). Chávez provides a novel twist on the traditional folktale in her play: the person who knows the language of the animals is a woman, not a man. Chávez has just finished her second novel, *Women in the State of Grace,* which is yet to be published.

Pat Mora is another Chicana professional writer and poet who is now writing for children, in addition to preparing wroks for adult readers. Mora, whose third book of poetry, *Communion* was published in 1991, will soon have three children's books published, all of them focusing on your Mexican-American characters. Mora, originally from El Paso, Texas but now living in Cincinnati, has drawn on her own family and culture for these books — an aunt and grandmother who actually lived with her family during her childhood years, her grown sister's family, and events in her own recent life. First on the publication schedule is *A Birthday Basket for Tía,* due out from Macmillan in fall 1992. The story is about "Cecilia, a young Mexican-American girl, who with her cat is trying to decide what to give her great aunt, Tía, for her ninetieth birthday." The characters were inspired by Mora's own daughter, Cecilia, and a great-aunt of Mora's children (P. Mora, personal communication with the first author, December 8, 1991).

Her other two books in press are scheduled for publication in 1993; they are *Tomás and the Library Lady,* by Knopf, and *Pablo's Tree,* by Macmillan. The former book is dedicated to the memory of Tomás Rivera, a major figure in the Chicano literary movement of the 1960s and 1970s, whose novel about migrant life, "*. . . y no se lo tragó la tierra"/"and the earth did not part,"* was awarded the first national Chicano literary award, Premio Quinto Sol, in 1970. Mora has taken a particular incident about Rivera that was in a news account after his death, and has used it as a springboard for a fictional story "about a boy from Texas who, like Tomás [Rivera], every year journeys with his family to the Midwest" as part of the fluid population of migrant workers in the U.S. *Pablo's Tree* tells the story of Pablo, his grandfather, and a tree that is decorated by the grandfather in special ways every year in honor of Pablo's birthday. It is about the "relationship between an older, caring adult, and a young person basking in the caring."

A collection of works by Carmen Tafolla, *Sonnets to Human Beings and Other Selected Works by Carmen Tafolla: A Critical Edition,* will be published in mid-1992 by Santa Monica Press of California, with one part of that five-part book devoted to works for children previously published by Tafolla, many of them taken from *Patchwork Colcha.* To be included will be three children's poems ("Mari and the Moon," "The Discovery," and "Las Gotitas Presumidas" [The Presumptuous Raindrops]) and two children's stories, "Tacho, el Tacuache" and "El Dulcero." Other parts of the book will consist of selected poems from Tafolla's earlier book of poems *Curandera* (1983), essays she has written, selected short stories, and critical essays on her work by a number of different individuals. In addition to a full schedule of poetry readings and dramatic performances, Tafolla has done extensive storytelling with school children from elementary to secondary levels since the early 1970s, in Texas, Arizona, and California. Several of her works are in school textbooks. Her latest poems, to be included in *Sonnets,* will also be published in a three-language edition in Germany in fall 1992 (C. Tafolla, personal communication with the first author, February 1992).

Another Chicana who is moving into children's literature from the adult literature field is Helena Maria Viramontes, a Los Angeles-born writer now living in Irvine, California. Viramontes, author of *The Moths and Other Stories* (1985), is presently in the process of writing a book-length collection of stories about a young female character named Cousin Cucita (an invented childhood spelling for "Cuquita"), a fictional East Los-Angeles child based on a real-life cousin of hers. The main character, a rambunctious, independent *Chicanita* (young Chicana), has been part of stories Viramontes has been telling her two children for several years now. The projected work is tentatively titled "Making Tortillas and Other Cousin Cucita Stories."

Rudolfo A. Anaya, who devotes some of his time to various literary projects with schoolchildren in and around the Albuquerque, New Mexico, area where he teaches at the University of New Mexico, is another Chicano writing more regularly now for children. Anaya has recently completed at least three manuscripts of stories for young readers; one of them is a revision of a short story previously published in Switzerland. "The Challenge." The story, about an episode in the schooling of a Mexican-American child, reinforces the value of language and culture in peoples' lives. The other two manuscripts are versions of two classics in Mexican and Mexican-American folklore, "La Llorona: The Story of the Wailing Woman" and "El Cucuí," a traditional bogeyman for children in the Mexican-American community. Anaya has written about La Llorona before in works for adults; in his recent work, he has taken the original gloomy and scary folktale and transformed it into an innovative version that reaches far back into Chicanos' cultural past.

The current and emerging contributions of Chicano writers such as the preceding tend to be in fiction and poetry, two genres in Mexican-American children's literature that clearly are in need of revitalization. The need for drama and poetry on Chicano themes and topics, however, has barely begun to be addressed. Writers such as Soto, Mora, and Tafolla have demonstrated considerable ability in navigating between poetry and prose for adult readers and youth; talent such as theirs is needed in the area of materials for younger readers. At the same time, there is potential in revisiting the large volume of Spanish-language works that were produced during the 1970s — the decade of bilingual education — for literary gems that are still relevant and appealing today, and may lend themselves to dual-language (Spanish and English) presentation. The folkloric emphasis that flavored those materials is still one of many potential directions for pursuit within Mexican-American children's literature in the 1990s. It is not the only one, however, as there is a pressing need for contemporary fiction depicting the varied experiences of growing up Mexican American.

In the nonfiction area, more balanced and accurate treatment of the Mexican-American community became evident during the 1980s and continues in the 1990s; most of these works were written by non-Chicanos. However, there are still many biographies to be written and many histories to be rewritten, plus other nonfiction works, before Mexican-American personages, life, culture, and history gain their rightful place in children's literature. We will briefly mention here some of the nonfiction materials that were produced in the past decade about the Mexican American; this is not intended to slight their importance. We will discuss them again in the next section.

In the historical area, the following works provide informed discussions of the Mexican-American community and experience: *The Hispanic Americans* (1982) by Milton Meltzer, an edition that needs updating but still contains sensitive and insightful information about the Mexican American in several chapters; *Famous Mexican Americans* (1989) by Janet Morey and Wendy Dunn; *The Mexicans in America* (1989) by Jane Pinchot, revised edition from 1973 and 1979; and a focused historical reenactment, *Spanish Pioneers of the Southwest* (1989) by Joan Anderson with photographs by Mexican-American photographer George Ancona. Biographies and other single-person treatments that provide children with adequate insights into contemporary Mexican Americans include *Scientist with Determination, Elma Gonzalez* (1985) by Mary Ellen Verheyden-Hallard, *Señor Alcalde: A Biography of Henry Cisneros* (1988) by John Gillies, *Vilma Martínez* (1990) by Corinn Codye, and *Getting Elected: The Diary of a Campaign* (1989), an account of Gloria Molina's California political bid by Joan Hewett.

The literary potential of the Mexican-American experience has barely begun to be tapped by children's literature, whether one is talking about fiction or nonfiction works, and the possibilities for expansion and enrichment of Mexican-American children's literature are just beginning to be envisioned. That Chicano writers such as the ones mentioned in this section are now writing for children and have caught the attention of major publishers does not automatically mean that the road ahead in the 1990s will be a smooth or easy one for Mexican-American children's literature. The lack of cultural awareness and understanding that we have been speaking about throughout this chapter still prevails in the children's literature arena, both in publishing and education, and poses a variety of problems for Chicano writers and their potential contributions to the field, as well as to the overall development of Mexican-American children's literature.

At the production and publication stage, here are some practices and conditions, past and present, that do not help the growth and development of children's literature about the Mexican-American experience:

- The re-issuance of questionable Chicano-themed materials from past years, as a means for satisfying the present need for Mexican-American children's literature. This only perpetuates gross misrepresentation of the Mexican-American experience.

- The translation of books from foreign Spanish-language countries, as a means for satisfying the present need for Mexican-American children's literature. These materials are not about the Mexican-American experience.

- The translation of English-language texts to produce bilingual (English-Spanish) editions, as a means for satisfying the present need for Mexican-American children's literature. Use of Spanish does not make a dominant-culture text multicultural.

- The assumption that the literature about other Hispanic Americans will satisfy the present need for Mexican-American children's literature. There is no generic Hispanic experience, and the different Latino groups are not interchangeable.

- The lack of editors sensitive to the language and culture of the Mexican-American community. Even editors from Spanish-language countries may not have the cultural or linguistic knowledge to effectively edit children's literature about Mexican-American life, culture, and history. Editors of Mexican-American background are sorely needed, as are illustrators.

- Unscrupulous efforts to standardize the language and culture of natively-written texts on Chicano content to fit standard-language or dominant-culture expectations. Tampering with the language and content of a text can infringe on its cultural authenticity and integrity.

Conditions and practices such as these must be recognized as problematic to the future of Mexican-American children's literature and subversive to the goals of multicultural literature overall. The makers of the literature have a social responsibility to improve them. Members of the Mexican-American community, in particular literature educators, have a responsibility to speak out on these conditions and practices until they are improved.

A SOURCE OF LEARNING FOR ALL CHILDREN

Literature about the Mexican-American experience is literature about the human experience. When written with authenticity and skill, such literature has the same potential for expanding and enriching the lives of children that all literature has. Its emotional, cognitive, and social benefits are no different from those benefits to be derived from all good literature. Assumptions that its value and appeal are limited or fleeting have no validity. Literature about Mexican-American life and culture is not only for Mexican-American children; all children need to read it. Nor is it literature to be used only for special occasions or special units of study; it needs to be an integral part of the school curriculum.

Students do not have to be from California, or Mexican American, or bilingual to understand and enjoy the stories in Gary Soto's *Baseball in April*. Readers from diverse backgrounds can relate to Lupe's desire in "The Marble Champ" to persevere and do well at something new and challenging. Regardless of their backgrounds, readers are likely to be amused by Alfonso in "Broken Chain," as he spends hours trying to straighten his front teeth until the time comes when he can get braces. Despite background differences, readers will appreciate Gilbert's realization in "The Karate Kid" that things are not always like they are made out to be, especially by the movies.

Likewise, students do not have to be from South Texas, or part of a Mexican-American family, or know both English and Spanish in order to find interest and learning in Carmen Lomas Garza's *Family Pictures/Cuadros de familia.* Regardless of their backgrounds, they will have an intuitive sense of people and family and social relationships to bring to the book that will help them to explore it. Their explicit or implicit sense of the basic needs of people, for example, love, shelter, health, food, tradition, and such, will help them to interpret the book's content and images. As they learn about Lomas Garza's family and community, there is potential for them to learn about themselves and humanity.

All students stand to learn about the political process by reading about the campaign efforts of Gloria Molina and her staff in Joan Hewett's *Getting Elected: The Diary of a Campaign.* The fact that the politican is Chicana does not alter the basic array of manifold and complex activities that a candidate must go through from the time of announcement of candidacy to election. However, the candidate's personal background plus the diversity of her district and supporters do provide a unique dimension to the basic campaign story. This combination of basic and unique angles only enhances the potential for learning from the book; the art and science of campaigning in a culturally pluralistic society is equally important for all children.

We could devote more space to explaining why Mexican-American children's literature should be shared with all children, but that explanation would be similar to one that might be given about multicultural literature in general, and to some degree, about *all* literature as a whole. Instead, in the rest of this section we explain some of the professional and instructional steps teachers might take so that literature about Mexican-American life and culture does indeed become a source of knowledge and learning for all children.

VALUE OF BACKGROUND KNOWLEDGE

Because teachers have an important role to play in mediating literature for children, especially in the early grades, it is important for them to have some factual knowledge about Mexican Americans if they are going to share literature on the Mexican-American experience with children. To teach from a multicultural perspective — literature or any other part of the curriculum — implies that teachers have multicultural awareness and knowledge. Moreover, teachers cannot critically evaluate multicultural literature without some sense, general and specific, about human diversity. Therefore, to do justice to Mexican-American children's literature, especially fiction, teachers should lern something about the real Mexican Americans in our society before or as they share such literature with children.

It is here where we see nonfiction materials on the Mexican American as being very important, namely, histories and biographies. Teachers have long known that children's literature is not just for children, and in the case of nonfictional works on the Mexican American, such materials can, and should, be read by teachers so as to gain a better sense of Mexican Americans. This is necessary because until recently the Mexican-American experience and community were not treated accurately or substantively in U.S. history books. We suspect that many teachers know little about the historical and contemporary lives of Mexican Americans. Books such as Meltzer's *The Hispanic Americans* can give teachers an overall sense of Hispanic Americans, and Mexican Americans in particular. A book such as Pinchot's *The Mexicans in America* can provide an historical overview, and a book such as Morey & Dunn's *Famous Mexican Americans* can provide biographical profiles on contemporary Mexican Americans. At the same time, it would be extremely valuable for teachers to also read historical works by Mexican Americans themselves; *Occupied America: A History of Chicanos* (1988) by Acuña could be helpful. Then teachers would be able to mediate literature for children from a more informed perspective.

USE OF ORAL TRADITION

Because books about Mexican-American themes and topics are still such a small part of the larger body of children's literature, it is important that teachers take an expanded perspective on multicultural literature and literature in general. This means that teachers ought to consider the oral tradition which is an important part of many cultures, including the Mexican-American culture, and make the oral literary heritage and oral literature of the Mexican-American community a part of the literature curriculum. Teachers in literature-based programs need to understand that just as there are multiple forms of literacy (Eisner, 1991), so too, there are multiple forms of literature (Barrera, 1992). We think the academic divide between folklore and literature (Rosenberg, 1991) has led to educator perceptions that the former is inferior and the latter superior. School-centric notions that literature, literacy, and literateness are only about written expression (Eisner, 1991), and not oral expression, are antithetical to a multicultural literature perspective. This is not to say that the written word, written literacy, and written literature are not important, but it is saying that to reject or ignore children's oral literary traditions is to devalue an important part of their knowledge and humanness.

Therefore, in the case of Mexican-American children's literature, it would be culturally enriching to invite people of Mexican origin, particularly if they are part of the school community, to share their oral literature in the classroom. The oral tradition in our ethnic community includes many forms, such as animal tales, ghost stories, fairy tales, nursery rhymes, fables, tongue twisters, riddles, jokes, proverbs and sayings, among others. It would be shortsighted, for example to leave kids (or teachers) with the impression that there is only one version of La Llorona, as implied in *La Llorona: The Weeping Woman* (1990) by Joe Hayes, when there are many versions of this tale. Sometimes, because literature in the schools has been defined only as (a) written, (b) in English, and (3) commercially-produced, diverse literary expressions and forms not fitting that description have been ignored. Until, and even after, Mexican-American children's literature is more plentiful within U.S. children's literature, the community's oral literature is an important resource for school literature and literacy instruction.

LITERATURE STUDY GROUPS

Literature study groups and circles are a regular instructional feature in many literature-based classrooms today. What teachers are asking their students to do, we are recommending that teachers do themselves, that is, that they undertake literature study, of diverse literature in order to gain a better understanding about cultural diversity. In other words, all of us, as education professionals in a culturally pluralistic society, ought to read literature written by individuals from diverse cultural and ethnic communities in this country. Just as the history of diverse peoples have been omitted from the school curriculum, so, too, has their literature. Therefore, many teaches are not aware or knowledgeable about the ethnic literatures that are often left out of the literary canon. In the case of the Mexican American, some teachers are not even aware that there is a robust body of literature written by Chicanos and a long literary tradition undergirding the Mexican-American community (Martínez & Lomeli, 1985; Tatum, 1982).

For some time now, in our talks about multicultural literature with education professionals and university students, we have made it a point to share Chicano literature with them (and literature from other cultural groups), and the responses have been consistently positive. For many in our audiences, it has been the first time that they have heard or read such works. It seems that if literature is a powerful way of knowing and learning — about oneself and the world — then it makes sense for us to turn to diverse literatures as sources for building multicultural awareness and knowledge. We have turned repeatedly, for example, to the poetry of Pat Mora to express to our audiences facets of the Mexican-American experience. From *Chants,* Mora's poems such "Elena," "Legal Alien," and "Mexican Maid" have said in a few words what we would take longer to say. Romero & Zancantella (1990) have described the instructional use they make of "1910," another poem from *Chants.* And, a colleague of ours who employs the poem "Tomás Rivera" from Mora's *Borders* to open her talks on Mexican-American children's literature, has found that the poem evokes much discussion and strong, but positive emotional responses.[5]

Whereas earlier, we mentioned the importance of turning to nonfiction materials for building knowledge about the Mexican-American experience, here we are referring mostly to works of fiction, poetry, and drama. Teachers of multicultural literature can gain important cultural insights by reading, individually or collectively, Chicano-written works such as *Barrio Boy* (1971) by Ernesto Galarza, *George Washington Gómez* (1990) by Américo Paredes, Pat Mora's three poetry books, *Borders, Chants,* and *Communion, The House on Mango Street* (1989) by Sandra Cisneros, Gary Soto's *Small Faces* (1986) and *A Summer Life* (1990), and Rudolfo A. Anaya's *Bless Me, Ultima,* and any of the many other contemporary writings by Chicanos. Our recommendations here are only suggestive, and not in any way comprehensive.[6]

When teachers of literature pursue the three areas of activity we have described above, they will be much more informed about Mexican-American life and culture — therefore, they will be in a better position to critique children's literature on the Mexican-American experience, will be better able to share it with breadth and depth in the classroom, and will be more inclined to serve as advocates for its continued growth, development, and use. In essence, they will have gained all the five understandings we set out at the beginning of this chapter.

CONCLUSION

Teaching multicultural literature is ultimately not about texts and stories, it is about people. This means knowing that literature is only as culturally enlightened as the people who create it and use it. The successful use of multicultural texts and stories with children depends greatly on the multicultural awareness and understanding of the teacher and the classroom environment he or she promotes, during and beyond the sharing of such literature. We should not count on books alone to engender and sustain cultural understanding and appreciation for children.

If literature is to do all the extraordinary things literature professional are presently saying it can do, namely to empower and transform human minds, then the present corpus of children's literature must first be transformed into a literature that represents all the cultural diversity in this country. If not, then literature will be empowering only in a selective way, more for children from some cultural groups than others. Given that a "new world" and a "new America" are unfolding before our eyes, it makes sense that a new literature for children, one grounded in human diversity and human understanding, be promoted.

ENDNOTES

1. Reimer (1992) cites several studies that provide publication figures on multiethnic literature, primarily African-American literature which has been the most carefully documented of the ethnic literatures in the U.S. She notes that "by the mid-1980s only 1% of the children's literature published was about African Americans; there was less about Asian Americans, Hispanics, and Native Americans." For that estimate, she cites Rudine Sims Bishop's 1987 work, "Extending multicultural understanding through children's books" in B. Cullinan (Ed.), *Children's literature in the reading program* (pp. 60-67), Newark, DE: International Reading Association.
2. We will use the terms "Mexican American" and "Chicano" interchangeably in this chapter, although they do have a history of different connotative meanings, stemming from a complex of historical, cultural, and political factors.
3. Mexican-American content in children's literature has not been documented as carefully as that of African-American content. Most of the writings in this area have been content/thematic analyses, not necessarily systematic analyses of publication patterns. Based on the 1975 CIBC survey, we can conclude that about six books a year on Mexican-American themes and topics were published between 1940 and 1973. That figure is likely to be inflated, however, because the Council found that of the 140 fiction books collected for its survey, many were not about Chicano people, culture or concerns per se; instead, they were "books about Mexicans, about Mexico, about Mexicans 'adventuring' in the United States, about characters with Spanish names," (p. 7) and so forth. Of the 60 nonfiction books gathered from the same time period, only 15 could be said to be about Chicanos and the Southwest. A more valid estimate might be an average of 1-3 books a year, counting both fiction and nonfiction.

From the work of Isabel Schon (1980, 1985, 1988), one of the few researchers to provide regular content/thematic analyses of children's and young adult literature on Hispanic people and cultures, we have calculated the following figures: of the 48 books surveyed by Schon in *Hispanic Heritage* (1980) under the category of "Mexico," (in-print books in English published in the U.S. from 1942 to 1978), 10 appear to be about Mexican American content. In *Hispanic Heritage II* (1985), of the 90 entries under the section titled "Mexico," (in-print books with publication dates roughly from 1977 to 1983), 23 are about Mexican-American content. In *Hispanic Heritage III* (1988), of the 58 titles in the section "Mexico," (in-print books published from 1984 to 1987), 7 deal with Mexican-American themes and topics. These last two Schon publications yield an average of about 2-3 books a year on Mexican-American content (fiction and nonfiction), a figure not too different from the estimate above. If we assume that anywhere from 3,000 to 5,000 children books might be published annually, then the proportion of books with Mexican-American content is about one-tenth of 1 percent (.1%) or less!

4. Both Reséndez (1985) and Barrera (in press) provide a fuller discussion of this corpus of materials produced by Mexican Americans during the 1970s. In this new era of multicultural literature, there is a need for further research of these materials.
5. We extend our appreciation to Laura Rodriguez for sharing this information with us.
6. Interested individuals might begin by looking at the literary offerings of Arte Público Press, one of the leading publishers of Latino materials, including the works of Mexican-American writers cited here and others.

Acknowledgements: Partial financial support for this study was provided by a grant from the Minority Recruitment and Retention Committee at New Mexico State University.

CHILDREN'S BOOKS REVIEWED

Anderson, J. (1989). *Spanish pioneers of the Southwest.* Lodestar Books/E. P. Dutton.

Anaya, R. A. (1987). *The farolitos of Christmas: A New Mexico Christmas story.* Sante Fe: New Mexico Magazine.

Brown, T. (1986). *Hello, amigos!* New York: Henry Holt and Company.

Codye, C. (1990). *Vilma Martinez.* Milwaukee: Raintree.

Garcia, M. (1978). *The adventures of Connie and Diego/Las aventuras de Connie y Diego.* San Francisco: Children's Book Press.

Gillies, J. (1988). *Señor alcalde: A biography of Henry Cisneros.* Minneapolis, MN: Dillon Press, Inc.

Griego, M. C., Bucks, B. L., Gilbert, S. S., & Kimball, L. H. *Tortillitas para Mamá and other nursery rhymes, English and Spanish.* New York: Holt, Rinehart and Winston.

Hayes, J. (1990). *La Llorona: The weeping woman.* El Paso, TX: Cinco Puntos Press.

Hayes, J. (1982). *The day it snowed tortillas: Tales from Spanish New Mexico.* Santa Fe, NM: Mariposa Publishing.

Hewett, J. (1989). *Getting elected: The diary of a campaign.* New York: Lodestar Books/E. P. Dutton.

Hewett, J. (1990). *Hector lives in the United States now: The story of a Mexican-American child.* New York: J. B. Lippincott.

Lomas Garza, C. (1990). *Family pictures / Cuadros de familia.* San Francisco: Children's Book Press.

MacMillan, D. & Freeman, D. (1986). *My best friend, Martha Rodriguez. Meeting a Mexican-American family.* New York: Julian Messner.

Meltzer, M. (1982). *The Hispanic Americans.* New York: Thomas Y. Crowell.

Morey, J. & Dunn, W. (1989). *Famous Mexican Americans.* New York: Cobblehill Books/E. P. Dutton.

Paul, P. G. (1980). *You can hear a magpie smile.* New York: Elsevier/Nelson Books.

Peña, S. (Ed.). (1981). *Kikiriki: Stories and poems in English and Spanish for children.* Houston, TX: Arte Publico Press.

Peña, S. (Ed.). (1986). *Tun-ta-ca-tun: More stories and poems in English and Spanish for children.* Houston, TX: Arte Publico Press.

Pinchot, J. (1989). *The Mexicans in America.* Minneapolis, MN: Lerner Publications Company.

Rohmer, H. & Gomez, C. (1989). *Mr. Sugar came to town/La visita del Sr. Azúcar.* San Francisco: Children's Book Press.

Soto, G. (1987). *The cat's meow.* San Francisco: Strawberry Hill Press.

Soto, G. (1990). *Baseball in April.* San Diego, CA: Harcourt Brace Jovanovich.

Stanek, M. (1989). *I speak English for my mom.* Niles, IL: Albert Whitman & Company.

Tafolla, C. (1987). *Patchwork colcha: A children's collection.* Flagstaff, AZ: Creative Educational Enterprises.

Taha, K. T. (1986). *A gift for Tía Rosa.* New York: Bantam Skylark.

Taylor, T. (1986). *The Maldonado miracle.* New York: Avon Books.

Ulibarrí, S. (1987). *Pupurupú: Cuentos de ninos: Children's stories.* Mexico, D. F.: Sainz Luiselli Editores.

Verheyden-Hillard, M. (1985). *Scientist with determination, Elma Gonzalez.* Bethesda, MD: The Equity Institute.

REFERENCES

Acuña, R. (1988). *Occupied America: A history of Chicanos* (3rd ed.). New York: Harper Collins.

Alvarez, R. (1985). The psycho-historical and socioeconomic development of the Chiano community in the United States. In R. O. de la Garza, F. D. Bean, C. M.

Bonjean, R. Romo, & R. Alvarez (Eds.), *The Mexican-American experience: An interdisciplinary anthology* (p. 33-56). Austin: University of Texas Press. (Original work published 1973).

Anaya, R. A. (1987). An American Chicano in King Arthur's court. *New Mexico English Journal, 2,* 16-20.

Barrera, M. (1979). *Race and class in the Southwest: A theory of racial inequality.* Notre Dame, IN: University of Notre Dame Press.

Barrera, R. B. (in press). The Mexican-American experience in children's literature: Past, present, and future. *Oregon English Journal.*

Barrera, R. B. (1992). The cultural gap in literature-based literacy instruction. *Education and Urban Society, 24,* 227-24.

Campos, A. J. (1977). *Mexican Folk Tales.* Tucson: University of Arizona Press.

Cortes, O. G. de. (1992). United States: Hispanic Americans. In L. Miller-Lachman (Ed.), *Our family, our friends, our world: An annotated guide to significant multicultural books for children and teenagers* (pp. 121-154). New Providence, NJ: R. R. Bowker.

Council on Interracial Books for Children. (1975). Chicano culture in children's literature: Stereotypes, distortions, and omissions. *Interracial Books for Children's Bulletin, 5,* 7-14.

Duran, D. F. (1979). The Latino literary renaissance: Its roots, status, and future. In D. F. Duran, *Latino materials: A multimedia guide for children and young adults* (pp. 3-12). New York: Neal Schuman, Publishers.

Eisner, E. (1991). What really counts in schools. *Educational Leadership, 48,* (5), 10-17.

Garcia, J., Hadaway, N. L., & Beal, G. (1988). Cultural pluralism in recent nonfiction tradebooks for children. *The Social Studies, 79,* 252-255.

Gómez-Quiñones, J. (1990). *Chicano politics: reality and promise, 1940-1990.* Albuquerque: University of New Mexico Press.

Gonzales, M. G. (1989). *The Hispanic elite of the Southwest.* El Paso, TX: Texas Western Press.

Martínez, J. A. & Lomeli, F. (Eds.). (1985). *Chicano literature: A reference guide.* Westport, CT: Greenwood Press.

Matute-Bianchi, M. E. (1991). Situational ethnicity and patterns of school performance among immigrant and nonimmigrant Mexican-descent students. In M. A. Gibson & J. U. Ogbu (Eds.), *Minority status and schooling: A comparative study of immigrant and involuntary minorities* (pp. 205-247). New York: Garland Publishing, Inc.

McLemore, S. D. & Romo, R. (1985). The origins and development of the Mexican-American people. In R. O. de la Garza, F. D. Bean, C. M. Bonjean, R. Romo, & R. Alvarez (Eds.), *The Mexican-American experience: An interdisciplinary anthology* (pp. 3-32). Austin: University of Texas Press.

McWilliams, C. (1990). *North from Mexico: The Spanish-speaking people of the United States* (rev. ed. by M. S. Meier). New York: Praeger Publishers.

Reimer, K. M. "Multiethnic literature: Holding fast to dreams." *Language Arts, 69,* 14-21.

Reséndez, G. A. (1985). Chicano children's literature. In J. A. Martínez & F. Lomelí (Eds.), *Chicano Literature: A reference guide* (pp. 107-121). Westport, CT: Greenwood Press, 1985.

Romero, P. A. & Zancanella, D. (1990). Expanding the circle: Hispanic voices in American literature. *English Journal, 79* (1), 24-29.

Rosenberg, B. A. (1991). *Folklore and literature: Rival siblings.* Knoxville: University of Tennessee Press.

Schon, I. (1978). *A bicultural heritage: Themes for the exploration of Mexican and Mexican-American culture in books for children and adolescents.* Metuchen, NJ: The Scarecrow Press, Inc.

Schon, I. (1980). *A Hispanic heritage: A guide to juvenile books about Hispanic people and cultures.* Metuchen, NJ: The Scarecrow Press, Inc.

Schon, I. (1989). Recent children's books about Hispanics. *Journal of Youth Services in Libraries, 2(2),* 157-162.

Sims, R. (1982). *Shadow and substance: Afro-American experience in contemporary children's fiction.* Urbana, IL: National Council of Teachers of English.

Tapahonso, L. (1990). [Interview by J. F. Crawford & A. O. Erysturoy]. In W. Balassi, J. F. Crawford, & A. O. Eysturoy (Eds.), *This is about vision: Interviews with Southwestern writers* (pp. 194-202). Albuquerque: University of New Mexico Press.

Tatum, C. M. (1982). *Chicano literature.* Boston: Twayne Publishers.

U.S. Bureau of the Census. (1991). *The Hispanic population in the United States, March 1991.* Current Population Reports, Series P-20, No. 455. Washington, DC: U.S. Government Printing Office.

CREATIVE LITERATURE CITED

Anaya, R. A. (1972). *Bless me, Ultima.* Berkeley, CA: Tonatiuh International.

Chávez, D. (1988). *The last of the menu girls.* Houston, TX: Arte Público Press.

Cisneros, S. (1989). *The house on mango street.* Houston, TX: Arte Público Press.

Galarza, E. (1971). *Barrio boy.* Notre Dame, IN: University of Notre Dame Press.

Mora, P. (1985). *Borders.* Houston, TX: Arte Público Press.

Mora, P. (1984). *Chants.* Houston, TX: Arte Público Press.

Mora, P. (1991). *Communion.* Houston, TX: Arte Público Press.

Paredes, A. (1990). *George Washington Gómez: A Mexicotexan novel.* Houston, TX: Arte Público Press.

Rivera, T. (1970). *". . . y no se lo tragó la tierra"/". . . and the earth did not part".* Berkeley, CA: Quinto Sol Publications, Inc.

Soto, G. (1990). *A summer life*. Hanover, NH: University Press of New England.

Soto, G. (1986). *Small faces*. Houston, TX: Arte Público Press.

Tafolla, C. (1993). *Curandera*. San Antonio, TX: M & A Editions.

Viramontes, H. M. (1985). *The moths and other stories*. Houston, TX: Arte Público Press.

8

Caribbean American Children's Literature

Yahaya Bello

INTRODUCTION AND HISTORICAL BACKGROUND

Demographics

Brathwaite, noted West Indian historian and literary critic, has described the Caribbean as:

> a 2,000-mile arc of jewel-islands; brown and green; jumping like porpoises from Florida, outward and south to the South American coast; some 5,000 fragments, varying in size from Cuba (44,218 sq miles) through Jamaica (4,411 sq miles) and Trinidad (1,978 sq miles) to sand spits the size of Friday's footprint. . . . The island/fragments are themselves the tops of sunken cordillera; an ancient mountain range, once part of mainland America, which swung out catastrophically from that double continent's western spine: Rockies and Andes; out into the Atlantic through the gape of Yucatan to end, perhaps, in what was once Atlantis. (Brathwaite, 1985, p. 57)

During the last four decades the population of the Caribbean Basin has more than tripled, growing from about 55 million to approximately 166 million people. "Such growth over an extended period was the highest ever recorded in the Americas and possibly the highest ever recorded on the planet earth" (Bouvier & Simcox, 1986, p. 15). Given the present population trends, by the year 2,000 the projected population of the Caribbean Basin — 250 million, will be close to the projected population of the United States — 266 million. This rapid growth in the region's population creates high rates of unemployment and underemployment and brings about tremendous pressures on young adults to seek work in neighboring countries, especially the United States. Some of the smaller English speaking islands lose over one percent of their populations annually to migration to the U.S.A. "Since independence, St. Kitts-Nevis has regularly sent at least 2.5 percent of its total population of 40,000 as immigrants to the U.S. More than 60,000 Jamaicans were on the waiting list for U.S. visas in early 1986, nearly 3% of its population" (Bouvier & Simcox, 1986, p. 46).

Upon arrival in the United States, many of the West Indian immigrants settle in major cities; New York, Miami, Palm Beach, Chicago, Boston, and Los Angeles. In 1988, the New York Metropolitan Area was the intended destination of over 30,000 West Indian immigrants legally admitted into the United States while Miami received approximately 15,000. Not only are the schools in these metropolitan areas being called upon to educate a growing number of West Indian children, but as the number of Americans of West Indian descent increases, it becomes increasingly important for all of us, especially educators, to have a some familiarity with the culture and literature of the region.

HISTORICAL DEVELOPMENT OF CARIBBEAN LITERATURE

When Columbus came to the West Indies in 1492, he found the islands populated by two major Amerindian groups: the Caribs and Arawaks. However, within 50 years the Europeans had virtually exterminated the Amerindian population. The Europeans enslaved African peoples and imported them wholesale to work the mines and plantations of the islands. Upon arrival, these Africans were not a homogeneous people speaking one language and observing one set of customs and traditions; they were Hausa and Kanuri, Tiv and Fanti, Yoruba, Ibo, Ashanti, and Congo. Each spoke their own language, had their own customs and cultures, and each worshipped their own gods in their own way. These captured and enslaved Africans were deposited on islands and lands controlled by the English, French, Spanish, the Dutch, the Danes, and the Portuguese. Beginning shortly after the abolition of slavery by the English in 1834, large numbers of Chinese and Indian indentured laborers were brought to the West Indies to perform the agricultural work previously done by the enslaved Africans.

In addition to the Africans, the Chinese, and East Indians, many Middle Eastern merchants came to settle in the West Indies, creating in the region a rich melange of races and ethnic groups. However, even though the population of the Caribbean is made up of people whose ancestors come from India, China, the Middle East, and many European countries, the vast majority of the region's people are of African descent. Dawes (1977) points out that "you will have heard, no doubt, the Caribbean described as a great melting-pot of races and cultures. Well, something must have gone wrong with the mixing and cooking because, whatever might bubble to the surface in the tourist brochures (to speak politely), the majority element in the pot is unmixed black African" (p. 1). It is this dominant African presence that forms the basis of what is unique in West Indian culture and gives Caribbean literature its distinctive content and flavor.

The predominant historical force informing the literature of the West Indies is that of struggle and resistance. The people of the region have struggled for centuries, first against a system of slavery and the ravages left in its wake, and more recently against the continuing social, cultural, political, and economic domination of their former colonial rulers. In short, Caribbean "society has been wrought in struggle and resistance against dehumanization" (Nettleford, 1989, p. 7). This theme of resistance is noted also by Brathwaite (1985). He says that "since all Caribbean territories were colonized (made dependent and imitative) since 1492, it follows that the greatest thought/action concerned in the Caribbean has been anti-colonialism: political in the first instance; then combined with cultural independence" (p. 60).

The struggle for political independence began with the Africans enslaved in the Caribbean who managed to escape from captivity and set up independent, self-governing communities in various West Indian territories (Dathorne, 1981). Examples of this can be found in Haiti, Jamaica, and Surinam. In Jamaica the Maroons set up their own settlements and waged an ongoing war with the British until 1739, when a treaty was signed ending the hostilities. In Surinam, the Djuka "attacked the Dutch so intensely that it caused the Dutch to beg for peace, and so a treaty was concluded between the African leader, Adoe, and the Dutch governor, Mauricus, in 1749" (Cudjoe, 1980, p. 11). In 1792, the enslaved Africans of Haiti under the leadership of Toussaint L'Ouverture would defeat the forces of Napoleon and eventually set up of the first independent black state in the New World.

Cudjoe (1980) in his book, *Resistance and Caribbean Literature,* defines resistance as "any act or complex of acts designed to rid a people of its oppressors, be they slave masters or multinational corporations" (p. 19).

He terms as cultural that resistance which "emanates from the beliefs, mores, or indigenous ways of life and is expressed in religion or the arts" (p. 19). He goes on to say that "resistance is that ideological content that is embodied in the artistic form, creating the political aesthetic of Caribbean literature . . . In the Caribbean, then, cultural resistance is synonymous with the cultural reaffirmation of the people" (pp. 65-66). Cudjoe maintains that an understanding of the role played by cultural resistance is indispensable in understanding and analyzing Caribbean literature. The theme of resistance in Caribbean literature has been spawned not only by the struggles of the captured Africans against the system of slavery, but also by the freed slaves and their descendants against continued rule by the various European colonial powers. Embodied in much of West Indian Literature is the struggle of the common people for democracy, for the right to their own language, for their freedom to worship as they please, and for the right to their own culture and way of life.

Anansi Stories

Of all the characters in Caribbean children's literature, Anansi is the one that most clearly embodies the struggle of the masses of the common people first against the ravages of slavery and later against the oppression wrought by colonialism. In addition, of all the tales told in the West Indies, none are as common or as widespread as the stories about that West African god and trickster, Anansi the Spiderman. Although his ancient association with the sky god of the Akan peoples of Ghana has been all but forgotten, Anansi is known throughout much of the Caribbean as a surprisingly benevolent trickster par excellence. The stories of Anansi the Spiderman reached the shores of the New World with the first shipload of kidnapped Africans and have been told and retold in most of the islands of the Caribbean ever since. "The original Akan-Asante name of Kwaku-Anansi has been shortened to Anansi, but the word still means 'spider' as in the original Twi" (Tanna, 1984, p. 78). The name also has many variant spellings. You may see it spelled Anansi, Anansee, Anancy or Ananci. Also, in some of the islands Anansi will be known by other names. For instance, "in Haiti which is French-speaking, he is Ti-Jean, which means Uncle John. In the islands of St. Lucia and Grenada, where the language of the people is based largely on French, he has yet another name, Compe Czien [or] Brother spider" (Sherlock & Sherlock, 1988, p. xv).

Anansi can be either a man or a spider. He usually takes the form of a spider to aid his escape after he has duped one of the larger and more powerful creatures. This happens often since he constantly uses his guile and cunning to defeat the strong and powerful creatures of the world. In his African homeland, Anansi, like many other creatures in the animal stories, is used to demonstrate how the small and weak through intelligence can defeat the large and strong. In the New World, "Anancy takes on the role of the downtrodden victim in his efforts to survive" (Dathorne, 1984, p. 102). He becomes the embodiment of the will to resist, through intelligence, guile, and cunning, the will of the slave master (Dathorne, 1981, p. 44). According to Carew, for both the Africans who were struggling against the cataclysm of slavery and the Amerindians who were fast disappearing in the conflagration of extermination:

> Anancy with his agile brain and his invincible instinct for survival, became the foremost symbol of wish-fulfilment. For Anancy the trickster, no matter how impossible the odds against him seemed to be or how mighty his opponents, inevitably came out on top, winning for himself food, women, land, respect, and liberty without the cruel tasks that those escaping with him vicariously were compelled to perform for such trifling rewards. (Carew, 1978, p. 253)

The trickster, Anansi the Spiderman, is so much a part of Caribbean folklore that no collection of Caribbean children's literature would be complete without at least one Anansi story. Phillip Sherlock, a major figure in the publication of West Indian folklore, presents us with 15 Anasi stories in his book *Anansi the Spider Man* (1954). The stories are presented at a level which should be suitable for average readers in the middle elementary grades. In this collection, there are stories that tell us how Anansi managed to dupe Snake into letting himself be tied up. We also find out how Anansi got Tiger to change the names from Tiger stories, which were their original names, to Anansi stories. In "The Quarrel" we find out why Anansi the spider lives in a web. All the fun-filled stories in this collection are accompanied by black and white drawings and will open up for the middle and upper elementary student a window onto the most popular form of authentic Caribbean children's literature.

The Caldecott honor book, *Anansi the Spider: A Tale from the Ashanti* (McDermott 1986), affords teachers the opportunity to introduce Anansi in the early primary grades. The text is short and many of the words should be within the sight vocabulary of the early primary student. Striking Ashanti patterns done in brilliant colors are used in the illustrations that enliven every page. In the story itself, "Anansi went a long way from home.... He fell into trouble" (p. 10). His six sons "they went fast, those six brothers gone to help Anansi" (p. 15). They rescue Anansi and, naturally, have several adventures along the way.

Not only does Anansi speak the African languages Twi and Fanti, but now Anansi has become fluent in Spanish as well as English. In *Brother Anansi and the Cattle Ranch: El Hermano Anansi y el Rancho de Ganado,* (Rhomer 1989) we are given an Anansi story with both English and Spanish text. Once again Tiger is the dupe and this time gets tricked out of his cattle by Anansi. According to the author, this version of the story comes from the town of Pearl Lagoon on Nicaragua's Atlantic coast. The story seems to have been brought to the region by the many people of African descent who had settled there in the past. The level of difficulty should be no trouble for the middle primary student, and perhaps could be used by some of the more ambitious readers in the early primary grades.

Folk Tales, Legends, and Animal Stories

West Indian folk tales, legends, and animal stories, like its people, are composed of a basic African stock liberally spiced with additional elements from all over the world. Tales from India, England, France, Spain, Holland, as well as the Amerindians, all add flavor and variety to the basic African stock. The people of the Caribbean have filled their myths and legends with an array of ogres, ghouls and monsters, tricksters, heroes and gods, equal to those of any people in the world.

The folk tales and legends of the Caribbean were preserved orally over the centuries. These tales were passed on from generation to generation by the village elders and storytellers. People like the now renowned Jamaican poetess and storyteller, Louise Bennet, have labored for years among the common people to keep the oral tradition alive. However, "The voice of the Folk, of the People was not recorded. Nor respected neither. But it told tales and sang, stories and song from dark-night to dawn, day-clean, in every crevice of our tiny, black, ridden societies" (Keens-Douglas, 1989, p. xiv). The performance of oral narratives was one of the main forms of community entertainment (Tanna, 1984). Among the common people, the storyteller, like the African griot of old, became a local celebrity. Carew (1978) tells us that the

> storytellers were invariably older folks. . . . The tales would amuse,
> instruct and at times fill the young listeners with a delicious sense of

terror, for the family storytellers were like maestros, educators handing down cultural secrets from one generation to the other, and instructors in the basic moral and ethical canons by which the family was supposed to live. (p. 242)

At the time when English-educated writers couldn't find an audience large enough to support themselves and their literary efforts in the West Indies and had to migrate to Europe and North America, local storytellers, poets, and calypsonians (the singers of the popular West Indian music) using the vernacular as the medium of communication found not only wide audiences, but they also found fame.

It wasn't until the late 60s that the oral literature told in the vernacular began to gain official recognition. Since the Caribbean Cultural Festival, Carifesta '76, in Jamaica, there has been such an upsurge in use of the vernacular in literature that it has now "become not the exception but the rule" (Brathwaite, 1984, p. 49). As the vernacular gained increasing status and official recognition, the folk tales and legends preserved in the oral tradition began to be transcribed and recorded.

The myths and legends of the West Indies have always functioned as vehicles to instill in the children basic lessons in resistance, survival and identity. Even though Jan Carew sees his duty as an author as creating "authentic works of imagination that will reach anyone who reads," when asked why he rewrote African and Amerindian myths and legends as children's stories, he replied:

> Because there is is a dearth of material for our children which would give them images of themselves. When I say 'our children,' it is the Black children everywhere who need this. And I'm interested giving the children's stories a kind of ideological underpinning. This is a tradition we inherited from Africa which should be maintained in the folk tales. For instance, Afro-American folk tales are lessons in survival by Black people. Brer Rabbit has a great fear of enemies. He survives best in a community. If he goes off by himself he is the victim of predators. . . . So I'm interested in transforming visions through stories. . . . For instance . . . I attempt to bring back a kind of African Aesthetic about age and beauty to counter the Western idea that all beauty must be young, have a toothpaste smile, high bosom, long legs, blond hair. When you get older they fade you out. Whereas in Africa the tradition was for the aged to acquire more status and respect. (Wamer-Lewis, 1987, p. 39)

Illustrated by Caldecott Medal winning illustrators Leo and Diane Dillon,

Carew's book, *Children of the Sun* (1980), is a retelling of an Guayanese Amerindian legend. In it the Sun, reckless and wild, is shorn of his wings by the Great Spirit and forced to keep to a fixed path in the sky. He eventually fathers twin sons by the beautiful maiden Tihona; Makunaima is wild and rebellious and often beats his gentle brother, Pia. In time the Great Spirit calls the children of the Sun to himself and poses a question to them. When they hesitate in answering, the Great Spirit then sends them to search the earth for the answer. The question posed is, "Would you like to be good men or great men?" The events of their search and its dramatic outcome makes up the remainder of this enchanting tale and is sure to generate numerous issues for discussion in any middle elementary class.

Many collections of Caribbean folk tales, legends and animal stories are available for inclusion in the elementary literature program. Two collections of legends and folk tales are *Tales of the Immortelles* (McCartney, 1989); and *Caribbean Folk Legends*, (Lewis, 1990). Animal stories and additional legends are presented in *Cric Crac* (Hallworth, 1990) and *Ears, Tails, and Common Sense* (Sherlock & Sherlock, 1988). The collection, *Anansesem,* (Pollard, 1985), treats us to a smorgasbord of West Indian poems, tales, legends and animal stories.

Tales of the Immortelles is a potpourri of West Indian and Amerindian tales. In the story "The Caribs and the Birds," we are told the Amerindian legend of how Trinidad's famous pitch lake was formed. In "The Witch of Kaiteur Falls" we are treated to a tale that explains the origin of Guyana's Kaiteur Falls. "The Legend of the Waterlilly" introduces up to Papa Bois, the guardian of the forests and its creatures, who appears in many of the region's legends. All in all, *Tales of the Immortelles* will expose children in the middle elementary grades to seven new, exciting, and entertaining tales.

Theresa Lewis's *Caribbean Folk Legends* (1990) take us into the eerie world of the Caribbean's supernatural where ghouls, ghosts, and specters flit through the mango trees on their way to haunt anyone bold enough to be out on moonless Caribbean nights. The denizens of these tales of the netherworld originate both in Africa and in Europe. The ancient African gods, Shango and Ogun, meet and mix with European vampires and werewolves, "thus creating a melange or, colloquially, a *Callaloo,* of rich mythical literature" (Lewis, 1990, p. 6).

The tales in this volume are all Trinidadian versions of familiar West Indian legends. The mythological figures in them can be found in many of the islands although by different names. In Trinidad and in other islands where French patois was spoken; the ghouls, spooks, and spirits retain their French names, in other islands English names are used. Nevertheless, even though the readers may not be able to recognize the names, they will no doubt recognize the characters, and to help us, Lewis also supplies us with a glossary of what may be, for some, unfamiliar West Indian names and terms such as: *cocoyea* (broom), *simidimi* (any type of ill defined ritual) and *cocorico* (a species of tropical bird). In America, we find the werewolves, vampires, and ghosts; we find their equivalent in the Caribbean, La Gahoo, Soucouya, and Jumbie.

The work, written for a West Indian audience, celebrates the African roots of the majority of the people of the Caribbean. In "The Seers," Mama Rose, one of the characters is described as "proud of her African ancestry — a descendant of the Ashantis' she proudly stated. This, no doubt, accounted for her regal bearing. Her son, Philip, whom everyone called Boyo, was a mixture of her own Ashanti and Zulu" (p. 8). Although Lewis emphasizes the African roots of her characters, she does not neglect the racial and ethnic mixtures which abound in the West Indies. This is clearly illustrated in the following passage:

> You were either Spanish or French; Mulatto or Bacchra — white-skinned Negro or indeterminate strains. You were Cheenwa — a dash or more of Chinese, or a Coolie — of East Indian descent. You were either a 'brown-skin' or light skinned, or 'very dark'. You were white or, if uncertainly so, you were Bacchra. (p. 17)

All the tales off the supernatural in this volume are sure to give the readers in the upper elementary grades many delightfully delicious scares with a Reggae beat.

Many of the children's stories told in the United States begin with "once upon a time," however, in the Caribbean the traditional story teller announces the beginning of a story with the words "cric crak." *Cric Crac* (Hallworth, 1990) is also the name of a collection of West Indian stories written by Trinidad-born author, Grace Hallworth. This collection of eight stories includes, naturally, several familiar Anansi stories, "The Magic Pot," "How Tocooma Found Trouble," and "How the Stars Came into the Sky." In this collection, Anancy is depicted both as a spider and as a man. When depicted as a man, Anancy is drawn as a Rastafarian. Rastafarians are members of a West Indian religious group who believe in the divinity of the late Ethiopian emperor, Haile Selassie. The Rastafarians reject Western values, seek a return to Africa and champion the cause of black nationalism. Perhaps the most well-known of the Rastafarians is the late Reggae music artist, Bob Marley. By depicting Anancy as a Rastafarian, the author gives recognition to this belief while celebrating the uniqueness of this distinctly West Indian life style and reaffirms the cultural independence of the Caribbean.

The collection also contains two stories from South America. The first story "Rabbit and Tiger," comes from the Amerindians of Guyana. In this tale, Konehu, the rabbit, tricks Tiger into believing that the sun's reflection in a pool is a golden ball. The second story, "The Greedy Brother," is also from Guyana and tells how the moon got into the sky. The stories should be of interest to children in all the elementary grades. Each of the stories has some moral to give such as: When you know trouble is coming, don't stay around to meet it; don't be greedy and selfish; through cunning and intelligence, the small and weak can overcome the large and strong; and pride goes before the fall. The judicious sprinkling of West Indian dialect throughout the text and a series of masterfully executed full-color illustrations transport the elementary student into the heart of Caribbean children's literature. The reading level should be appropriate for children in the middle elementary grades.

Veteran children's authors Philip and Hilary Sherlock bring us ten animal stories in their work, *Ears, Tails, and Common Sense* (Sherlock & Sherlock, 1988). The stories are told at a six-day party given by the animals who are celebrating the first anniversary of their deliverance from a drought. The right to tell a story must be earned by correctly answering a riddle. The first riddle, "Riddle me riddle, riddle me ree / Guess me this riddle and perhaps not. Two brothers are running a race. Not one can catch the other," is answered correctly by the Capucine monkey. Other riddles are given and answered and the order for the story telling is set. The animals tell their stories, and Tiger gets duped by the rabbit. We also learn how the animals got their ears, tails, and common sense. Naturally, Anansi is up to his tricks and the animals find out that "you have to watch Anansi all the time" (p. 120).

The final work reviewed is *Anansesem: A Collection of Caribbean Folk Tales, Legends, and Poems for Juniors* (1985) edited by Velma Pollard. The authors of the stories in this work come from Jamaica and Trinidad, from Guyana, Curacao, Barbados, the Bahamas, Belize, Monserrat, and St. Lucia. Their stories are familiar ones that are told, in one form or another, to children all over the Caribbean and many will appear in other collections of Caribbean children's stories. The poems presented are full of rhyme, rhythm, and humor and many easily lend themselves to some form of group recitation. Many of the tales that average three pages, are suitable for dramatic presentation. The material in this book will bring true pleasure to children in all of the elementary grades; the students in the middle and upper elementary grades will be able to read it to those in the lower grades. The book is illustrated with photographs and black and white drawings. Unfamiliar terms are included in a glossary.

Realistic Fiction

In addition to the traditional Anansi stories, folk tales, legends, and animal stories, there is a growing body of realistic fiction being written for students in the middle and upper elementary grades. For readers in the middle elementary grades there is *Business at Boon Farm* (Gilroy, 1983), *Chris and Fred* (Waterman, 1983), and *Manie the Manicou Goes Traveling* (Dyer, 1975).

Business at Boon Farm (Gilroy, 1983) contains two stories both set in rural West Indian villages. In the title story, strangers come to the village and begin renovations at the rundown Boon Farm. As their work progresses, an air of mystery begins to surround the farm and its new owners. The village children start to observe what they consider to be strange goings on. They attribute these strange happenings to the newcomers and their imagined helpers, a host of malevolent creatures known in the Caribbean as Duppies. Frightened and at a loss as to what to do, the children turn to the village elder and are able to convince him to investigate the strange business at Boon Farm. In the second story, "The Luck of the Village," the runt of the litter of pigs is adopted by the children and raised as a pet. The trouble starts when the father decides to sell the pig. The children once again turn to the village elder for advice and guidance.

The Caribbean's diversity of culture, color, ethnicity, and religion is presented in both of these superb stories as a natural part of the Caribbean milieu. In one scene Mr. Rufus, the father, tells his daughter, Rita, that "a pig is a useful animal; its bristles make good brushes. The bones make good glue. The flesh makes bacon and pork. The insides make tripe and black pudding. Everybody likes bacon." Rita responds, "The Muslims don't; they say pigs are unclean" (p. 22). Nothing else is said about the matter; the story moves right along. However, religious differences are acknowledged, respected, and communicated to the young readers. In a similar manner, lessons in mutual respect, toleration and cooperation are subtly and skillfully interwoven throughout the text.

For the older, more accomplished elementary school reader there is *Backfire* (1988) edited by two long-established West Indian writers, Neville and Undine Giuseppi. This collection of 17 short stories by both new and well-known Caribbean writers is used extensively throughout the West Indies and is one that definitely should be included in any program touching on West Indian children's literature. The stories focus on a variety of West Indian themes and reflect the diversity found in Caribbean life and culture. Included are stories about Chinese shopkeepers, East Indian farmers, and young Trinidadian boys flying kites.

The story, "Paradise Lost," vividly depicts the yearnings that contribute to so many young West Indians migrating to Canada and the U.S.A. in search of a what they believe will be a better life; it also shows the rude awakening experienced by so many of these migrants once they arrive. "The New Teacher," a story written by an 18-year-old Trinidadian of East Indian descent, is focused on the question of dialect. In it the main character, a Trinidadian secondary school student, was "forced to wonder which posed the greater problem — translating 'English-as-written' into the 'mudder-tongue' for the purposes of speech or translating the 'mudder-tongue' into 'English-as-written for exams" (p. 77). However, the question of the use of the vernacular was, for the new teacher, no problem at all. He had concluded that "fuh in English we hah to convey ideas to each odder. An' we mus' convey dem in we mudder-tongue. Leave de fancy style fuh writin'. In any case, yuh won't hah much uses fuh dat wen yuh leave school, cause is here in yuh own country we wants yuh to stay." The issues raised by "The New Teacher" have relevance and immediacy for teachers in many ethnic American communities where non-standard varieties of English are spoken. Each of the stories in this collection are followed by comprehension questions, vocabulary exercises, as well as questions for discussion and suggestions for writing.

Climbing Clouds: Stories and Poems from the Bahamas (1988), edited by noted Caribbean poet and author of numerous works for children, Telcine Turner, is another collection of stories and poems that the upper elementary grade student will be sure to benefit from and enjoy. Since many of the stories in this collection were originally intended for radio presentation, they are ideal for readers' theater type activities. Written mainly by students at the College of the Bahamas, these stories cover a number of genres and are sure to engage the interest of the upper elementary student. In addition to suggested activities, each story has accompanying comprehension and vocabulary exercises.

The works of C. Evrard Palmer are sure to appeal to upper elementary and junior high school readers. Palmer, who has been publishing books for upper elementary students for almost 30 years, presently has nine books in print including *My Father, Sun-Sun Johnson* (1984) and *The Sun Salutes*

You (1984). Set in small Caribbean villages, these short novels both have themes of maturation from youth to adulthood, cooperation, conflict between traditional and modern values, and the little man's struggle against social and economic injustice.

Palmer sensitively and delicately touches on such realistic subject matter as separation and divorce, splitting up of the children, custody battles, courtship and remarriage of parents, the ups and downs of business, boy-girl relationships, and social class conflict. In *My Father, Sun-Sun Johnson,* one of the problems the main character Rami, a 16-year-old boy, has to work through while trying to assume the new role of an adult is his parents' divorce. He wonders "What was happening? I couldn't get much out of it at all. I didn't mind Miss Hilcher having come to see Father, so why did I hate Jake's being at Ma's house? I guess it was different. I guess for men everything was different" (p. 36). Rami's father experiences a series financial setbacks at the hands of an unscrupulous business rival. Rami is forced to choose between the human values of his father and the position and wealth of his father's rival. Rami decides on human values and concludes that "Father has the values. And by Jingo I'd help him to have the others back, the money and the position, if he wanted it" (p. 77). In spite of the problems encountered by his youthful characters, there is a clear sense of gaiety and joy in Palmer's work; conflicts are resolved, truth and justice triumph, and the child matures into the strong, upright young adult despite all of the vicissitudes of life.

Illustrated Books for Early Primary Grades

Of the many illustrated children's books with Caribbean themes and settings, we found six that were especially excellent: *Caribbean Canvas* (1987), *My Little Island* (1984), and *Caribbean Alphabet* (1989), all by American-born writer/artist Frane Lessac; *Calypso Alphabet* (1989) by John Agard, a Guayanese now living in England; *Coconut Kind of Day* (1990) by Trinidadian, Lynn Joseph; and *Rain Falling Sun Shining,* (1975) by Trinidad-born author Odette Thomas.

In Lessac's *Caribbean Canvas,* vivid paintings grace and enliven every page. Limbo dancers going under flaming bars, West Indian village cottages, coral colored churches, vegetable markets and ladies selling sheep, school boys and policemen, barber shops and government houses quickly place the reader in the center of the variegated Caribbean scene. Scenes of island life in Barbados, Antigua, St. Kitts-Nevis, Grenada and Monserrat make this work a genuine Caribbean canvas. Each painting is coupled with a short poem or West Indian proverb forming matched pairs that not only delight the eyes and ears, but also bring the readers, both young and old, additional glimpses of island life and culture. Teachers using this book may need to read the proverbs and poems to some children. Even though some of the poetry used is written in the West Indian dialect, it's all very understandable and the dialect only adds a bit of a calypso beat to the rhyme and rhythm of the poems and proverbs.

In *My Little Island,* written and also colorfully illustrated by Lessac, a child returns with a friend to visit the island of her birth. The children's trip through the island that includes a trip to town, a visit to her auntie's house in the country for lunch, a stop at the market and the seashore, and her former school, will help American primary schoolers get a hint of island life. *My Little Island* is sure to create many teachable moments as the children encounter such things as guava, soursop, pawpaw, and pepper sauce.

The two alphabet books, Lessac's *Caribbean Alphabet* and Agard's *Calypso Alphabet,* are worthwhile additions to any collection of books for the early elementary student. In addition to serving as marvelous resources to reenforce learning the sounds of the letters, these two books introduce the children a multitude of things West Indian. Each letter of the alphabet has its own brightly colored page and each is illustrated by paintings of things West Indian. Each letter in *Caribbean Alphabet* has its own brief vignette. This one followed the letter "P": "A **pretty parrot** is **perched** on a **pirate's** shoulder. A **peckish pelican parades past** the **palm trees. Delicious fruits like pineapples** and **pawpaws** are plentiful here. This must be **paradise**." Agard, true to his West Indian roots, begins his *Calypso Alphabet* with "A is for Anancy Spiderman of tricky-tricky fame" and then proceeds to immerse us in things Caribbean: Amerindians, Caribs, cricket, and curry, flying fish, iguanas, and roti.

Lynn Joseph says that she wants "to give boys and girls who aren't familiar with the Caribbean a glimpse into another child's world." This she does in splendid fashion in *Coconut Kind of Day: Island Poems.* Vibrant images and melodious poetry take us vicariously through the day of a young school girl in Trinidad. The day begins with "Coc-a-toodle-too from the galvanized gate. / Whoo-too-too, from the sea. / 'G'mornin Miz Rosie,' from the ebony man / selling mangoes and pawpaws / in the street." Through the day we accompany our young guide to the sea, the market, school, and a cricket game. We buy coconuts in the savannah with her daddy, and hear the steel pans play; we met the Jumbi-man and finally end our day with sounds of the Caribbean night.

Summary

West Indian children's literature is represented by a wide range of genres: legends, folk tales, fairy tales, animal stories, illustrated children's books, poetry, historical, and realistic fiction. The literature, in varying degrees, reflects the struggle of the region's people to define and develop for themselves their culture and language now freed from the restraints imposed by colonialism. The region's struggle for political maturity is also reflected in the struggles of many of the adolescent characters in the realistic fiction written for the children of the Caribbean. A growing sense of regionalism and Caribbean unity has fueled the demand for children's books by and about West Indians. Many such works are being published by Macmillan Caribbean, Longman's Jamaica, and Heinmann Jamaica.

STRATEGIES FOR PRESENTATION

A Supplement for Units in Social Studies & History

All the materials described can be used to supplement units in Social Studies/History, especially those dealing with Central and South America. With the 500th anniversary of the arrival of Columbus in the Islands at hand, it is an opportune time to explore, from a West Indian literary perspective, the lands that he found. Perhaps some historical works written by West Indian authors for West Indian children would be appropriate at this juncture. Several historical works published by Handprint Publications would both supplement units on European exploration of the West Indies, and also provide a West Indian perspective on these events.

Handprint's *The Arawaks of Jamaica* (1990), although historical in content, is written in a clear straightforward style and will be as appealing to the elementary and junior high school student as any good work of fiction. It is an excellent source for any unit on European exploration in the New World. In broad strokes it gives the history of Jamaica's discovery, the origin, culture, and life style of the Arawaks, the island's original people, and their fate at the hands of the Spaniards. The book is written from a totally West Indian perspective and will give American students a clear idea of history as seen through the eyes of other than Americans and Europeans.

Nanny of the Maroons (1990) is another historical work in the Handprint series. Like *The Arawaks of Jamaica*, it is exciting history written in an uncomplicated, swiftly moving style that not only will hold the attention of young readers, but will also expose them a good bit of Caribbean history. The Maroons were those Africans who escaped from their captors and established separate territories in the island of Jamaica. This short history of the Maroons tells of their fight for freedom against the British, and the circumstances leading up to the treaty of peace signed in 1739. One leader of the Maroons was the woman, Nanny, who led over 800 free Africans in Jamaica for close to 50 years. In 1975 Nanny became Jamaica's first National Heroine. Any multicultural study of the history of the Americas must include Nanny among those who, like George Washington, loved freedom enough to shed their blood in its defense. Nanny's is a classic story of humanity's continuing struggle for freedom and should be an inspiration to all Americans.

A Means to Explore Attitudes Concerning Language and Cultural Diversity

The West Indian literature presented in this chapter can form the basis for examining a number of attitudes: attitudes toward varieties of English different from the one we speak, and attitudes about people who have a different history, customs, and cultures. In many places Caribbean literature provides the teacher with excellent opportunities to explore themes of cooperative effort and tolerance for differences in ethnicity, religion, family structure, color and language variety. One such instance is demonstrated in Lessac's book *Caribbean Canvas* by Susan Wallace's poem "Ilan Life"

> Ilan life ain' no fun less ya treat errybody
>
> Like ya brudda, ya sister, or ya frien'
>
> Love ya neighbour, play ya part, jes remember das de art
>
> For when ocean fence ya in, all is kin (p. 10).

Examples of West Indian dialect, either on the audio tapes or in the literature reviewed in this chapter can be used in the class as focal point to discuss dialect differences. This can be the springboard to explore the judgements we make about people based on the dialect that they speak and how our reactions to people can be affected by our attitudes toward their dialects. For instance, we could use the audio tape accompanying the book *The People Could Fly* (Hamilton, 1985) or some other with stories told in the Black Southern vernacular and compare the dialects of the West Indies to the regional and ethnic dialects of America. A useful resource teachers can use is *Ways With Words* by Shirley Brice-Heath.

A Means to Explore the Similarities in the Responses of African People to their Experiences in the Western World

Many literary similarities can easily be found between the West Indian folk tales and tales told by African Americans. We can help the children search for the common African link between, for example, the Anansi stories and the African-American tales of Brer Rabbit. We can use Caribbean literature as a means to explore the ways in which the Africans held captive in the United States and the Africans help captive in the Caribbean might have had similar responses to their captivity. Both groups had continuing rebellions. Perhaps various slave narrative such as *Incidents in the Life of a Slave Girl* (Brent, 1973) and *Great Slave Narratives* (Bontemps, 1969) could be explored at this point.

CONCLUSION

West Indian literature presents a wealth of material for American children of all ages. Books by Caribbean authors about Caribbean themes range in reading and interest level from picture books for preschool children to short stories and novels for junior high school learners. These works will not only provide valuable literary experiences for American youngsters, but will also expand their cultural literacy and make it easier for them to live in an increasingly multicultural society. West Indian literature used skillfully and creativity in the Social Studies can also help more American children to see the similarities in the human response to inhuman conditions. Hopefully, this can help all of us to find ways in which we, as human beings can remove such conditions for all and perhaps our collective struggle to do so will make better humans of us all.

LIST OF RECOMMENDED BOOKS

Oral Literature

Keens-Douglas, P. (1989). *Twice upon a time.* Port of Spain, Trinidad: Keensdee Productions. (UE, JH)·

Keens-Douglas, P. (Speaker). (1982). *Is town say so* [Cassette Recording]. Bridgetown, Barbados: Audio Magnetics.

Tanna, L. (1984). *Jamaica folk tales and oral histories.* Kingston, Jamaica: Institute of Jamaica Publications.

Tanna, L. (1984). *Jamaica folk tales and oral histories.* [Cassette Recording]. Kingston, Jamaica: Institute of Jamaica Publications.

Anansi Stories

McDermott, G. *Anansi the spider: A tale from the Ashanti.* New York: Henry Holt. (IC, EE)

Rhomer, H. (1989). *Brother Anansi and the cattle ranch: El hermano Anansi y el rancho de ganado.* San Francisco, CA: Children's Book Press. (IC, EE, ME)

Sherlock, P. (1954). *Anansi the spider man: Jamaican folk tales.* New York: Thomas Y. Crowell. (ME, UE)

Folk Tales, Legends and Animal Stories

Carew, J. (1980). *Children of the sun.* Boston, MA: Little, Brown. (IC, EE, ME, UE)

Hallworth, G. (1990). *Cric Crac: A collection of West Indian stories.* Kingston, Jamaica: Heinmann Caribbean. (IC, ME)

Joseph, L. (1990). *A wave in her pocket.*

Lewis, T. (1990). *Caribbean folk legends.* Trenton, NJ: Africa World Press. (UE, JH)

McCartney, N. (1989). *Tales of the immortelles: A collection of Caribbean fairy tales.* London: Macmillan Caribbean. (UE, JH)

Pollard, V. (Ed.) (1985). *Anansesem: A collection of Caribbean folk tales, legend, and poems for juniors.* Kingston, Jamaica: Longmans Jamaica. (ME, UE)

Sherlock, P. & Sherlock, H. (1988). *Ears, tails, and common sense.* London: Macmillan Caribbean. (ME)

Realistic Fiction

Dyer, P. (1975). *Manie the manicou goes traveling.* London: Macmillan Caribbean. (ME, UE)

Gilroy, B. (1983). *Business at Boon farm.* London: Macmillan Caribbean. (ME, UE)

Giuseppi, N. & Giuseppi, U. (1988). *Backfire: A collection of Caribbean short stories.* London: Macmillan Caribbean. (UE, JH)

Palmer, C. E. (1984). *My father, Sun-Sun Johnson.* London: Macmillan Caribbean. (UE, JH)

Palmer, C. E. (1984). *The sun salutes you.* London: Macmillan Caribbean. (UE, JH)

Turner, T. (1988). *Climbing clouds: Stories and poems from the Bahamas.* London: Macmillan Caribbean. (UE, JH)

Historical Works

Bontemps, A. (1969). *Great slave narratives*. Boston: Beacon Press. (UE, JH)

Brent, L. (1973). *Incidents in the life of a slave girl*. New York: Harcourt Brace Jovanovich. (UE, JH)

Phillpotts, K. (1990). *The Arawaks of Jamaica*. Birmingham, England: Handprint Publications. (ME, UE, JH)

Phillpotts, K. (1990). *Nanny of the Maroons*. Birmingham, England: Handprint Publications. (ME, UE, JH)

Illustrated Books for the Early Primary Grades

Agard, J. (1989). *Calypso alphabet*. New York: Henry Holt.

Joseph, L. (1990). *Coconut kind of day: Island poems*. New York: Lothrop, Lee and Shepard.

Lessac, F. (1984). *My little island*. New York: Lippencott.

Lessac, F. (1987). *Caribbean canvas*. London: Macmillan Caribbean.

Lessac, F. (1989). *Caribbean alphabet*. London: Macmillan Caribbean.

Thomas, O. (1975). *Rain falling, sun shining*. London: Bogle-L'Overture.

Key

IC-illustrated children's book
UE-upper elementary
EE-early elementary
ME-middle elementary
JH-junior high school

REFERENCES

Allis, J. (1981). *West Indian literature: An index of criticism 1930-1975*. Boston, MA: G.K. Hall & Co.

Arnold, A. (1981). *Modernism and Negritude: The poetry and poetics of Aime Cesaire*. Cambridge, MA: Harvard University Press.

Birbalsing, F. (1988). Jan Carew *Interview*. *Journal of Caribbean Studies, 6,* 117-141.

Bouvier, L., & Simcox, D. (1986). *Many hands, few jobs: Population, unemployment and emigration in Mexico and the Caribbean*. Wash., DC: Center for Immigration Studies. (ERIC DRS No. ED300 308).

Brathwaite, E. (1985). World order models — a Caribbean perspective. *Caribbean Quarterly, 31,* 53-64.

Brathwaite, E. (1984). *History of the voice: The development of national language in anglophone Caribbean poetry.* London: New Beacon Books.

Brathwaite, E. (1976). The love axe: Developing a Caribbean aesthetic, 1962-1974. In Houston A. Baker (Ed.) *Reading Black: Essays in the criticism of African, Caribbean and black American literature.* pp. 20-36.

Carew, J. (1978). The fusion of African and Amerindian folk myths. *Bim, 16,* 241-257.

Carty, D. (1978). *Selected West Indian novels: Thematic and stylistic trends from the nineteen-fifties to the early nineteen-seventies. Ph.D.* Dissertation, University of Michigan.

Cobb, M. (1979). *Harlem, Haiti and Havana: A comparative critical study of Langston Huges, Jacques Roumain, Nicholas Guillen.* Wash., DC: Three Continents Press.

Coulthard, G. R. (1962). *Race and color in Caribbean literature.* London: Oxford University Press.

Cudjoe, S. (1980). *Resistance and Caribbean literature.* Athens, OH: Ohio University Press.

Dash, M. (1974). Towards a West Indian literary aesthetic — The example of Aime Cesaire. *Black Images, 3,* 21-28.

Dathorne, O. R. (1981). *Dark ancestor: The literature of the black man in the Caribbean.* Baton Rouge, LA: Louisiana State University Press.

Dathorne, O. R. (1984). Toward synthesis in the New World: Caribbean literature in English. In William Luis (Ed.) *Voices from under: Black narratives in Latin American and the Caribbean.* Westport, CT: Greenwood Press. pp. 101-112.

Dawes, N. (1977). *Prolegomena to Caribbean literature.* Kingston, Jamaica: Institute of Jamaica for the African-Caribbean Institute.

Decraene, P. (1983). Aime Cesaire: Black rebel. *Callaloo, 6,* 63-69.

DuBois, W. E. B. (1990). *The soul of black folks.* New York: First Vintage Books.

Franklin, J. (1989). *Race and history: Selected essays 1938-1988.* Baton Rouge, LA: Louisiana State University Press.

Ismond, P. (1987). West Indian literature as an expression of national cultures: The literature of St. Lucia. *New West Indian Guide, 61,* 23-37.

Jacques-Garvey, A. (Ed.). (1982). *Philosophy and opinions of Marcus Garvey.* New York: Atheneum.

London, C. (1988). Educational theorizing in an emancipatory context: A case for a Caribbean curriculum. *Journal of Caribbean Studies, 6,* 163-177.

Luis, W. (1984). History and fiction: Black narratives in Latin America and the Caribbean. In William Luis (Ed.) *Voices from under: Black narrative in Latin America and the Caribbean.* Westport, CT: Greenwood Press. pp. 3-32.

Nettleford, R. (1989). The Caribbean: The cultural imperative. *Caribbean Quarterly, 35,* 4-13.

Nettleford, R. (1990). Communication with ourselves: the Caribbean artist and the society. *Caribbean Affairs, 3,* 30-38.

Rawlings, R. (1958). Migrants with manuscripts. *Black Orpheus, 4,* 46-50.

Saakana, A. (1987). *The colonial legacy in Caribbean literature.* Trenton, NJ: Africa World Press.

Safa, H. (1987). Popular culture, national identity, and race in the Caribbean. *New West Indian Guide, 61,* 115-126.

Wamer-Lewis, M. (1987). Jan Carew interviewed by Maureene Wamer-Lewis Prague, 1984. *Journal of West Indian Literature, 2,* 37-40.

Wright, R. (1937). Introduction: Blueprint for Negro writing. In Addison Gayle, Jr. (Ed.) *The black aesthetic.* New York: Doubleday.

Sources for Multicultural Children's Literature

Violet J. Harris

$\mathbf{P}$arents, teachers, and librarians want information about multicultural literature. Many are not familiar with the journals devoted to children's literature that periodically include multicultural children's literature, the organizations that promote it, or the bookstores that sell it. This chapter tries to fill that void. The listings contain various sources that parents, teachers, and librarians can consult. The information is divided into five sections: small or independent presses, large presses, organizations, journals, and a small sampling of bookstores.

The small presses are crucial to the existence of multicultural literature. These publishers are willing to take changes with first-time authors. Often, they publish books that portend new trends. They deserve a much broader readership, and are worth seeking out.

SMALL PRESSES

All information is accurate at the time the book went to press.

Africa World Press
PO Box 120470
East Haven, CT 06512
800-253-3605

Arte Público
University of Houston
4800 Calhoun
Houston, TX 77204
713-749-4768

Black Classic Press
PO Box 13414
Baltimore, MD 21203
301-486-5917

Children's Book Press
6400 Hollis Street
Suite 4
Emeryville, CA 94608
415-655-3955

Children's Press
5440 North Cumberland Ave.
Chicago, IL 60656

Greenfield Review Literary Center,
2 Middle Grove Rd.
PO Box 308
Greenfield Center, NY 12833
518-584-1728

Ward-Hill Press
PO Box 04-0424
Staten Island, NY 10304
718-816-9449

Just Us Books
301 Main Street
Suite 22-24
Orange, NJ 07050
800-762-7701

One World-Ballantine
400 Hahn Road
Westminster, MD 21157
800-733-3000

Open Hand Publishing, Inc.
PO Box 22048
Seattle, WA 98122

Pathfinder Press
410 West St.
New York, NY 10014
212-741-0609

Red Sea Press
15 Industry Ct.
Trenton, NJ 08638
609-771-1666

Third World Press
7524 S. Cottage Grove
Box 730
Chicago, IL 60619
312-651-0700

William Ruth Company
2404 Owens Road
Oxon Hill, MD 20745

Winston-Derek Publishers, Inc.
PO Box 90883
Nashville, TN 37209
800-826-1888

LARGE PRESSES

Large presses have the advantages of experienced staffs, advertising budgets, established relationships with distributors and bookstores, and rosters of major authors. Most have some writers of color; a few have strong lists such as Bantam Doubleday Dell, Harcourt Brace Jovanovich, Harper Collins, Macmillan, Scholastic, and Franklin Watts. However all can devote more resources to the identification and publication of their writers of color.

Arcade (See Little, Brown)
800-343-9204

Atheneum (See Macmillan)

Bantam Doubleday Dell
666 Fifth Avenue,
New York, NY 10103
800-223-6834

Bradbury (See Macmillan)

Carolrhoda Books, Inc.
241 First Ave. North
Minneapolis, MN 55401
800-328-4929

Chelsea House
95 Madison Ave.
New York, NY 10016
800-848-2665

Clarion (See Houghton Mifflin)
Cobblehill (See Penguin USA)
Coward-McCann & Geoghegan
  (See Putnam)
Crestwood House (See Macmillan)
Crowell (See HarperCollins)
Crown (See Random House)
Delacorte (See Bantam Doubleday
  Dell)
Dian Books (See Penguin USA)
Doubleday (See Bantam Doubleday
  Dell)
Dutton (See Penguin USA)

Farrar, Straus & Giroux
Sales Department
19 Union Square West
New York, NY 10003
800-631-8571

Four Winds (See Macmillan)
Greenwillow (See William Morrow)
Grosset & Dunlap (See Putnam)

Gulliver (See Harcourt Brace
  Jovanovich)

Trade Order Entry
465 South Lincoln Dr.
Troy, MO 63379
314-528-8110

Harmony (See Crown)
Harper & Row (See HarperCollins)

HarperCollins Children's Books
HarperCollins, Pub.
Keystone Industrial Park
Scranton, PA 18512
800-242-7737

Holiday House
425 Madison Ave.
New York, NY 10017
212-688-0085 (not toll free)

Henry Holt
115 W. 18th St.
New York, NY 10011
800-488-5233

Houghton Mifflin
Trade Order Dept.
Wayside Road
Burlington, MA 01803
800-225-3362

Johnson Publishing Co., Inc.
820 South Michigan Ave.
Chicago, IL 60605
312-322-9248

Joy Street (See Little, Brown)
Knopf (See Random House)

Lerner Publications
241 First Avenue North
Minneapolis, MN 55401
800-328-4929

Lippincott (See HarperCollins)

Little, Brown and Co.
200 West Street
Waltham, MA 02254
800-343-9204

Lodestar (See Penguin USA)

Lothrop, Lee & Shepard (See William Morrow

Macmillan Children's Books
Order Dept.
Macmillan Pub. Co.
Front and Brown Streets
Riverside, NJ 08075
800-257-5755

McElderry Books (See Macmillan)
Julian Messner (See Silver Burdett)

William Morrow & Co.
Wilmor/Order Department
39 Plymouth Street
Box 1219
Fairfield, NJ 07007
800-237-0657; 201-227-7200

Mulberry (See William Morrow)
Orchard Books: (See Franklin Watts)
Pantheon (See Random House)

Penguin USA
Order Dept. - Box 120
Bergenfield, NJ 07621-0120
800-526-0275

Philomel (See Putnam)
Platt & Munk (See Putnam)
Potter (See Random House)

Putnam Publishing Group
200 Madison Ave.
New York, NY 10016
800-631-8571

R & S Books (See Farrar, Straus & Giroux)

Random House, Inc.
400 Hahn Road
Westminster, MD 21157
800-726-0600

Reader's Digest (See Random House)

Scholastic, Inc.
2931 East McCarty St.
Jefferson, MO 65102
800-325-6149

Scribners (See Macmillan)

Sierra Club (See Little, Brown)

Silver Burdett Press
Box 1226
Westwood, NJ 07675
800-843-3464

Simon & Schuster Trade
7230 Ave. at Americas
New York, NY 10020
212-698-7000

Times Books (See Random House)

Viking (See Penguin USA)

Frederick Warne (See Penguin USA)

Franklin Watts
387 Park Ave. S.
4th floor
New York, NY 10016
800-672-6672

Albert Whitman & Co.
6340 Oakton St.
Morton Grove, IL 60053
800-255-7675

ORGANIZATIONS

Pioneer organizations such as the Association for the Study of Afro-American Life and History and the Council on Interracial Books for Children were often lone voices that strongly advocated diversity in children's literature and other educational materials. Because of their tenacity, multiculturalism never died. Other organizations emerged to help shoulder the work.

American Black Book Writers Assoc. Inc.
4109 Via Marina
PO Box 10548
Marina del Rey, CA 90291

American Booksellers Association
137 W. 25th St.
New York, NY 10001
800-637-0037

American Library Association
50 E. Huron St.
Chicago, IL 60611
312-944-6780

Association of Caribbean Studies
PO Box 22202
Lexington, KY 40522

Association for the Study of Afro-American Life and History
1407 14th St. NW
Washington, DC 20005
202-667-2822

The Children's Book Council
568 Broadway
New York, NY 10012
212-966-1990

Children's Literature Association
22 Harvest Lane
Battlecreek, MI 49015
616-965-8180

Cooperative Children's Book Center
4290 Helen C. White Hall
University of Wisconsin-Madison
600 N. Park St.
Madison, WI 53706
608-263-3720

Council on Interracial Books for Children
1841 Broadway
New York, NY 10023

International Reading Association
PO Box 8139
800 Barksdale Rd.
Newark, DE 19714-8139
301-731-1600

National Association for Asian and Pacific American Education
c/o ARC Associates
310 8th St. Suite 220
Oakland, CA 94607

National Association for the Education of Young Children
1834 Connecticut Ave. NW
Washington, DC 20009

National Association of Hispanic Publications
PO Box 2285
Orlando, FL 32802
407-425-9911

National Council for Black Studies
Ohio State University
115-A Independence Hall
1923 Neil Ave. Mall
Columbus, OH 43210

National Council of Teachers of English
1111 Kenyon Road
Urbana, IL 61801
800-369-6283

Oyate (Native American)
2702 Mathews Street
Berkeley, CA 94702
510-848-6700

Society of Children's Book Writers
PO Box 296
Mar Vista Station
Los Angeles, CA 90066

United States Board on Books for Young People
c/o International Reading Assoc.
800 Barksdale Rd.
PO Box 8139
Newark, DE 19714

JOURNALS

Currently, no journal devoted exclusively to multicultural children's literature exists. Journals concentrating on early childhood education, literacy, book reviewing, and so forth, occasionally feature articles and annotated bibliographies about multicultural children's literature. The following will prove helpful.

ABBWA Journal
American Quarterly
Black American Literature Forum
Book Links
Booklist
CBC Features
Children's Folklore Newsletter
Children's Literature Association Quarterly

Children's Literature in Education
Five Owls
Horn Book Magazine
Langston Hughes Review
Language Arts
Lion and the Unicorn
New Advocate
Publisher's Research Quarterly
Publishers Weekly

Reading Teacher
Research in the Teaching of English
School Library Journal
Top of the News

The Web
Wilson Library Bulletin
VOYA
Young Children

BOOKSTORES

The limited sampling profiles a few activist bookstores whose owners are knowledgeable about children's literature and who exhibit a certain missionary zeal. Consult the organizations listed in the previous section for others, or visit your local library to review a listing of bookstores, or contact your local chamber of commerce.

African-American Book Center
7524 S. Cottage Grove
Chicago, IL 60619
312-651-0700

Black Books Plus, Inc.
702 Amsterdam Ave.
New York, NY 10025
212-749-9623

Global Village
2210 Wilshire Blvd.
Box 262
Santa Monica, CA 90403
800-955-GLOBAL

Hue-Man Experience Bookstore
911 23rd St.
Denver, CO 80205
303-293-2665

Liberation Bookstore Inc.
421 Lenox Ave at 131st St.
New York, NY 10037
212-281-4615

Nkiru Books
68 St. Marks Ave.
Brooklyn, NY 11217
718-783-6306

Index ─────────────────────

Entries are filed word-by-word. Locators followed by *n* indicate endnotes.

Abby (Caines), 88
Abrahamson, R., 116, 133
Abuela (Dorros), 45
Acuna, R., 209, 210, 233, 238
Ada, Alma Flor, 189, 200
Adams, Janus, 69
Adams, 164 *n*.4
Adler, David, 25, 27, 29, 33
Adoff, Arnold, 74, 187, 189, 197
Adventures of Connie and Diego
    (Garcia), 223-224
African American authors
    the reinforcements, 75, 86-91
    the reinterpreters, 75, 91-95
    the vanguard, 75-86
African-American children's literature
    beginnings, 64-68
    and cultural consciousness, 69-95
    current status of, 68-75
    genres other than fiction in, 71-73
    historical information, 99
    African-American cultural traditions in,
    71
    and increased role of small presses,
    70-71
    and independent publishers, 65-66
    for intermediate grades, 97-98
    and mainstream publishers, 66-68
    for pre-school and primary ages, 96-97
    realistic content, 70-74
    recurring and new trends and themes
        in, 70-74
    recommended readings, 100-101
    strategies for classroom use, 96-99
    recurring and new trends and themes
        in, 70-74
    statistics for, 68
    strategies for classroom use, 96-99

    for upper elementary, 98-99
African-American Read-In Chain, 69
African Americans in literature
    stereotypes of, 60-64
African-American writers
    of children's literature, 57-108
    as storytellers and griots, 57-108
African Heroes and Heroines (Woodson),
    66
Afro-Bets 123 (Hudson), 72
Afro-Bets ABC (Hudson), 72
Agard, J., 257-258, 263
Aida (Price), 58-59
ALA Notable Children's Books award, 88
Algarin, M., 196 *n*.14, 200
Algonquin, 146
Alligators All Around (Sendak), 151, 152
Allis, 4
Allis, J., 263
Allis, S., 33
All-Jahdu Storybook, The (Hamilton), 72,
    97
All Night All Day (Bryan), 87
All Us Come Cross the Water (Anderson),
    77
All-White World of Children's Books, The
    (Larrick), 67
Alvarez, R., 209-210, 238
American Booksellers Association, 95
American Girls series, 73
Amifika (Anderson), 77
Amon, A., 165
Amos Fortune, Free Man (Yates), 7
Anansesem (Pollard), 252, 254-255
Anansi the Spider (McDermott), 249-250
Anansi the Spider Man (Sherlock), 248
Anaya, Rudolfo A., 213, 217, 220-221, 228,
    235, 237, 239, 240

Ancona, George, 33, 229
Anderson, J., 17-18, 33, 77, 229, 237
Animal-Indians, 164 *n.*3
Annie and the Old One (Miles), 127
Antebellum south, 7
Anthony Burns (Hamilton), 7, 72, 96, 99
Anti-Slavery Alphabet, The, 63
Apple, 31 *n.*2
Apple & Christian-Smith, 8, 31 *n.*2
Apple, M.W., 33, 36
Arawaks of Jamaica (Phillpotts), 259
Arbuthnot, M., 77, 101
Arnez, N.L., 128, 133
Arnold, A., 263
Arte Público Press, 192, 237 *n.*6
Aruego, Jose, 115-116
Ashley, L.F., 36
Asian American Children's Book Project
   Committee, 122
Asian Pacific American children's
   literature, 111-135
   another look at history, 128
   covert censorship in, 116-118
   criteria for selecting quality literature,
      122-123
   cross cultural experiences comparisons,
      127
   evolution of Asian Pacific American
      authors and illustrators, 114-155
   folktales, 125-126
   playing with language, 126
   point of view, 126-127
   rationale and goals for, 120-122
   recommended list of, 128-132
   role playing, 128
   role of educators in promoting,
      132-133
   statistics for, 113
   and stereotypes, 111-113
   and teaching ideas and strategies,
      123-128
   teaching ideas and strategies for
      folktales, 125-126
   what is being promoted in, 116-119
Associated Publishers, 65
Atariba and Niguayona (Rohmer),
   190-191
Atlantic Monthly, The, 3
Atlantic Slave Trade, 13-14
Auchincloss, K., 31 *n.*4, 33
*Aunt Flossie's Hats (And Crab Cakes
   Later)* (Howard), 45, 70, 94-95
Austin, M.C., 118, 133

Baby Says (Steptoe), 82, 84
Baby Sitter Club series, 72
Backfire (Neville), 255-256
Baker, Augusta, 67
Baldwin, James, 51
Ballad of Belle Dorcas, The (Hooks), 97
Banks, Dennis, 158
Banks, J.A., 119, 124, 133, 200
Banks, Lynne Reid, 145-146, 165 *n.*8
Bannerman, H., 62, 104
Barbour, Karen, 187
Barrera, Rosalinda 207, 209-210, 219,
   233, 239
Barrera, M., 237 *n.*4
Barrio Boy (Galarza), 235
Bartolome de Las Casas, 16
Baseball in April (Soto), 224-225, 231
Beal, G., 210-211, 239
Beat the Story Drum, Pum, Pum (Bryan),
   87
Belsey, C., 8, 33
Berelson, B., 135
Berg, Charles Ramirez, 223
Berg-Cross, 133
Berkhofer, Jr., R.F., 163, 165
Beyond the Divide (Lasky), 7
Bielke, P.F., 196 *n.*7, 200
Bigelow, 7, 13-15, 18- 20, 31 *n.*3, 33
Big Friend, Little Friend (Greenfield), 72
Big Thunder Magic (Strete), 152
Birbalsing, F., 263
Birthday Basket for Tia (Mora), 227
Bishop, 70
Bishop, C.H., 113, 116, 133
Bishop, Rudine Sims, 37-53, 39-53, 101
Bjorkman, Steve, 19, 35
Black Butterfly Children's Books, 79
Black History Month, 100
Black Star, Bright Dawn (O'Dell),
   147-148
Black Vernacular English, 77-78, 83
*Bleeding Man and Other Science Fiction
   Stories* (Strete), 149
Bless Me Ultima (Anaya), 220, 235
Bloomsbury Review, The, 226
Boat Ride with Lillian Two Blossom
   (Polacco), 151
Bone Wars, The (Lasky), 7
Bonfante, J., 4, 33
Bontemps, Arna, 61, 66, 104, 261, 263
Booth, C., 4, 33
Borders (Mora), 223, 235
Boston Globe-Horn Book Award

Bouvier, L., 263
Boyd, Candy Dawson, 86, 96, 98, 104
Boy's Life Magazine, 84
Boy Who Didn't Believe in Spring, The
 (Clifton), 78
Bradshaw, F., 120, 135
Braithwaite, William, 60, 102
*Brambleberrys Animal Book of Big and
 Small Shapes, The* (Mayer), 152
Brathwaite, E., 245, 247, 263-264
Brent, L., 261, 263
Bright Eyes, Brown Skin (Hudson &
 Ford), 69, 71
Brink, C.R., 6, 33
Broderick, D., 11, 33, 61, 102
Broker, I., 165
Brooks, C.K., 52, 158
Brother Anansi and the Cattle Ranch
 (Rhomer), 250
Brown, Sterling A., 61, 102
Brown, T., 216-217, 237
Brownies' Book, The, 65
Bruchac, Joseph, 155, 165
Bryan, Ashley, 75, 86-88, 90, 104
Buchanan, Patrick, 3, 7
Bucks, B.L., 237
Buffalo Knife, The (Steele), 142-143
*Building Bridges of Learning and
 Understanding* (Perez-Selles), 197 *n.*
 18
Business at Boon Farm (Gilroy), 255
Byler, M.G., 165

Caddie Woodlawn (Brink), 6
Caines, Jeanette, 75, 86, 88-90, 104
Caldecott Honor Books, 84, 115, 249, 251
Caldwell-Wood, 142, 147, 151, 153, 160,
 164 *n.*2, 165
Calhoun, M., 104
Calypso Alphabet (Agard), 257-258
Campbell, P.B., 72, 104, 133
Campos, A.J., 227, 239
Cannon, A. E., 150, 165
*Captivity of the Oatman Girls, Being an
 Interesting Narrative of Life Among
 the Apache and Mohave Indians*
 (Stratton), 144
Carew, Jan, 251-252, 262, 264
Caribbean Alphabet (Lessac), 257-258
Caribbean-American children's literature,
 243-265
 African influences on, 247-248
 Anansi stories, 262

 attitudes concerning language and
  cultural diversity in, 260
 fiction, 255-257
 folk tales, legends and animal stories,
  262
 historical development of works,
  246-262
 illustrated books for early primary
  grades, 263
 oral literature, 261-262
 oral tradition of, 250-251
 publishers of, 259
 realistic fiction, 262
 recommended book list, 263
 and responses of Africans toward the
  western world, 261
 strategies for presentation, 259-261
 struggle and resistance theme in,
  247-259
 supplement for units in social studies
  and history, 259-260
Caribbean Canvas (Lessac), 257
Caribbean Connections (Menkart), 197
 n. 18
Caribbean Folk Legends (Lewis), 252-253
Caribbean population
 statistics of, 245-246
Carifesta '76, 251
Carlson, L., 187, 197
Carty, D., 264
Casey, K., 5, 33
Cat's Meow, The (Soto), 220-221
Chagoya, Enrique, 224
Chall, J., 68, 102
Challenge, The (Anaya), 228
Chants (Mora), 223, 235
Charlie Pippin (Boyd), 96
Chavez, Denise, 226-227, 240
Cherokee, 143
Chicano, 236 *n.*2
 See also Mexican-American
Chickamaugas, 142-143
Child, I.L., 120, 133
Child of the Owl (Yep), 45, 112, 128
Children of Long Ago (Little), 97
Children of the Sun (Carew), 251-252
Children's Book Press, The, 192, 223-224
Children's Choice Award, The, 117
Children's literature
 criticism and analysis of, 8-12
 politics of, 8-12
 politics of multiculturalism and
  Christopher Columbus, 3-35

Children's Literature in Education, 95
Children's Literature in the Reading Program (Cullinan), 236 *n*.1
Children's Theater Festival, 226
Child's Story of Dunbar, A (Henderson), 66
Child's Story of the Negro, The (Shackelford), 66
Chilly Stomach (Caines), 89
Chin, F., 133
Chinn, P., 116, 134
Chita's Christmas Tree (Howard), 70, 94
Chris and Fred (Waterman), 255
Christian-Smith, L., 33, 35-36
Christopher Columbus
    in children's literature, 8, 12-26
    critics of revisionist approaches to, 7-8
    genocide of the native population by, 13, 16
    myth of, 13-26
    and the politics of multiculturalism, 3-35
    and the selective tradition of facts, 26-30
Christopher Columbus, Great Explorer (Adler), 25
Christopher Columbus, Mariner (Morison), 27
Christopher Columbus and the World Around Him (Meltzer), 15-16, 28
Christopher Columbus: From Vision to Voyage (Anderson), 17-18
Chronicles of American Indian Protest (Council on Interracial Books for Children), 163
Chubb, I., 62, 104
Cinderella (McKissack), 90
Cisneros, S., 235, 240
Clarence And Corinne (Johnson), 64
Classic Slave Narratives, The (Gates), 99
Class President (Hurwitz), 189
Clean Your Room Harvey Moon (Cummings), 97
Clifton, Lucille, 75, 77-78, 85, 98, 102, 104-105
Climbing Clouds (Turner), 256
Cobb, M., 264
Cockburn, A., 3-4, 8, 33
Coconut Kind of Day (Joseph), 257-258
Codye, Corinn, 229, 237
Cohen, Miriam, 152, 165
Collier, C., 7, 33

Collier, J., 7, 33
Columbus (Ingri & Edgar Parin D'Aulaire), 16
Columbus Day, 29-30
Communion (Mora), 227, 235
Compadres, 214
Connolly, J.E., 154, 165
Contemporary Women Authors of Latin America (Meyer), 196 *n*.14
Cooper, F., 52
Cooperative Children's Book Center, 102, 201
Coretta Scott King Award, 88
Cortes, 207, 210-211, 213, 224-225, 239
Coulthard, G.R., 264
Council on Interracial Books for Children, 196 *nn*.8-10, 12, 200-201
Council on Interracial Books for Children (CIBC), 49, 51, 80, 163, 165-166, 175-176, 192, 211, 213, 239
    and Chicano themes in children's lit, 175-176
    and Puerto Rican themes in children's lit, 175-176
    report on Mexican American-themed books, 206
Country Mouse and City Mouse (McKissack), 90
"Cousin Ann", 105
Cousin Ann's Stories for Children, 63
Coutant, 127
Crews, Donald, 72
Cric Crac (Hallworth), 252-254
Crisis, The (Du Bois), 60
Crocodile's Tale (Aruego), 115
Crow Chief (Goble), 153
Cruz, Victor Hernandez, 181
Cucui, El (Anaya), 228
Cudjoe, S., 247-248, 264
Cuentos (Wagenheim), 182
Cullen, Countee, 61
Cullinan, B., 102
Cultural authenticity, 40-43
Cultural awareness
    and development and use of multicultural literature, 205-237
Culturally conscious writers
    the reinforcements, 75, 86-91
    the reinterpreters, 91-95
    the vanguard, 75-86
Cumming, P., 97, 105
Curanderas, 215

Curandera (Tafola), 228

Daddy and I (Greenfield), 72
Daddy (Caines), 88
Daddy is a Monster . . . Sometimes
    (Steptoe), 82
Daiches, D., 60, 102
Dances With Wolves, 6
Dancing Granny, The (Bryan), 87
Dancing Teepees (Sneve), 155
Dark Way, The (Hamilton), 72
Dash, M., 264
Dathorne, O.R., 247, 264
D'Aulaire, Edgar Parin., 16-17, 33
D'Aulaire, Ingri., 16-17, 33
Dawes, N., 264
Day It Snowed Tortillas (Hayes), 214
DeAngula, J., 154, 166
DeChiara, E., 133-134
Decraene, P., 264
Defoe, Daniel, 147
Delacre, Lulu, 190-191, 197-198
Deloria, Jr., V., 166
De Luca, G., 82-83, 103
DePaola, Tomie, 19-21, 34
Diane Dillon, 251
Dill, Augustus G., 65-66
Dogsong (Paulsen), 147-148
Do Like Kyla (Johnson), 70, 91-92
Don't Explain (De Veaux), 72
Dorros, A., 45, 52
Double Life of Pocohontas (Fritz), 159
Douglass, Frederick, 99
Dragonwagon, Crescent, 74
Dragonwings (Yep), 115
Drinnon, R., 139, 163, 166
D'Souza, Dinesh, 5, 33
D'Souze, 31 *n.*1
Du Bois & Dill Publishing Company,
    65-66
Du Bois, W.E.B., 60, 65-67, 74, 86-87,
    264
Dunbar, Paul L., 64, 99-100, 105
Dunn, Wendy, 229, 233, 238
Duran, D. F., 206, 211, 217, 239
Dyer, P., 255, 262

Ears, Tails, and Common Sense (Sherlock
    and Sherlock), 252, 254
Earth Did Not Part, And the (Rivera), 227
Earth is Sore (Amon), 156

Eastman, Charles, A. (Ohiyesa), 153-154,
    166
Edmonds, Walter D., 6, 33, 145, 166
Egoff, S., 36
Eifler, D., 135
Eisenberg, L., 166
Eisner, E., 233, 239
El Bronx remembered (Mohr), 182, 190
Elliot, R., 102
Elsie Dinsmore series, 61
Encountered, 31 *n.*4
Encounter (Yolen), 31
Epstein, B., 31 *n.*1, 33
Erdoes, Richard, 154, 158, 164 *n.*1, 166
Ericson, Lief, 29
Everett Anderson books (Clifton), 72
*Extending Multicultural Understanding
    Through Children's Books* (Bishop),
    236 *n.*1

Facing West (Drinnon), 139, 163
Fallen Angels (Myers), 72, 85, 96
False Face (Katz), 146
Faludi, S., 12, 34
Family Pictures (Lomas Garza), 224,
    231-232
Famous Mexican Americans (Morey &
    Dunn), 229, 233
Farolitos of Christmas, The (Anaya),
    220-221
Fast Sam, Cool Clyde and Stuff (Myers),
    84
Fauset, Jessie, 61, 65
Feelings, Muriel, 86
Feelings, Tom, 45, 51
Fences (August Wilson), 41
Ferdinand and Isabella, 17
Ferre, Rosario, 188
*Finding the Center; Narrative Poetry of
    the Zuni Indians* (Tedlock), 155,
    164-165 *n.*7
Finkelstein, N., 32, 34 *n.*7
First Biography Series (Adler), 25
First Snow (Coutant & Vo-Dinh), 127
Fitzgerald, Patricia, 75
Five Chinese Brothers (Bishop and
    Wiese), 113, 116, 133
Flamboyan (Adoff), 187, 189
Flor, Alma, 189
Flossie and the Fox (McKissack), 89
Flournoy, V., 71, 96, 105
Floyd, S., 65, 105

Floyd's Flowers or Duty and Beauty for Colored Children (Floyd), 65, 105
Follow the Dream (Sis), 23, 28
Foner, E., 4-8, 34
Forbes, E., 7, 34
Forbes, J.D., 163, 166
Ford, B., 69, 71, 106
Foster, D.W., 201
Franklin, J., 264
Fraser, J., 63-64, 102
Freedman, R., 158, 166
Freeman, D., 238
French, V., 102
Friedman, Judith, 217
Friendship, The (Taylor), 82
Fritz, Jean, 19-21, 34, 142, 144, 159, 162, 166
Frymer, M., 133

Galarza, Ernesto, 219, 235, 240
Garcia, J., 210-211, 239
Garcia, Maria, 223-224, 237
Garcia, Richard, 190-191, 197, 199
Gates, Henry Louis Jr., 42, 99, 51, 102
Gayle, A., 64, 102
Gender stereotyping in children's books, 11-12
George, Jean Craighead, 147, 165 *n*.8, 166
George Washington Gomez (Paredes), 235
Geronimo, 158
Getting Elected (Hewett), 229, 232
Gift for Tia Rosa (Taha), 215-216
Gilbert, S.S., 237
Gilles, J., 229, 237
Gilroy, B., 255, 262
Gimmestad & De Chiara, 124
Gimmestad, B.J., 133-134
Giovanni, N., 97, 105
Girion, B., 150, 166
Girl Called Boy, A (Hurmence), 74
Giuseppi, N., 262
Giuseppi, U., 262
Gladiola Garden (Newsome), 66
Goble, Paul, 6, 34, 153, 155, 162, 166
Going home (Mohr), 190
Gold Cadillac, The (Taylor), 82
Golden Indian, The (Adams), 164 *n*.4
Gollick, D., 134
Gollnick, 116
Gomez, Cruz, 224, 238
Gomez-Quinones, Juan, 210, 239

Gone With the Wind (Mitchell), 7
Gonzales, R., 49, 52, 209, 226
Goodard, C., 102
Graham, Lorenzo, 62, 67, 72, 105
Grandpa's Face (Greenfield), 45
Grant & Sleeter, 116
Grant, C., 134
Gray, P., 13, 31 *n*.4, 34
Great Adventure of Christopher Columbus, The (Fritz), 19-21
Great Age of Exploration, 13
Great Slave Narratives (Bontemps), 261
Green, M., 105
Greenfield, Eloise, 10, 34, 45, 52, 59, 70, 72, 75, 78-79, 85, 98, 102, 105
Greenlaw, M.J., 116, 135
Gregory, Kristiana, 140-142, 166
Griego, M.C., 237
Griots, contemporary, 57-108
Grossman, Virginia, 151, 166
Guadalupe Cultural Arts Center, 226
Guerrero Rea, Jesus, 200
Gunsmoke, 7

Hadaway, N.L., 210-211, 239
Hale, S.J., 52
Haley, A., 34, 102
Hall, C., 102
Hallworth, G., 252-254, 262
Hamilton, Virginia, 7, 17, 34, 59, 69-72, 75, 76-77, 85, 93, 96-97, 99, 102, 105
Handprint Publications, 259
Hansen, Joyce, 98, 124
Hanson, Rick, 29, 35
Happily May I Walk; American Indians and Alaska Natives Today (Hirschfelder), 157
Harambee Bookclub, 69
Harlem Renaissance, 60-61
Harris, 62, 64-65, 70,
Harris, Violet, J., 102
Haskins, J., 105
Hayes, J., 214, 234, 237
Hayley, 7, 82
Haynes, E., 66, 106
Hazelby Family, The (Johnson), 64
Hazel (Ovington), 63
Hector Lives in the United States Now (Hewett), 216-217
Hello Amigos! (Brown), 216-217
Henderson, J., 66, 106
Hepler, S., 47, 52

Herbst, Laura, 145, 166
Hewett, J., 238
Hewett, Richard, 216-217, 229, 232
Hickman, J., 47, 52
Highwater, Jamake, 152, 166
Hill, B., 65, 103
Hirschfelder, Arlene B., 148, 150-151, 157, 155, 166-167
Hispanic, definition of, 177
Hispanic Americans (Meltzer), 189, 229, 233
Hispanic Community Mobilization for Dropout Prevention, 196 *n*.4
Hispanic Heritage, A (Schon), 196 *n*.6
Hispanic Heritage III (Schon), 237 *n*.3
Hispanic Heritage II (Schon), 237 *n*.3
Hispanic Heritage (Schon), 236-237 *n*.3
History of the Indies, The (Las Casas), 16
Hogan, 62
Hokada, E., 135
Holman, F., 183-186, 197
Honey, I Love (Greenfield), 78-79
Hooks, W., 97, 106
Hoops (Myers), 84
Horning, K.T., 47, 52
House on Mango Street, The (Cisneros), 235
Howard, Elizabeth Fitzgerald, 43, 45, 52, 106
Howard, Patricia Fitzgerald, 70, 72, 91, 94-95, 102
Huck, C., 52
Huck, 47
Hudson, C., 69-70, 72, 102, 106
Hudson, W., 70, 101, 102
Hughes, Langston, 61, 66, 104
Hundred Penny, The (Mathis), 72
Hurmence, B., 74, 102
Hurston, Zora Neale, 61
Hurwitz, J., 189, 197

Ignoble Savage, The (Moore & MacCann), 165 *n*.8
Igus, T., 71, 103
Ihejirika, M., 69, 103
"I" is not for Indian (Caldwell-Wood & Mitten), 164 *n*.2
Iktome and the Berries (Goble), 153
I Make Music (Greenfield), 72
I'm Going to Sing (Bryan), 87
In 1492 (Marzello), 18-19, 21

Incidents in the Life of a Slave Girl (Brent), 261
Indian Boyhood (Eastman), 153
Indian Chiefs (Freedman), 158
Indian in America's Past, The (Forbes), 163
Indian in the Cupboard, The (Banks), 145
Indian Summer (Girion), 150
Indian Summer (Monjo), 6
Indian Tales (deAngulo), 154
I Need a Lunch Bow (Caines), 88
In Nueva York (Mohr), 191
Inter-American Bookfair and Literary Festival, 226
International Reading Association, 95
International Reading Association's Children's Choice, 117
Interracial Books for Children Bulletin, 92, 133, 162
In the Beginning (Hamilton), 72
Invasion of America, The (Jennings), 163
Irene's Big Fine Nickel (Smalls), 71
Iroquois Stories (Bruchac), 155
Ismond, P., 264
I Speak English for My Mom (Stanek), 216-217

Jackson, Jessie, 67
Jacques-Garvey, A., 264
Jahn, J., 103
Jake and Honeybunch Go To Heaven (Zemach), 75
Jassem, K., 159-160, 166
Jay, G.S, 134
Jean, 19-21
Jenkins, E.C., 118, 133
Jennings, F., 163, 166
Jessi and the Superbrat (Martin), 73
Jessi's Baby-sitter (Martin), 73
Johnny Tremain (Forbes), 7
Johnson, 73
Johnson, A.D., 167
Johnson, Angela, 59, 64, 70, 75, 91-92, 95, 106
Johnson, D. W., 101, 103, 106, 159, 134
Johnson, Mrs. A. E., 99
Johnson, R., 103
Jones, J., 106
Jones, Lois Mailou, 66
Joseph, L., 257-258, 262-263
Journey Home (Uchida), 114, 128
Journey to Topaz (Uchida), 114, 128

Joy, The (Johnson), 64
Jubilee (Walker), 7
Justice Trilogy (Hamilton), 72
Just My Luck (Moore), 92
Just Us Women (Caines), 88
Juvenile Poems for the Use of Free
    American Children of Every
    Complexion, 63

Kanellos, N., 201
Katz, Jane B., 158, 167
Katz, Welwyn Wilton, 146, 167
Keats, Ezra Jack, 45, 52, 74
Keens-Douglas, P., 261
Kelly, 10
Kelly, R.G., 34
Kikiriki (Pena), 181-182, 223
Kimball, L.H., 237
Kimmel, E.A., 134
King, M., 73, 103
Kirkus Reviews, 92
Klein, G., 49, 52
Kleven, E., 52
Kogawa, Joy, 128
Kopkind, A., 3, 34
Kruse, G.M., 47, 52
Kummel, 120

Lach, M.A., 11, 35
Lacy, Virginia, 67
Lampman, Evelyn Sibley, 144, 149, 165
    *n.*8, 167
Langstaff, J., 106
Larrick, Nancy, 34, 67-68, 103,
Larsen, Nella, 61
Las Casas, 16
Lasky, K., 7, 34
Last of the Menu Girls (Chavez), 226
Latino children's literature in the United
    States
    review of, 175-176
Latino themes in children's literature
    statistics, 173
    stereotypes in, 173-176
Leaving Morning, The (Johnson), 92
Legend of Jimmy Spoon, The (Gregory),
    140-142
Legend of Tarik, The (Myers), 84
Leo Dillon, 251
Lessac, F., 257-258, 263
Lester, Julius, 7, 13, 34, 71, 97, 106
Let Me Be A Free Man (Erdoes), 158

Let the Circle Be Unbroken (Taylor), 44,
    82
Levine, E.M., 120, 133
Levinson, N.S., 32 *n.*6, 34
Lewis, T., 262
Lieberman, M., 11, 34
Liestman, V., 30-31, 35
Life Magazine, 82
Lindgren, M., 51-52
Lion and Ostrich Chicks (Bryan), 87
Lion and the Unicorn, The, 95
Lippincotts, 62
Litcher, J.W., 134
*Literature and Society of the Puerto Rican
    People* (Marquez), 197 *n.* 18
Little, L., 33 *n.*16, 105
Little Brown Baby (Dunbar), 64
Little Girl With Make-Believe Hair
    (Pietri), 193
Little House on the Prairie (Wilder), 145
Little Pickaninies (Chubb), 62
Little Red Hen, The (McKissack), 90
Liverwurst is Missing (Mayer), 151
Llorona, La (Anaya), 228
Llorona, La (Hayes), 234
Locke, Alain, 60, 103
Log of Christopher Columbus, The
    (Lowe), 21
Lomas Garza, C., 224, 231-232, 238
Lomeli, F., 234, 239
London, C., 264
Long Hard Journey, The (McKissack), 72,
    90
Long Journey Home (Lester), 7
Lost Garden (Yep), 115
Lost Lake, The (Say), 112
Lovell, Donna, 164 *n.*5
Lowe, S., 22, 35
Lucky Stone, The (Clifton), 78
Luis, W., 264
Lukens, R., 47, 52
Lurie, 164 *n.*1

McBrown, G., 66, 106
MacCann, Donnarae, 8, 11, 34-35, 165 *n.*8
McCartney, N., 252, 262
McDermott, G., 249-250, 262
McKissack, Frederick, 89
McKissack, Patricia, 72, 75, 86, 89-91, 97,
    106-107
McLemore, S.D., 239
McLemore and Romo, 209

McMillan, B., 46, 52
MacMillan, D., 211, 238
McWilliams, C., 209-210, 239
Magical Adventures of Pretty Pearl, The
   (Hamilton), 97
Magical Encounter (Ada), 196 *n.*16
Malonado Miracle, The (Taylor), 217-218
Mango, K.N., 185-185, 197
Manie the Manicou goes Traveling
   (Dyer), 255
Margarita, 226
Mariah Keeps Cool (Walter), 96
Mariah Loves Rock (Walter), 96
Marin, 196 *n.*5
Marley, Bob, 253
Marquez, Roberto, 195, 197. *n.*18
Martel, Cruz, 192, 195, 199
Martin, A., 73, 106
Martinez, J.A., 234, 239
Mary Had a Little Lamb (McMillan), 46
Marzello, Jean, 18-19, 21, 35
Matchlock Gun, The (Edmonds), 6, 145
Mathis, S., 72, 106
Matsuyama, U.K., 118-119, 134
Matute-Bianchi, M.E., 210, 239
Mayer, Marianna, 152, 167
Mayer, Mercer, 151
M.C. Higgins, the Great (Hamilton), 76
Me and Neesie (Greenfield), 78
Meltzer, Milton, 7, 14-19, 21-22, 28, 30-
   31, 31 *n.*3, 32 *nn.*6, 8, 33 *n.*16, 35,
   74, 120, 134, 189, 229, 233, 238
Methodological fallacies when studying
   Hispanics (Marin), 196 *n.*5
Mexican-American children's literature
   defining the Mexican-American
      experience, 208-212
   fiction and poetry, 220-229
   insights into the Mexican-American
      experience in, 205-241
   insights for future development of, 208
   literature study groups for teachers of,
      234-235
   necessity and challenges of authentic
      portrayal in , 212-218
   nonfiction, 229
   nonnative writers of, 213-218
   potential and future directions of,
      226-231
   source of learning for all children,
      231-232
   stereotypes and biases in, 210-218

underrepresentation and
   misrepresentation in, 206-208
use of oral tradition in literature
   curriculum, 233-234
value of background knowledge for
   teachers of, 232-235
vital role of Mexican-American authors
   in, 218-225
Mexican-American content in children's
   literature
statistics for, 236 *n.*3
Mexicans in America, The (Pinchot), 229,
   233
Meyer, D., 201
Miles, 127
Miller, L., 33
Million Fish . . . More or Less, A
   (McKissack), 89, 97
Mirandy and Brother Wind (McKissack),
   71, 89
Mississippi Bridge (Taylor), 82
Mitchell, M., 7, 35
Mitten, A., 142, 147, 151, 160, 164 *n.*2,
   165
Mobley, Jane, 152-153, 167
Mohr, Nicholasa, 181-182, 190-192, 197,
   199
Momo's Kitten (Yashima), 126
Monjo, F.N., 6, 35
Monson & Shurtleff, 124
Monson, D., 134
Montoya, Malaquais, 224
Moonsong Lullaby (Highwater), 152
Moore & Hirschfelder, 152
Moore, Emily, 59, 75, 91-93, 95
Moore, Robert B., 150, 151, 165 *n.*8, 167
Mora, Pat., 223, 227, 229, 235, 240
Moreland, J.K., 124, 134
Morey, J., 229, 233, 238
Morison, Samuel Eliot, 26-28, 32 *n.*15
Moths and Other Stories, The
   (Viramontes), 228
*Mountain Wolf Woman, Sister of
   Crashing Thunder* (Lurie), 164 *n.*1
Mouse Rap, The (Myers), 45, 84
Mr. Sugar Came To Town (Rohmer),
   224
Mufaro's Beautiful Daughters (Steptoe),
   71, 82-84, 97
Mujica, Barbara, 187
Multicolored Mirror, The (Kruse &
   Horning), 47

Multicultural children's literature, sources
for
small presses, 269-270
large presses, 270-272
organizations, 273-274
journals, 274-275
bookstores, 275
Multiculturalism, critics of, 3-8
Multicultural literature
defined, 39-40
Multicultural literature for children
need for cultural authenticity, 40-43
making informed choices about, 39-53
selection guidelines, 47-51
strategies for becoming informed about,
43-47
types of, 44-46
Muse, D., 63-65, 103
My Aunt Otilia's Spirits (Garcia), 190-191
My Best Friend Martha Rodriguez
(MacMillan), 211
My Brother Fine with Me (Anderson), 77
My Brother Sam is Dead (Collier &
Collier), 7
My Doll Keisha (Greenfield), 72
Myers, Walter Dean, 45, 53, 59, 72, 75,
84-86, 96, 98-99, 103, 107, 124, 134,
186, 189, 197
My Father Sun-Sun Johnson (Palmer),
256-257
My Friend Jacob (Clifton), 78
My Little Island (Lessac), 257-258
My Special Best Words (Steptoe), 82

Nanny of the Maroons (Phillpotts),
259-260
Naomi's Road (Kogawa), 128
Narratives, as value-laden selections, 22-23
Nathaniel Talking (Greenfield), 72, 79
National Book Award, 76, 220
National Council of Teachers of English,
95
Native American children's literature,
137-169
recommended titles, 168-169
selection guidelines, 160-163
Native Americans
genocide of, 7
Native Americans in children's literature,
137-169
in folklore and poetry, 153-157
in history novels, 140-146

in novels about modern times, 146-150
in picture books, 150-153
and cultural assimilation, 149-150
discussion questions, 163, 163-164
in histories and biographies, 157-160
recommended titles, 168-169
and the "virgin land" myth, 139
and white bias, 139-163
Natov, R., 82-83, 103
Navaho Sister (Lampman), 149
Ned, N., 107
Negro Art Music and Rhyme, Book II
(Whiting), 66
Negro Folk Tales, Book I (Whiting), 66
Nettie Jo's Friends (McKissack), 89
Nettleford, R., 247, 264-265
Neville, 255-256
Newbery Honor Medal, 76, 80, 85
"New Negro", 60-61
New Nigger Nursery Rhymes, 62
New Republic, The, 3
Newsome, E., 66, 107
Newsweek, 3, 31 *n.*4
New Western historians, 7
New West History, 7
Nicholas, C., 66, 103
Nicodemus books (Hogan), 62
Nieto, Sonia, 134, 201
Night Flying Woman (Broker), 158
Night on Neighborhood Street
(Greenfield), 72, 79
Nilda (Mohr), 191
Nisei Daughter (Sone), 128
Norton, D., 49, 52
Now Is Your Time! (Myers), 84, 99
Nuyorican Poetry (Algarin), 196 *n.*14

Occupied America (Acuna), 233
O'Dell, Scott, 147-148, 162, 167
Office of Superintendent of Public
Instruction, State of Washington, 134
Olmos, M.F, 201
One of Three (Johnson), 70, 92
Ortiz, Fran, 182, 190, 216
Ortiz, S., 157, 167
Ortiz Cofer, Judith, 197, 199
Other 1492, The (Finkelstein), 32 *n.*7
"Others," concept of
and genocide, 32 *n.*9
Outside Shot, The (Myers), 84
Ovington, Mary White, 63, 107

Pablo's Tree (Mora), 227
Page, T., 107
Palmer, C. Evrard, 256-257, 262
Paredes, A., 240
Patchwork Colcha (Tafolla), 220, 222-223, 227-228
Patchwork Quilt, The (Flournoy), 71, 96
Pate, G., 128, 134
Pau, P.G., 238
Paul, 214-215
Paul Robeson (Hamilton), 99
Paulsen, Gary, 147-148, 167
Pelta, K., 32 *n.*6, 35
Pena, Sylvia Cavazos, 181-182, 198, 200, 223, 238
People Could Fly, The (Hamilton), 71
People Shall Continue, The (Ortiz), 157
Perkins, 61
Petersham, Maud, 152, 167
Petersham, Miska, 152, 167
Peterson, S.B., 11, 35
Phillpotts, K., 259-260, 263
Pichilinguis, 226-227
Picture Book Biographies (Adler), 25
Picture Book of Christopher Columbus (Wallner), 25
Picture Poetry Book, The (McBrown), 66
Pietri, Pedro, 193
Pinchot, J., 229, 233, 238
Pinero, M., 200
Pinkney, Jerry and Bryan, 70
Pinky Marie (Graham), 62
Pioneers of Long Ago (Roy & Turner), 66
Pleasant Company, The, 73
Polacco, Patricia, 151, 167
Political correctness, 4, 7-8
Pollard, V., 252, 254-255, 262
Popo and Fifina, (Hughes), 66
Portable North American Indian Reader, The (Berkhofer), 163
Potter, E.H., 120, 133
Premio Quinto Sol award, 227
Price, Leontyne, 57-59, 107
Print and Prejudice (Zimet), 124
Puerto Rican American children's literature
  absence and disparagement of the Puerto Rican family in, 182-188
  based on tenets of Puerto Rican adult literature, 190
  case study of, 177-178
  changes in genres and images, 178-191

characteristics of, 189-191
classroom use of, 193-195
demeaning misuse of language in, 186
depiction of multiple realities in, 190
emergence of, 188-191
future of, 178, 191-193
guidelines for use of, 194-195
inauthentic illustrations in, 187
invisibility of, 179-182
mis-classification of, 182
and publishing companies, 192
Puerto Rican authors of, 192
and the Puerto Rican community, 193
and roles of teachers and schools, 193
since 1983, 178-191
stereotypes in, 182-188
unspoken dilemmas in, 190
Puerto Rican Literature (Foster), 196 *n.*14
Puerto Ricans and the Media (Vazquez), 196 *n.*15
*Puerto Ricans (Rodriguez), 196-197 n.*17
Puerto Ricans in children's books (literature), 173-201
Puerto Ricans in Children's Literature and History Texts (Nieto), 196 *n.*11
Puerto Rican Writers at Home in the U.S.A. (Turner), 196 *n.*13
Pupurupu (Ulibarri), 220-222
Pytowska, E., 201

Rain Dance People; The Pueblo Indians, Their Past and Present (Erdoes), 158, 164 *n.*1
Rain Falling Sun Shining (Thomas), 257
Ransome, J., 52
Rashburn, E., 102
Rastafarian(s), 253-254
Rawlings, R., 265
Rea, J.G., 198
Reading Teacher, The, 117
Red Dog, Blue Fly (Mathis), 72
Reed, Adolph, 4
Reimer, K.M., 236 *n.*1, 240
Resendez, G.A., 206, 211, 219, 237 *n.*4, 240
Resistance and Caribbean Literature (Cudjoe), 247-248
Rethinking Schools, 13, 32 *n.*10, 35
Return of the Indian, The (Banks), 145-146
Rice Cake that Rolled Away, The, 118

Richie, D., 118, 134
Ringgold, Faith, 57-59, 107
Rivera, Tomas, 227, 240
Road to Memphis, The (Taylor), 45, 82
Roback, D., 68, 103
Robe, Rosebud Yellow, 155
Robinson Crusoe (Defoe), 147
Robleda Moguel (Margarita), 226
Rockwood, J., 14, 35
Rodriguez, C.E., 201
Rodriquez, Laura, 237 *n*.5
Rohmer, Harriet, 200, 224, 238, 250, 262
Rohmer, S.C., 190-191, 198
Rollins, Charlmae, 67
Roll of Thunder, Hear My Cry (Taylor),
    44, 68, 80-82
Roman & Christian-Smith, 8
Roman, L., 35
Romero & Zancanella, 217
Romero, P.A., 235, 240
Romo, R., 239
Roney, R.C., 134
Roosevelt, Franklin, 29
Rooster Crows, The (Petersham &
    Petersham), 152
Roots (Haley), 7, 82
Rosa Parks (Greenfield), 72
Rosebud, Yellow Rose, 155
Rosenberg, B.A., 233, 240
Ross, C., 135
Rothenberg, Jerome, 164-165 *n*.7
Roy, J., 66, 107
Rudman, M.K., 49, 52, 134

Saakana, A., 265
Sabuda, Robert, 21-22, 35
Sacajewea, Wilderness Guide (Jassem),
    159
Safa, A., 265
Sambo and the Twins (Bannerman), 62
Sam (Scott), 46
Samurai of Gold Hill (Uchida), 114
San Souci, R., 97, 107
Saul, E., 65, 103
Say, 112
Schon, Isabel, 175, 201, 206, 210, 236 *n*.3,
    236-237 *n*.3, 240
School Library Journal, 92
Schubert, W., 36
Sciara, Frank J., 200
*Scientist with Determination, Elma
    Gonzalez* (Verheyden-Hillard), 229
Scorpions (Myers), 85, 186

Scott, A.H., 46, 53
Scott, C.J., 116, 135
Sea Glass (Yep), 128
Seale, Doris, 49, 52, 152, 161-162, 167
Sebesta, S.L., 126, 134
Secret City (Holman), 183-186
Secret Valentine (Stock), 46
Selassie, Haile, 253
*Selecting Materials For and About
    Hispanic and East Asian Children
    and Young People* (Bielke), 196 *n*.7
Selective Bibliography and Guide
    (Caldwell-Wood & Mitten), 142
Seminole, 147
Sendak, Maurice, 151-152, 167
Senich, G., 103
*Senor Alcalde: a Biography of Henry
    Cisneros* (Gillies), 229
Shackelford, J., 66, 107
Shadow Brothers, The (Cannon), 150
Shadows of the Indian (Stedman), 161
Shaftel, F., 128, 134
Shaftel, G., 128, 134
Shannon, D., 36
Shannon, P., 116-117, 133, 134
Sherlock, H., 248, 252-254, 262
Sherlock, P., 248, 252-254, 262
Shor, I., 5, 35
Shurtleff, C., 134
Silas, Daphne , 164 *n*.6
Silent Dancing (Ortiz), 182, 190
Simcox, D., 263
Sims, R., 5, 11, 35, 41, 52, 67-68, 74, 103,
    213, 240
Sinnette, E., 61, 65, 103
Sis, P., 23-24, 28-29, 31, 32 *n*.14, 35
Sitting Bull, 158
Slapin, B., 49, 52, 161-162, 167
Slavery, 7
Sleeter, C., 134
Small Faces (Soto), 235
Smalls-Hector, I., 71, 107
Smith, Henry Nash, 139, 167
Smith, N.J., 116, 135
Smithsonian Institution's National
    Museum of Art (Smithsonian) and
    controversy over *West as America*
    exhibition, 4-8
Sneve, V.D.H., 155, 167
Snowy Day, The (Keats), 45
Something to Count On (Moore), 92
Somewhere Green (Mango), 185-186
Sone, Monica, 128

Song of the Trees (Taylor), 80
Sonnets to Human Beings and Other Selected Works (Tafolla), 227-228
Sonora Beautiful (Clifton), 78
Soto, Gary, 220-221, 224-226, 229, 231, 235, 238, 241
Soule, Gardner, 13, 15, 32 n.6, 35
Sound of Flutes and Other Indian Legends, The (Erdoes), 154
Spanish Pioneers of the Southwest (Anderson), 229
Speare, Elizabeth George, 162
Spin a Soft Black Song (Giovanni), 97
Squanto, The Pilgram Adventure (Jassem), 160
Stanek, M., 216-217, 238
Star Husband (Mobley), 152
Stedman, R.W., 161, 167
Steele, W.O., 142-144, 161, 167
Steptoe, John, 70, 75, 82-85, 107
Stevie (Steptoe), 82
Stock, C., 46, 53
Stories From El Barrio (Thomas), 192-193
Story of Jumping Mouse, The (Steptoe), 82
Story of Little Black Bohtail (Bannerman), 62
Story of Little Black Quasha, The (Bannerman), 62
Story of Little Black Quibba, The (Bannerman), 62
Story of Little Black Sambo, The (Bannerman), 62
Story of Little Kettle Head, The (Bannerman), 62
Story of Sitting Bull, Great Sioux Chief (Eisenberg), 160
Story of The Teasing Monkey, The (Bannerman), 62
Stratten, 144
Strete, Craig Kee, 149, 152, 167-168
Stubbs, G.T., 36
Summer Life, A (Soto), 235
Sun Salutes You, The (Palmer), 256-257
Sutherland, Z., 77, 101
Sweet Dreams, 12
Sweet Valley High, 12

Tafolla, Carmen, 220, 222-223, 227-229, 238, 241
Taha, K.T., 215-216, 238
Takaki, R., 135

Taking Care Of Yoki (Campbell), 72
Tales of the Immortelles (McCartney), 252
Talking Earth, The (George), 147
Talking Eggs, The (San Souci), 97
Tangalin, A.B., 135
Tanna, L., 248, 261-262
Tannenbaum, F., 13, 35
Tapahonso, L., 213, 240
Tar Beach (Ringgold), 58, 59
Tarzan, 70
Tate, Eleanora, 59
Tatum, C.M., 234, 240
Taxel, Joel, 1-35, 5, 7-8, 11-12, 32 *n*.10, 33 *n*.16, 36, 60, 103
Taylor, Mildred, 53, 59, 68, 72, 75, 79-82, 85, 103, 107-108
Taylor, T., 217-218, 238
Teaching Strategies for Ethnic Studies (Banks), 197 *n.* 18
Tedlock, Dennis, 162, 164-165 *n*.7, 168
Tell Me a Story Mama (Johnson), 70, 91, 92
Ten Little Rabbits (Grossman), 151
Thomas, Joyce Carol, 98
Thomas, O., 263
Thompson, K., 198
Thorndyke, 118
Through Indian Eyes (Slapin & Seale), 161-162
Time Magazine, 3-4
Times They Used to Be, The (Clifton), 78
To Be A Slave (Lester), 99
Toby, 107
Tomas and the Library Lady (Mora), 227
Tonweya and the Eagles and Other Lakota Indian Tales (Rosebud Yellow Robe), 155
Tortillitas Para Mama and Other Nursery Rhymes (Griego), 212
To Spoil the Sun (Rockwood), 6, 20
Townsend, J.R., 9, 36
Train Ride (Steptoe), 82
Train to Lulu's, The (Howard), 70, 94
Treaty of Guadalupe Hidalgo, 209
Tun-ta-ca-tun (Pena), 182, 223
Turner, D., 48, 52
Turner, F.W. III., 168
Turner, G., 66, 107
Turner, T., 256, 262
Two Little Confederates, 61

Uchida, Yoshiko, 113-114, 116

Udry, J., 97, 108
Ulibarri, Sabine, 220-222, 238
Umbrella (Yashima), 126
Uncle Remus Tales (Lester), 71, 97
Under the Sunday Tree (Greenfield), 79
Unlearning Indian Stereotypes (film), 162
Un Nueva York (Mohr), 182
Unsung Heroes (Haynes), 66
Uptown (Steptoe), 82
U.S.A. Today, 196 *n*.3
U.S. Bureau of the Census, 196 *n*.2
U.S. News and World Reports, 3

Value of Adventure; The Story of Sacagawea, The (Johnson), 159
Varela-Perez, Franklyn, 181
Vargas, Cirilo Toro, 181, 190
Vaughn-Roberson, C., 65, 103
Vazquez, Blanca, 185, 201
Ventura, C.L., 187, 197
Verheyden-Hillard, M., 229, 238
Vilma Martinez (Codye), 229
Vine Deloria, 158
Viramontes, Helena Maria, 228, 241
Virgin Land myth, 140
Vo-Dinh, 127

Wagenheim, Kal, 182, 200
Walker, M., 7, 36
Walker, P.R., 198
Walk Together Children (Bryan), 87
Wallner, A., 25, 33
Wallner, J., 25, 33
Walter, Mildred Pitts, 86, 108
Wamer-Lewis, M., 265
Waples, D., 120, 135
Waterman, 255
Watkins, M., 51-52
W. E. B. Du Bois (Hamilton), 99
Weekly record, American books publishing record data base and children's books statistics, 196 *n*.1
Weiner, J., 4-8, 34
Weitzman, L.J., 11, 120, 135
West & West, 15, 32 *n*.6
West, D., 36
West, J., 36
West as America exhibition, 4-8
Wexler, P., 12, 36
What a Morning (Bryan), 87
What Kind of Babysitter Are You? (Shelby), 71
What Mary Jo Shared (Udry), 97

What Reading Does to People (Waples, Berelson & Bradshaw), 120
When Grandfather Journeys into Winter (Strete), 149
When I Am Old With You (Johnson), 70, 92
Where Angels Glide at Dawn (Carlson and Ventura), 187
Where Do You Think You're Going Christopher Columbus? (Fritz), 19
White, E. B., 120
White Captives, (Lampman), 144
White Man's Indian (Berkhofer), 163
Whiting, H., 66, 108
Whose Side Are You On? (Moore), 92, 93
Why the Possum's Tail is Bare and Other North American Indian Nature Tales (Connolly), 154
Wiese, K., 133
Wilder, Laura Ingalls, 145, 168
Willett, G.P., 201
William Ruth Company, The, 73
Williams, Vera, 74
Willie Bea and the Time the Martians Landed (Hamilton), 76
Willie Pearl (King), 73
Will I Have a Friend? (Cohen), 152
Wills, Gary, 31 *n*.1, 36
Wilson, August, 42, 45, 52
Window Wishing (Caines), 88
Wirtenberg, J., 133
Woman Who Knew the Language of the Animals (Chavez), 226-227
Women in the State of Grace (Chavez), 227
Woodson, Carter G., 65-67, 108
Woodward, G., 8, 11, 34-35
Wright, R., 265

Yagua days (Martel), 192, 195
Yamashita, D.J., 135
Yarbrough, Camille, 59, 86
Yashima, Taro, 126
Yates, E., 36
Yellow Robe, R., 168
Yep, Laurence, 45, 112-113, 115-116, 128, 135
Yolen, J., 31, 36
You Can Hear a Magpie Smile (Paul), 214-215
Young Abolitionists; or Conversations on Slavery, The, 63
Young Landlords, The (Myers), 84

Yuill, P., 62, 103

Zancanella, D., 235, 240
Zeely (Hamilton), 69-70, 76
Zeke (Ovington), 63

Zemach, M., 75, 108
Zimet, S.G., 120, 124, 135
Zinn, Howard, 16, 19, 26-28, 32 *nn.*11, 12, 36

Contributors ─────────

Violet J. Harris received her Ph.D. from the University of Georgia. She is currently an Assistant Professor at the University of Illinois at Urbana-Champaign. Her research interests include children's literature, multiethnic children's literature, and literacy materials created for African-American children prior to 1950.

Elaine Aoki received her Ph.D. from the University of Washington. She is currently an acting principal at Bagley Elementary School, Seattle. She has also been a district K-12 reading/language arts coordinator. Her research interests include Asian Pacific American literature, comprehension, response to literature, and assessment.

Rosalinda B. Barrera received her Ph.D. from the University of Texas at Austin. She is currently Associate Professor in the Department of Curriculum and Instruction at New Mexico State University at Las Cruces. Her many journal articles and book chapters reflect her interests in Mexican-American children's literature, the reading performance of Mexican-American bilingual elementary students, and cultural foundations of literature-based literacy education.

Yabaya Bello received his Ph.D. from the University of Illinois. He has taught at all levels and in many countries, including the United States and Nigeria; and founded a school in Haiti. He is currently assistant principal at Cancryn School and has taught at the University of the Virgin Islands.

Rudine Sims Bishop received her Ed.D. from Wayne State University in Detroit. She is a professor of education at The Ohio State University, where she teaches courses in children's literature. She is author of Shadow and Substance: *Afro-American Experience in Contemporary Children's Fiction* and *Presenting Walter Dean Myers*.

Olga Liguori is currently doing doctoral work in curriculum and instruction with an emphasis on bilingual education at New Mexico State University at Las Cruces. Her current research focuses on Mexican-American literature for children and adolescents and teachers' multicultural awareness

Donnarae MacCann earned her Ph.D. in American Studies from the University of Iowa. Currently a columnist for *The Wilson Library Bulletin* and *The Children's Literature Association Quarterly,* she is coauthor, editor, and coeditor of numerous books, including *Cultural Conformity in Books for Children, The Child's First Books: A Critical Study of Pictures and Texts,* and *Social Responsibility in Librarianship: Essays on Equality.*

Sonia Nieto is Associate Professor and Program Director of the Cultural Diversity and Curriculum Reform Program in the School of Education at the University of Massachusetts at Amherst. She received her Ed.D. from the University of Massachusetts. In addition to numerous articles and book chapters, she is author of *Affirming Diversity: The Sociopolitical Context of Multicultural Education.*

Loretta Salas is a doctoral student with an emphasis on bilingual education at New Mexico State University at Las Cruces. Her current research focuses on the Mexican-American experience in children's literature and higher education of Mexican-American students.

Joel Taxel received his Ph.D. from the University of Wisconsin at Madison. He is a Professor in the Department of Language Education at the University of Georgia and Director of the UGA Education Initiative, a project that is seeking to link school-based reform with the reform of the University of Georgia's teacher education program. Editor of *The New Advocate,* he has published articles on topics ranging from the social and political values in children's fiction to censorship.